A SQUARE PEG IN BUSH HOUSE
Memories of a BBC man

Also by David Perman

Cublington
A Blueprint for Resistance (1973)

Change and the Churches
An Anatomy of Religion in Britain (1977)

Scott of Amwell
Dr Johnson's Quaker Critic (2001)

A New History of Ware
its people and its buildings (2010)

Stranger in a Borrowed Land
Lotte Moos and her writing (2012)

Islington Born and Bred
A Memoir of Childhood (2014)

David Perman

A SQUARE PEG IN BUSH HOUSE
Memories of a BBC man

Rockingham Press

Published in 2020 by
Rockingham Press
11 Musley Lane
Ware, Herts SG12 7EN

Copyright © David Perman, 2020

The right of David Perman to be identified as the author of this work has been asserted by him in accordance with Section 77 of the Copyright, Designs and Patents Act, 1988

British Library Catalogue-in-Print Data

A catalogue record for this book
Is available from the British Library

ISBN 978-1-904851-80-6

CONTENTS

Foreword by William Oxley		7
1.	Bush House	9
2.	A Talks Writer	21
3.	*Cublington: a Blueprint for Resistance*	33
4.	*The World Today*	41
5.	*World Today* features	51
6.	*Twenty-four Hours*	56
7.	Becoming a Civil Servant	67
8.	Arabic Programme Organiser	70
9.	A tour of Arab capitals	80
10.	Sacked!	97
11.	Interviewing the Ayatollah	106
12.	Greek Programme Organiser	115
13.	Nafplion in the Peloponnese	125
14.	*The True Cost of Sound Money*	131
15.	*America, Europe and the World*	143
16.	The Falklands Conflict	175
17.	Greeks and Turks	181
18.	'Are you really a Communist?'	192
19.	Two Bush House poets	217
20.	Then and Now	225

ILLUSTRATIONS

The Centre Block of Bush House, seen from Kingsway	8
Anatol Goldberg	20
FOC leaving card from The Observer	25
Members of the Roskill Commission	34
The Cublington Tractor Rollout in December 1970	38
Cublington: A Blueprint for Resistance	39

David and the belly dancer in Istanbul	44
Not with Europe: the case for staying out by William Pickles	47
Ightham Mote and Dodington Park	53
Hugh Leach	59
The Marsham Street towers	69
The Great Umayyad Mosque of Damascus	83
David on a horse at Petra	87
Two views of the Byzantine map at Madaba	88
Dr Hanan Ashrawi and Dr Gabi Beramki at Birzeit University	93
The Ayatollah in the garden at Neauphle-Le-Château	109
The new Greek PO with colleagues / his first words in Greek	117
Camilo Jose Cela and Anthony Burgess	121
Austen Kark and his wife, Nina Bawden	123
Palamidi Castle seen from Nafplion harbour	127
With Kostas Psomadarkis in the Yacht Club	130
J.K. Glbraith	133
Milton Friedman	137
Caravaggio: *The Rest on the Flight into Egypt*	139
Caravaggio: *The Conversion on Way to Damascus*	140
Lord Carrington	145
Zbigniew Brzezinski and Cyrus Vance	153
Mrs Jeanne Kirkpatrick	157
Greeting and interviewing Robert Mugabe of Zimbabwe	161
Abba Eban and King Hussein of Jordan	166
Georgiy Arbatov	170
Casper Weinberger	173
Turgut Özal and Andreas Papandreou	183
Mario Modiano	187
US Navy Admiral William N. Small	189
Malcolm Billings and Brigid O'Hara	195
Monemvasia: the rock and the causeway	197
The Greek Section outside Bush House in 1981	199
'Eleni' of Crete	207
Sir Jeremy Thomas at the brains-trust in Thessaloniki	210
The Mayor and the Opposition leader visit the BBC stand	211
Management of the BBC World Service 1992	216
Feyyaz Kayacan Fergar	220
Mahmud Kianush	223

FOREWORD
by William Oxley
1939-2020

For countless numbers of humanity world-wide, the BBC has been the preeminent Media of public communication. As a consequence, this is a vital book because it covers a definite period in the history of that institution.

Not only does it inform about the various technical practices involved in broadcasting, but it provides a fascinating, wide-ranging memoir of a BBC employee's various experiences of running the Greek and Arabic departments at Bush House. All of which involved worldwide travel, interviewing politicians and leaders like Margaret Thatcher and the Ayatollah Khomeini. It also reveals the technical side of broadcasting, the innumerable experiences of travel – both the pleasure and hardship of it – and the frequent clash of personalities between the BBC journalists themselves.

This is a fascinating, readable and invaluable history of a period in the life of a remarkable institution.

The Centre Block of Bush House, seen from Kingsway

1.
Bush House

Bush House is a grand building with an illustrious past. It sits like a castle or minor cathedral across the bottom of Kingsway, so that anyone travelling down that Central London *Boulevard* cannot take their eyes off it before they are deflected into the one-way system known as Aldwych. Getting closer, the visitor sees the classical Corinthian columns hiding an entrance courtyard, and above them two figures grasping a torch and the dedication: TO THE FRIENDSHIP OF ENGLISH-SPEAKING PEOPLES.

Bush House is now part of the Strand Campus of King's College London and looks sparkling clean and bright – and so it should, for £35 million was spent on refurbishing it after the last tenant left and the college moved in. That last tenant was the External Services of the BBC or – to give it its later, better known title – the BBC World Service.

This book has three protagonists. The first is Bush House itself, not in its shiny new incarnation as part of a college but as a BBC building – crowded with broadcasting equipment and people of different nationalities, many of them habitually smoking even in studios, a building always busy but ill-maintained because there was never time or money even to give it a lick of paint, yet a place of fond memories by all who used its offices, studios, canteen and Club. The second protagonist is the World Service – internationally renowned for the veracity of its News Bulletins, but undervalued and often salami-sliced by its paymasters in the British government, an institution of the highest ideals but also strange, even Byzantine, in its managerial practices. The third protagonist is the author, who spent twenty years working for the World Service in Bush House, praised for his journalistic skills but also officially 'reprimanded' and then abruptly sacked, yet rescued and resettled – a veritable 'square peg' in this august institution of neat round holes. And all this against the backcloth of disputes and issues uncomfortably similar to the disputes and issues of forty years later – Harold Wilson's European referendum of 1975, the form of austerity which went under the name of 'monetarism', the international shock and concern which greeted the election of a right-wing President in the United States.

Bush House was built between the two world wars by the Bush Terminal Company, the business vehicle of the New York entrepreneur, Irving T. Bush. He had inherited a fortune from his father, Rufus T. Bush, who sold his waterfront oil refinery in Brooklyn to Standard Oil and promptly retired to devote the remainder of his life to ocean sailing. Irving was also a keen yachtsman, but his main interests were his business empire and collecting paintings. In the mid-1880s he began building Bush Terminal, an enormous warehousing, storage and manufacturing facility on the site of his father's refinery, employing 25,000 people. From there he went on building – first the 30-storey Bush Tower on 42nd Street in Manhattan, just south of Times Square, then a winter mansion in Florida and finally Bush House in London.

Bush House, claimed by Irving to be the most expensive building in the world at £2,000,000, was intended to bring together displays of transatlantic trade and social space, but the Depression intervened. The Centre Block with its marble fittings and architectural features was formally opened in 1925 – the opening ceremony on 4 July 1925 was performed by the former Foreign Secretary, Lord Balfour, famous for the 'Balfour Declaration' which guaranteed the Jewish people 'a homeland' in Palestine. The ceremony included the unveiling of the two entrance statues *(above)* by the American artist Malvina Hoffman. The wings were finished later to less ambitious design and without the use of marble – the North-West Wing in 1928,

North-East Wing in 1929, South-East Wing in 1930 and South-West Wing in 1935 when the whole development was declared complete. Bush House remained a trade centre during the 1930s despite the slump in world trade but in 1938, as international tensions seemed to be leading to war, many of the American companies retreated across the Atlantic.

The BBC External Services

The BBC came late to international broadcasting, particularly in languages other than English. The Empire Service, broadcasting on shortwave, had been founded in 1932 and aimed principally at English speakers across the British Empire. In his first Christmas Message, King George V said the service was intended for 'men and women, so cut off by the snow, the desert, or the sea, that only voices out of the air can reach them.' The first foreign language service was Arabic, launched in January 1938 to counter broadcasts by Italian Fascist radio aimed at North Africa and the British Mandate in Palestine; two months later, the BBC began broadcasting in Spanish and Portuguese in response to German propaganda in Latin America. Foreign language broadcasts to Europe began in September of the same year at the height of the Munich Crisis – but almost as a government after-thought. Two days before the Munich Agreement was signed by Germany, Great Britain, France and Italy – permitting Adolf Hitler to annex the Sudetenland of Czechoslovakia – the Prime Minister, Neville Chamberlain, was due to broadcast to the nation and at the very last moment the government decided that the BBC should also broadcast his speech in French, German and Italian. In that haphazard manner the BBC's European Service was born. With the outbreak of war in September 1939, BBC broadcasts in European languages kept pace with Germany's occupation of the countries where those languages were spoken. Thus – as Gerard Mansell described in *Let Truth Be Told, 50 Years of BBC External Broadcasting* – by 1945 the BBC was broadcasting from 45 high-powered shortwave transmitters in 45 languages.

The Overseas Services, including the old Empire Service, and the European Services were located at first in Broadcasting House in Portland Place. However, on 15 October 1940 the building was hit by a delayed action bomb, which came through the seventh floor and fell two floors down to rest in the Music Library on the fifth floor.

Bruce Belfrage was reading the 'Nine O'clock News' on the Home Service when the explosion took place. Listeners heard a dull thud, there was a slight pause, a whispered "are you all right?" and Bruce Belfrage went on reading the news as if nothing had happened. Just at the same time, in a nearby studio, another news reader, Carl Brinitzer, was in the process of broadcasting a German news bulletin. He too carried on without detectable signs of alarm, and even the most attentive listener in Germany would not have known what had just happened. [Mansell, p. 113]

The building was evacuated but not before eight people were killed when the bomb eventually exploded.

Another evacuation took place over the following months. The Overseas Services relocated around the corner to 200 Oxford Street, the former Peter Robinson department store on the corner of Great Portland Street. The European Service went first to studios at a disused skating rink at Maida Vale and then from January 1941 to Bush House. All these locations were chosen because they had basement areas suitable for radio studios – those in the basement and lower ground of Bush House were still being built, and those below 200 Oxford Street had the disadvantage during certain recordings of picking up the noise of Central Line trains entering Oxford Circus underground station.

The move to Bush House was done in a hurry and there was no time – or government money – to redesign the interior for broadcasting operations. Rooms and corridors in the South-East Wing were not big enough to cope with the large numbers thrust into them. One senior government official, Robert Bruce Lockhart, who visited offices on the lower ground, found conditions 'terrible . . . forty to fifty feet below ground, no air-conditioning, too little space and very indifferent ventilation', he wrote. There were reports of people emerging from offices unable to breathe and reference was made in newspapers to 'slum conditions'. In the summer of 1941 the Labour MP, Philip Noel Baker, took up the cause of the broadcasters in Bush House or – as he called it in the House of Commons for the new location of the European Services was now a security issue – 'the Black Hole of Tooting Bec'. Whether that confused Goering and the Luftwaffe is not recorded. Life in Bush House gradually improved, but the feeling survived that a quart had been squeezed into a pint pot and that there were never enough resources to make the former marketing forum into a dedicated broadcasting centre. When I began working in the South-East Wing in 1969, the offices were still too small to accommodate all the desks, lockers, tape recorders and people crammed into them, and the studios were too few for the all the broadcasts and recordings required of them.

* * * * *

Once the problems were put right – or at least acknowledged – the European Service had a dramatic and fascinating war. Frenetic activity was the order of the day in Bush House as hundreds of newcomers from scores of different language services competed for studio and room space. There was also an invasion of different bodies seeking air time and control of the broadcasts. There was the Foreign Office which provided the funding and sought to influence how it was spent, as well as the newly-established Ministry of Information; there was the BBC management and the directorate of External Services, sometimes working against each other; there were all the egos represented in the different language services, especially the highly influential heads of services. Then there were the governments in exile of the occupied countries, some of which like the Free French actually attended editorial meetings in Bush House. There were also the cloak-and-dagger bodies established for white or black propaganda to occupied Europe – the Political Warfare Executive, set up in the autumn of 1941, actually had offices in Bush House.

Quite separate and insulated from these competing influences was the Newsroom which was charged with maintaining the credibility of the BBC in those crucial early years of the war. That credibility was founded on three pillars: accuracy, comprehensiveness and consistency – in other words, the truth must be told to everyone and there could be no question of the BBC broadcasting something in English but a quite different version in French or German. The independence of the Newsroom extended to the translators, who at that time formed a special department away from the foreign language programme organisers. The translators were constantly monitored by 'language supervisers'.

The French Service enjoyed a more exciting war than most. When the leader of the 'Free French', General Charles de Gaulle, began broadcasting to his occupied compatriots in June 1940, a keen eye was kept on what he said. The general never admitted it in his memoirs, but on occasion he was required to drop a sentence which offended BBC or Foreign Office policy. The broadcasts were made while the French Service was still in Broadcasting House, but the microphone he used – the chunky BBC-Marconi Type A mike – was still in use when I worked in Bush House.

Then there was the remarkable 'V' campaign. It was the idea of the Belgian programme organiser, Victor de Lavaleye – responding to a suggestion by a young refugee from Brussels that Belgians ought to be made aware of their feelings for the Allies. In a broadcast on 14 January 1941 he proposed that French-speaking Belgians should chalk up the letter 'V' wherever they could, to show they believed in an ultimate Allied victory. The idea was an immediate success not only in the French-speaking part of Belgium, but over the border in France as well as in Flemish-speaking areas and the Netherlands where the 'V' also stood for *Vrijheid* – freedom. As the 'V' campaign spread to other occupied countries, Douglas Ritchie, the deputy editor of European Service News, came up with the brilliant idea of transmitting the 'V' sign as sound. Thus the Morse code for the letter 'V' –*di-di-di-dah* which also happened to be the opening bars of Beethoven's Fifth Symphony – was pressed into service and the following day, 28 June 1941, the Morse letter 'V' on drums was introduced. It then became the call sign for the BBC's News throughout Europe. The 'V' for Victory campaign was praised in a speech in June 1941 by the Prime Minister, Winston Churchill, who thereafter began using it as his personal gesture – carefully showing supporters the palm of his hand, not the back.

In 1940 the BBC opened its studios for the Free French to launch 'Radio Londres'. It began with the words *'Ici Londres! Les Français parlent aux Français'* (*'This is London! The French speaking to the French'*) and was intended like the 'V' campaign to make people aware of their support for the Allies – important in France because of the existence of the collaborationist Vichy government in the South, headed by Marshal Phillipe Pétain. Radio Londres was also used to boost the nerve of the Resistance and to ferment unrest, including de Gaulle's call for the streets of Paris to be emptied for one hour.

Later they became a vehicle for the Special Operations Executive (SOE) to send coded messages to its agents and the Resistance at large. They were usually no more than one brief sentence, sometimes amusing but always obscure except to the agents for whom they were intended – such as 'Jean has a long moustache' or 'there is a fire at the butcher's store'. Occasionally, they were of a personal nature. Harry Rée – code named 'César' and celebrated for persuading the local director of a Peugeot car factory to cooperate in its sabotage – was told of the birth of his daughter, Janet, in 1943 with the message *'Clémentine ressemble à sa grand-mère'* [*www.messages-personnels-bbc-39-45.fr/pdf*]. Harry Rée was later a renowned educationalist, as head of Watford Boys Grammar School, a professor at York University and finally a comprehensive school teacher at Woodbury Downs in north London. His daughter, Janet, was a friend of my wife.

* * * * *

Eventually other parts of Bush House were occupied by the BBC. In November 1957 the Overseas Services vacated Oxford Street and moved into the spacious rooms of the Centre Block, thus bringing all parts of the External Services under one roof for the first time since 1940. The move enabled a new BBC canteen to be created under the carpark between the South East Wing and Centre Block. Some years later, with the move of the India Library Reading Room from the Lower Ground, the BBC Club was able to move into the Centre Block from its former site across the Strand in Surrey Street. For a while in the 1970s the BBC World Service occupied the North-East Wing, housing parts of the South European Service.

The move of the Overseas Services to Bush House came a year after the 'Suez Crisis' which posed a clutch of problems for the BBC, as it did for the nation at large. But the Overseas Services were expanding in response to the changes taking place in Britain's role as a colonial power. New nations – India, Pakistan and Burma (now Myanmar) – had emerged in Asia and there was the prospect of further independent governments in the Caribbean and Africa, especially after the 'Wind of Change' speech in 1960 by Prime Minister Harold Macmillan. In Europe, Britain and its allies in the NATO alliance were engaged in the 'Cold War' with the Soviet Union. I arrived in Bush House in 1969 and the mood in the

European Services was heavily obsessed with confronting the propaganda of Russia and the Soviet bloc. The Overseas Services and the World Service in English, on the other hand, were more up-beat. Away from Europe, new transmitters were operating and relay stations had been opened in what is now Malaysia, in Cyprus at Limassol and on Masirah Island at the mouth of the Persian Gulf.

From the 1970s, however, the trend of the World Service was not expansion but retrenchment and closures. With the British economy lurching from crisis to crisis, a number of commissions were set up to look at the future of the World Service. One of the more radical was carried out in 1977 by the Central Policy Review Staff, a think-tank based in Downing Street, which recommended that the BBC should concentrate on the parts of the world where freedom of information was restricted and cut back in other areas. The report wanted the External Services to stop broadcasting between 8pm and 4am each day and recommended that all broadcasting to Europe should cease except for those to the Communist bloc. The cuts would have amounted to 40 per cent of broadcast output and the BBC strongly resisted them. The opposition within Britain to the cuts was so strong that the Labour government under James Callaghan backed down.

But the reprieve did not last long: governments of both parties were intent on cutting back the overall expense of the BBC and its international broadcasts in particular. Transmissions in Italian, Spanish, Portuguese, Finnish and French for Europe were discontinued in the 1980s, following Dutch, Hebrew and Malay some years earlier. Broadcasts in German ended in March 1999, after research showed that the majority of German listeners tuned into the English service. In 2005 it was announced that broadcasts in Bulgarian, Croatian, Czech, Greek, Hungarian, Kazakh, Polish, Slovak, Slovene and Thai would end by March 2006, to finance the launch in 2007 of TV news services in Arabic and Persian. Romanian broadcasts ceased in 2008 and in 2011 the closure of the Albanian, Macedonian, Portuguese for Africa, Serbian, and English for the Caribbean services was announced. This reflected the financial situation the Corporation faced following the transfer of responsibility for the World Service from the Foreign Office, so that it would in future have to be funded from the BBC television licence fee. Following that change of responsibilities, the Russian,

Ukrainian, Mandarin Chinese, Turkish, Vietnamese, Azeri, and Spanish for Cuba services ceased all broadcasting by radio, and the Hindi, Indonesian, Kyrgyz, Nepali, Swahili services plus those in the languages of Rwanda and Burundi ceased shortwave transmissions. The British government announced that the three Balkan countries had wide access to international information, and so broadcasts in the local languages had become unnecessary.

The change in funding – from the 'Grant-in-Aid' which came out of the budget of the Foreign and Commonwealth Office to part of the BBC's television licence fee – took effect on 1 April 2014. It was a momentous change for an April Fool's Day, but it had been on the cards for some time. From 2010, when the coalition Conservative-Liberal Democrat government introduced the first of many austerity budgets, government funding on broadcasting had been under threat. The licence fee itself had seemed at times to be threatened. In many respects, the change in funding was to the advantage of the World Service since it was freed from government austerity. But, taken together with the end of the BBC's lease on Bush House, it was a major cultural shock. The last News bulletin was broadcast from the traditional home of the World Service on 12 July 2012; thereafter all the staff of the World Service in English and the other 27 languages worked from offices on the ground floor of the expanded Broadcasting Centre at Portland Place. No longer could they complain of pokey, ill-lit offices; now their complaints were of open-plan working and lack of privacy.

In a valedictory comment on these momentous changes, 'World Service Bush House' was the phrase used by John Tusa – managing director of the World Service from 1986-93 – to link the building with the broadcasts and broadcasters:

The symbiotic relationship between place, purpose and behaviour can be overstated; but the paradoxical possibility that a building unsuited for broadcasting and journalistic activities actually released a synergistic rush of creativity cannot be ruled out. Nor can the strong feeling of many that the sheer eccentricity, the individuality of Bush House fortified the World Service's sense of itself. However you define it, World Service Bush House was real.

Tusa's 'Farewell to Bush House' was published in a collection of reminiscences of 'Bushmen' and 'Bushwomen' – *Tales from Bush House*, collected by Hamid Ismailov, Marfie Gillespie and Anna Aslanyan, and published soon after the last broadcast from the home of the World Service since the 1940s. It is an amusing, affectionate, occasionally revealing collection, showing just what a vital, invigorating life it was – from the visits by kings, presidents and other notable interviewees and the occasional exhilarating contact with listeners to studio mishaps, equipment failures and unlikely friendships in the BBC Club or the sprawling subterranean canteen. It bore out how Tusa imagined that the rest of the BBC viewed Bush House: 'peopled by amiable well-intentioned and well-informed eccentrics'. At the same time, affirmed Tusa, 'the World Service was undoubtedly the most successful and most reliable international broadcaster; research said so, anecdotage said so, our competitors said so'. All of that was true and needed to be said to a nation which took the World Service for granted when it was funded by grant-in-aid from the Foreign Office, and would probably underplay its value even more when it was yet another adjunct of the BBC's sprawling empire.

* * * * *

And yet there was something else, something quite different that characterized working in Bush House. There was a tension existing not too far beneath the surface between the broadcast managers and the creative broadcasters, between the high purpose of projecting the best image of the United Kingdom and the often gritty reality of life in modern Britain. I experienced this tension whenever I wrote talks about the 'Troubles' in Northern Ireland. That particular tension was a product of the Cold War when Britain felt it had to project itself as a parliamentary democracy to listeners whose democracy had been taken from them by a totalitarian power. At times this was achieved by a committee or semi-secret body like the Information Research Department (IRD) of the Foreign Office looking over the shoulder of the broadcasters. *Commentary* – a five-minute programme of analysis or background following the News – was closely watched and vetted by these secret censors, particularly at times of crisis like the 1956 Suez affair when a Foreign Office official was stationed in Bush House – and given lots of cups of tea, but few scripts.

But paternal attitudes towards broadcasting went deeper and were survivals from the colonial past. From its earliest days in the 1930s, the External Services identified their regional managers as 'heads' – Head of the Eastern Service, Head of the European Service, Head of the Arabic Service, and so on – while the managers or editors of different language services were merely 'programme organisers' and the actual broadcasters 'programme assistants'. A professor of Gujerati, for example, might be the most literate exponent of that language in the world but if he was appointed to lead the Gujerati Section he could never be called 'Head of the Gujerati Service', only Gujerati Programme Organiser. Journalists of some years' standing in their own countries might find themselves managed or even censored by a Head with a background in the Colonial Service or university, whose main allegiance was to an ill-defined British view of the world. Often the censorship was self-censorship, applied in a very British spirit of persuasion – 'I say, old chap, don't you think?'.

I began to think of the people in Bush House who did not quite 'fit in', the 'square pegs' so to speak – and how the BBC management and Personnel (as we used to call Human Resources) handled them. I was fascinated by the case of Anatol Goldberg *(opposite)*, whose talks I often recorded for *Commentary*. Anatol as I knew him was the Chief Commentator of the World Service and very kind and generous to junior newcomers like me. I soon learned that he was one of the most talented linguists ever employed by the BBC, as well as a fount of good sense. He was born in St. Petersburg before the Communist Revolution and spent his childhood in Germany. Later he studied Chinese and Japanese at the Berlin School of Oriental Studies and, when he came to Britain on the outbreak of war in 1939, he joined the BBC Monitoring Service, working in German, Russian and Spanish. When the BBC Russian Service began broadcasting in 1946, he joined it and progressed through the ranks to become its Head.

In the 1950s, following the death of Stalin, Anatol was accused by the IRD (Information Research Department) at the Foreign Office of being 'ambivalent' towards the Soviet Union: articles attacking him appeared in the Press, a question was asked in the House of Commons, and eventually the management of the External Services

Anatol Goldberg MBE

replaced Anatol as Head of the Russian Service. But they then made him the Chief Commentator, thus extending his influence beyond the purely Russian Service and allowing him to tell the world of his more nuanced attitude towards the Soviets.

In a similar manner, though perhaps not so dramatic, BBC management and Personnel handled other 'square pegs'. My friend Feyyaz Fergar used often to write poetry instead of translating the News into Turkish: the BBC then made him Turkish Programme Organiser. Another friend, who had been born in Egypt and knew Arabic from childhood, was made Assistant Head of the Arabic Service but became the target of a newspaper campaign because he was Jewish; BBC Management promptly moved him to become Head of a different service. And when I was dismissed from the post of Arabic Programme Organiser, the Managing Director External Broadcasting affirmed that the action was not disciplinary and paid fulsome tribute to my competence as a journalist. I was then 'resettled' as Greek Programme Organiser and given a handsome budget to interview thirteen world leaders about their views on the US presidency of Ronald Reagan. Thus it was with many resettlement cases or, as I would label them, 'square pegs'.

2.
A Talks Writer

I came to Bush House in the Sixties as a freelance or, in BBC jargon, an 'Outside Contributor'. Outside Contributors (OCs) were people – men mostly at that time but also some women – who could amplify or fill out the News with background information or relevant comment. They were drawn from the ranks of the national newspapers, then still based in Fleet Street less than a mile from Bush House, or from the London School of Economics and Political Science (the LSE) just across the road in Aldwych, or Kings College on the opposite side of Bush House in the Strand. Other commentators were employed from farther afield, provided they did not claim exorbitant travel or accommodation expenses. The commodity required of them was a 'Talk', a scripted piece of prose, usually of four to five minutes duration when read in a normal voice, without too many long or obscure words or technical terms. The Outside Contributor might be expected to broadcast the Talk but in any event it had to be suitable for translation in up to 70 other languages. The Talk was infinitely more acceptable than an interview – interviews had to be transcribed before they could be translated and, besides, they were unpredictable and therefore potentially dangerous. Anyone who said: 'I haven't time to write a Talk, but I'll come in for an interview', was usually told: 'We'll get back to you'.

At the time I was employed by *The Observer* or, to be precise, the Observer Foreign News Service. The OFNS – often known by its telegraphic address 'Servob' – was the syndication service of the Sunday newspaper, permitting overseas clients such as *The Washington Post* or *Straits Times* to reproduce *Observer* material. This was supplemented Monday to Friday by specially commissioned articles by *Observer* staff writers and correspondents overseas. My job as assistant editor of Servob was to commission and sub-edit these Monday-to-Friday scripts before they were sent out by telex – this was long before the use of fax or email. It was not a job for a writing journalist, as the editor of my previous newspaper had warned me: 'You'll be essentially a subeditor and you'll be bored,' said Mark Barrington Ward of the *Oxford Mail* – and he was right. At the *Oxford Mail* I had been a reporter, leader writer and local political correspondent. One of my proudest assignments was reporting the declaration of the 1966 General Election in the constituency of Buckingham, where the winner was the Labour Party candidate, Captain Ian Maxwell MC – or Robert Maxwell, 'the bouncing Cheque' as the *Financial Times* dubbed him:

> *In Buckingham Market Square the crowds began to gather at about 11 o'clock. It was a damp morning but the sun had come out, illuminating the Labour supporters on the west side of the square and casting into shadow the Conservatives gathered within and just outside the White Hart Hotel. There was a rendition of 'The Red Flag' from the Labour side, many of whom were railway workers from Wolverton. Then a woman in a red anorak led her dog across the square and allowed it to piddle against the pillars of the Tories' hotel. Shouts of glee from her followers. At 12.35 the returning officer and candidates appeared at the Town Hall window. Labour had gained the seat with a majority of 1,481 and Maxwell said it was gratifying to have been able to help Harold Wilson increase the majority he needed to form a stable and effective government. Mrs Elaine Kellett, Conservative, surrounded by her family and in tears, conceded defeat while her supporters tried to sing 'Land of Hope and Glory' above the din. So Robert Maxwell became an MP, though not the honoured and influential one that he expected: his highest office was chairman of the House of Commons Catering Committee.*

There was little opportunity for such reportage at Servob, although the editor did allow me to write a few articles to add to the syndication packages. He was Ronald Harker and he was also Night Editor of *The Observer* on Saturdays, which meant that he was not in the Servob office on Mondays and on other days left much of the editing to me. I was fond of Ronnie Harker, a large and self-confident Yorkshireman, given to turning a fine phrase and pronouncing foreign names, like *Trafal-gár* and the *Himá-layas*, with the correctness that betrayed the true traveller – or perhaps a poseur. In late 1968 my frustration with my role at Servob was so great that I asked Ronnie Harker if he could arrange a transfer for me to *The Observer* proper. After a few weeks, a reply came down from the office of the Editor, the Hon. David Astor, who had taken advice from the Managing Editor, Ken Obank: 'There is no chance of Perman working for the Sunday paper – he cannot write!' I was devastated. Had I not been writing for Servob, with articles over my name published by the *New Zealand Herald*, the *New Nigerian*, the Jamaican *Daily Gleaner*, the *Jersey Post* and even the *Washington Post*? I was determined not to take this dismissal lying down.

One thing I did was to help form an *Observer* chapel of the National Union of Journalists (NUJ) and put myself forward to be elected Father of the Chapel. David Astor, true to his patrician liberalism, had long opposed the unionisation of the paper's journalists and called me to his office to explain myself. Journalists were not trade union material, he said, they were like barristers, novelists or Members of Parliament – independent practitioners of their professional craft. I replied that what we wanted was a fair wage and equity and that one of his reporters had a County Court summons against him for defaulting on his household rates. Astor replied that, if I gave him the name of the reporter, he would see that the rates bill would be paid. There was no meeting of minds between David Astor, the great champion of liberal causes, and the majority of his journalists who soon joined the *Observer* chapel of the NUJ. Years later, the Astor family sold the newspaper to the Atlantic Richfield oil company and the NUJ chapel had a vital role to play in negotiating redundancy terms for its journalists.

* * * *

My other response to David Astor's snub was to begin freelancing elsewhere. It was Neal Ascherson, the Eastern Europe affairs editor, who put the idea into my head. 'Why don't you go along to the BBC at Bush House and write for the African Service? They're crying out for people and will take almost anything.' I said I had never been to Africa but Neal, who had and had written a gripping book about Belgian colonial policy in the Congo, said lack of experience did not matter. So I duly presented myself at Bush House and was interviewed by Elliot Watrous, Head of the African Service. The openings, it seemed, were many. There were African language services, broadcasting in Hausa, Somali and Swahili, and they were all hungry for translatable four-minute Talks on world affairs. There were English-language programmes, particularly *Focus on Africa*, and they too wanted fresh commentators. Last but not least, there was a new programme aimed at Rhodesia and specially financed by the Foreign and Commonwealth Office to target and, I supposed, try to overthrow the rebel settler regime of Ian Smith. It was *The World and Rhodesia*, edited by a brash Yorkshireman called Frank Barber, and broadcast twice a day from a medium-wave transmitter in Francistown in Botswana. This was the programme that, in Neal Ascherson's words, would take almost anything. Week after week I went along to Bush House with scripts about anti-Smith feeling in Britain, the boom in sales of Japanese calculators to Zambia and so forth. It seemed an odd way of trying to bring down Ian Smith and his cronies, but that and economic sanctions were the only weapons available to Prime Minister Harold Wilson once he had decided not to send in British troops to fight their 'kith and kin'.

The World and Rhodesia was a token and doomed to an early end since the medium-wave transmitter on which it was carried reached only the suburbs of Bulawayo and not the capital, Salisbury (now Harari). However, I did make one live broadcast for the African Service. On 9 April 1968 I was just about to leave Bush House to return to Servob when the Ugandan-born editor of *Focus on Africa*, Israel Wamala, asked if I would stay on to describe the funeral of Dr Martin Luther King, the assassinated US civil rights leader. I agreed and waited by the television, and waited and waited. Eventually I made my broadcast but it was far too late to return to Servob.

In the same period, I also freelanced for the US magazine *Presbyterian Life*, edited in Philadelphia by the father of Kevin Cadigan, with whom I had shared digs in Oxford. All the articles had a religious angle though their tone was secular – for example, I interviewed Bruce Kenrick, the Free Church minister who had set up the Notting Hill Housing Trust which later evolved into the homelessness charity, Shelter. I also conducted interviews in Northern Ireland. The point was to explain to American Presbyterians why their co-religionists – the official Presbyterian Church in Ireland – were trying to calm religious tensions in the province, while Ian Paisley's Free Presbyterian Church was fanning the flames of sectarianism. I travelled up and down the Shankill and Falls roads of Belfast interviewing community leaders but could not interview Dr Ian Kyle Paisley – he was serving a three-month sentence in jail.

The 10½ x 14 ins leaving card for the FOC (Father of the Chapel) of the NUJ at The Observer, with inside "all those in favour" signed by 72 journalists, including the Editor, the Hon. David Astor.

Eventually the time came for me to leave *The Observer* and go, inevitably, to the BBC External Services at Bush House. In fact, I applied for two BBC jobs at the same time – one to be a producer in the English-language World Service, the other to be a Talks Writer on European affairs for the language services. I got the latter job which seemed the best use of my experience with the African Service, but the appointment may have been influenced by my performance at an odd preliminary interview. Seated outside a pub in Mortimer Street, near Broadcasting House, were Michael Sumner, a senior producer in the World Service, and Stanley Mayes, a senior Talks Writer, vetting a succession of candidates over drinks. It was my first experience of the *buddy-buddy* culture at the Beeb. Much of the meeting was devoted to Michael Sumner recounting and then laughing at jokes on *Rowan and Martin's Laugh-In*, a television programme I had never seen, which Sumner found incredible. I left the *Observer* in September 1969 and received a good luck card *(opposite)*, signed by virtually the whole editorial staff of the newspaper, including Ronnie Harker and David Astor himself. David Haworth who took over my trade union role later wrote: 'I am adding my personal thanks for the superb job you did in getting our Chapel established and put into good running order. Since I assumed your old duties temporarily – at least – I have come to appreciate the difficult work you did with such ease and humour'.

* * * * *

My first job at the External Services was to understudy a splendidly knowledgeable Talks Writer on European affairs named Josephine Gamon, who was about to retire. Our unit was called Central Current Affairs Talks and it was headed by an even more knowledgeable woman, Elizabeth Barker, who had been the BBC's first woman Diplomatic Correspondent – and who was also about to retire. At that time, Elizabeth had a Chief Assistant in Elliot Watrous, whom I had met when he was Head of the African Service. Other members of the unit included Stanley Mayes, whom I had met at the pre-interview, and Leslie Stone who had joined the External Services from Westminster Press where he had been Diplomatic Correspondent and chief leader writer. The *Oxford Mail* was part of Westminster Press and Leslie was somewhat miffed when he learned that, instead of using his leading articles, the editor had often commissioned alternatives from me. Leslie was the main Talks Writer on British politics; he was also a considerable expert on the United States, having spent a year in Washington following his Oxford DPhil thesis on President F.D. Roosevelt. He and I got on well together since we had both worked for the provincial Press and had both been born in Islington, although he boarded at Christ's Hospital School in Sussex while I went to the local grammar school. We even tried a family get-together, but his Jewish wife and my half Jewish wife did not hit it off.

Central Current Affairs Talks was on the first floor of the South-East Wing of Bush House, which it shared with part of the French Section and South European Service. There were five offices, all of them too small for the furniture they contained. To get to my seat I had to shuffle past my secretary's chair and then squeeze between her desk, my desk and a filing cabinet, which contained the back Talks written by Jo Gamon and two Outside Contributors, who also used the office from time to time. The day began with a Morning Meeting, held in the slightly larger office which Elizabeth Barker inhabited as Head. Here possible topics of the day were discussed, subjects allocated, and then a list of the day's Talks, with the times they were expected to be available, was agreed, quickly typed up on a Banda machine stencil so that the Head could take copies to the Controller's Meeting. Sometimes Elizabeth or Elliot Watrous would return to say: 'Sorry, they didn't like it. Instead you are to write about …'

When I arrived at Bush House in 1969, the News was dominated by events in Northern Ireland. There had been serious rioting in Londonderry (or Derry) in August – the so-called 'Battle of the Bogside' – and the provincial government at Stormont in Belfast had asked the British government for troops to be sent in. This made newspaper headlines throughout Europe and it was decided there should be a Talk explaining why the troops were there. As I had been in Belfast recently, I was asked to write it – which I did with the utmost concern for fairness to all parties: the Northern Ireland government, the British government, Protestants and Catholics, even the Irish government in Dublin. The Talk was to be broadcast in the sensitive *Commentary* slot, after the evening News bulletin. When I had finished writing it, a council of war was convened to see if it conformed to BBC policy and was indeed broadcastable. In attendance were Elizabeth Barker (my boss), two members of staff born in Northern Ireland (one Protestant, one Catholic) and the Chief Commentator, Maurice Latey, who had previously been Head of the East European Service, broadcasting to people behind the 'Iron Curtain'. They examined my Talk, argued about it a little and decided I could broadcast it – with one addition. At Maurice Latey's suggestion, I had to add that Northern Ireland was part of the United Kingdom and held elections to send Members of Parliament to the House of Commons at Westminster – which of course I did.

* * * * *

In 1969 the United Kingdom became a candidate for membership of the European Economic Community (EEC), usually known then as the 'Common Market'. Britain had first applied to join the EEC in 1961 but that application was vetoed by President Charles de Gaulle of France, who feared that British membership would weaken the influence of France and the close Anglo-American relations would lead to the United States increasing its influence in European affairs. De Gaulle resigned in April 1969 and Britain submitted a new membership application. As a result, I went with increasing frequency to Brussels to observe the EEC at work. This was the Community of the original six – Belgium, France, West Germany, Italy, Luxembourg and the Netherlands. Their ministers and other representatives met in the newly constructed Berlaymont Building and the business was conducted mainly in French (but also Dutch, Italian and German) but never in English. There was no European Parliament, no economic integration or euro currency, no 'single market' – but there was the Customs Union created in July 1968. I used to fly to Brussels (no Eurostar trains then) with the World Service News correspondent, Cliff Smith, a Canadian, and together we attended briefings given by ministers of various nationalities. What struck me most forcibly was how every statement and every question was slanted to public opinion back home in Paris, Rome, The Hague or wherever.

In Brussels I recorded an interview with the President of the European Commission, the very Anglophile Belgian lawyer, Jean Rey. He had been one of the founders of the European Coal and Steel Community, so important to the French-speaking part of Belgium from which he came, and had also worked with Jean Monnet and Robert Schuman on setting up the EEC. On the other side of the argument about British entry was one of our regular contributors to *Commentary* – William Pickles of the LSE, where he was a Senior Lecturer alongside his wife, Dorothy, a great expert on modern French history. Bill Pickles was a long-term opponent of British membership and in 1962 had written a Fabian Society pamphlet *Not with Europe – the political case for staying out*. His main argument was that the EEC was dominated by laissez-faire interests alongside federalists, and that the highly-trained bureaucrats who ran it were not effectively controlled by democratic institutions – this was before the creation of the European Parliament. He believed it was the wrong international grouping for Britain to join and that it would soon damage Britain's relations with the countries of the Commonwealth. The pamphlet had some fascinating insights, relevant to the debate which followed the 2016 referendum – for example, that in negotiations the British and Europeans were usually talking at cross purposes, the British believing it was mainly about economics and trade, the Europeans really talking about politics. Bill gave me a copy of the Fabian pamphlet and also a 1920s touring map of Hertfordshire, which I have always treasured. But nothing much happened about British membership until June 1970, when the General Election brought the Conservatives to power under the strongly pro-European Edward Heath.

In addition to writing about Europe, I was responsible for the recording of *Commentary*, the five-minute – or, to be precise, 4 minute 45 seconds – Talk in English which went out after the evening News on the World Service. This introduced me not only to the skills of editing recorded speech (with a razor blade and sticky tape) but also to many of the luminaries of the BBC External Services. There was Maurice Latey, whom I had met early on, his predecessor – both as Head of the Russian Service and Chief Commentator – Anatol Goldberg, the Head of the Polish Section Konrad Syrup, who was an expert on the Katyn massacre of the Polish officer corps, and Hugh Lunghi who had been Winston Churchill's personal interpreter at all of his meetings with Stalin. There were also Outside Contributors, the most colourful of whom was Hella Pick, a gravel-voiced expert on Communist affairs who was said to have taught Anatol Goldberg to dance the tango.

Occasionally, recording *Commentary* with an Outside Contributor could go sadly wrong. One frequent contributor was Sylvain Mangeot, a pleasant, quietly spoken man who had been Diplomatic Correspondent of Reuters news agency; Sylvain had a particular interest in India and the Himalayas, being a frequent visitor to the Kingdom of Sikkim and having written a biography of Lobsang Thondup, one of the leaders of the Dalai Lama's Tibetan government in exile. He liked to come in on a Saturday afternoon to write and record his Talk. One Saturday, I was on duty and went to see how Sylvain was getting on, but found him distraught and almost in tears. He had been dictating his Talk to an agency typist, but when he asked to see the script she showed him a page of gobbledegook: not a single word made sense. He asked her what she thought she had been doing – as I did when I arrived – and the woman said she thought she was typing a foreign language. Having dismissed her with a promise that the agency would hear of it, Sylvain cobbled together his notes for the recording and I typed up a version of sorts for distribution to the language services. It was a ridiculous event and I felt ashamed of the BBC's penurious use of cheap temps. Sylvain was worth so much better than that. Later I learned that he was the son of the famous French violinist, André Mangeot, and had first made his mark as an eleven-year old, illustrating a book of animal poems – *People one ought to know* – by Christopher Isherwood:

> *"It was one of the first things I wrote,"* Isherwood said. *"There was this mews house in Cresswell Place where I worked as secretary to the father, André Mangeot, for about a year. He was a violinist with the string quartet of the Music Society, a very distinguished club where many of the leading musicians, including Pablo Casals, performed.*
>
> *"This very artistic kid did the illustrations - cats and dogs, crocodiles, sharks, frogs, whales, butterflies, a small menagerie - and I wrote the words to go with them. I rattled off the verses for fun; wrote them as fast as my hand moved over the paper."*

* * * * *

In March 1970 Elizabeth Barker retired and was succeeded as Head of Current Affairs Talks by Frank Barber, who had formerly led the ill-fated *World and Rhodesia* programme. Frank was a journalist of the old school – a non-graduate who had worked his way up the profession to a leading role in the old *News Chronicle* newspaper. His particular outlook on life and journalism was a hatred of graduates. As his obituary in 1999 in *The Independent* put it: *Barber was perhaps the last of the old 'clear all wires' newspaper men. Tough as they come, printer's ink in their veins, giving way to modern media but never giving up.'* His son, Lionel Barber, editor of the *Financial Times* – in the Hugh Cudliff Lecture at London College of Communication 31 Jan 2011 – concurred:

> I come from a family of journalists. So does my younger brother, Tony. Our father left school at 15 and started as a copy boy on the Leeds Weekly Citizen *before graduating to Fleet Street and the* BBC World Service. *Frank Barber was a blunt, self-educated*

Yorkshire man, a dedicated sub-editor who never met a paragraph he couldn't cut. He regarded the News business not as a profession but as a vocation.

The *Independent* obituary also commented on Frank's bluntness:

His last period at the BBC was as head of current affairs talks, the political and news centre of overseas broadcasting. He had a remarkable team of experts to draw upon but their very expertise, their donnish – indeed prima-donnish – rather than journalistic approach to news made for many bruising exchanges.

The *'remarkable team of experts'* with whom Barber clashed included Leslie Stone, a Hungarian-born, Scottish-educated Talks Writer, George Schöpflin – later a European professor and Hungarian member of the European Parliament – a Russian-speaking barrister Robert Montgomery and myself. We would meet in the Bush House canteen and plot Barber's downfall. On one occasion in a self-op studio in the South-East Wing, where I was operating the tape-recorder for a *Commentary* by Leslie Stone, someone brought in a whip and symbolically chastised a desk.

Frank certainly lacked admirers, even among the senior members of the department. One such was Henry Barwick, a former soldier and one of the World Service's defence experts. Frank seemed to like him but the feeling was not reciprocated. He was due to retire and Frank insisted on giving him a leaving party, or rather a tea-time glass of sherry with speeches. Henry took this in good part, only rarely pulling a face at Frank's silver words. But afterwards, when Frank had locked the sherry bottle away, Henry beckoned two of us aside and led us across the courtyard, through the Centre Block and into the Aldwych. Still without any word of explanation, he led us to India Place and stood looking up at India House, home of the India High Commission. Henry then told us that his great uncle had been Sir Herbert Baker, the well-known architect and designer of India House. He pointed out the coloured raised medallions on the side of the building, each representing a state during the days of the British Raj. *"Just look at the rhinoceros of Assam,"* he shouted, unable to suppress a fit of the giggles. *"Who does that remind you of?"* It was Frank Barber to a tee and we all joined his laughter.

My major confrontation with Frank Barber came in 1971 when Britain's chief negotiator for EEC membership, Sir Con O'Neill, gave a press conference on the burning issue of the day – the 'Cost of Entry' for the British economy. I went along to the Foreign Office with Cliff Smith from the Newsroom. We heard Sir Con's briefing which was rather odd since the all-important 'Cost of Entry' was put at anything between £10 million and £100 million. Many years later, an unpublished report by Sir Con was revealed to state: 'What mattered was to get into the Community, and thereby restore our position at the centre of European affairs which, since 1958, we had lost.' Furthermore 'it would be in the interests of this country to join the EEC whatever the terms.'

Cliff and I went back to Bush House, clutching copies of Sir Con's statement, and I wrote my Talk on the 'Cost of Entry'. I took it to Frank's office for him to pass before it was reproduced on the Banda machine and distributed to the language services.

"That's no bloody good," said Frank. *"You can't say the cost is between £10 million and £100 million. Our listeners want to know the cost not some wishy-washy estimate."*

"But that's what Sir Con said. That's what his printed statement says."

"Well that's nonsense. You don't join a bloody golf club" – or words to that effect – *"not knowing if it will set you back ten quid or a hundred quid. Go away and work it out."*

"I can't. £10 million and £100 million is what Sir Con said."

"Well give it here – I'll write the effing Talk."

I left his office with Frank poring over Sir Con's handout, trying to work out the exact cost of Britain joining the Common Market. My Talk had been announced in the morning schedule to be available by 12.30 pm, and soon after one o'clock anxious translators began to appear from the language services. At about 2 pm, Maurice Latey arrived to ascertain the fate of the Cost-of-Entry Talk; I showed him the draft of what I had written and explained Frank Barber's objections – Frank himself remained *incognito* behind his office door. Cliff Smith was summoned from the Newsroom and agreed with what I had written. At last, at 5.30 pm, my Talk on the Cost of Entry was issued – as I had written it.

3.
Cublington:
a Blueprint for Resistance

One of the peculiarities – and proud traditions – of World Service Bush House was that it was a haven for writers. Dissidents arrived from Occupied Europe or totalitarian countries clutching manuscripts and were soon setting to work on further books. Zinovy Zinik from Russia, Zdena Tomin from Czechoslovakia and Georgi Markov, the murdered novelist from Bulgaria, are names that spring to mind. There were other famous names like V.S. Naipaul – though not George Orwell as is sometimes claimed, for he worked for the Eastern Service at 200 Oxford Street, not Bush House.

I joined the ranks of book writers almost by accident. It happened in my last months as a Talks Writer. Among the Outside Contributors I recoded in the self-op studio was an engaging character named Edward Ashcroft. He was the retired Head of the South European Service, a biographer of General de Gaulle and the older brother of the actor Dame Peggy Ashcroft. Over coffee in the canteen – or more likely a drink in the BBC Club – I learned that he lived part of the week in London and part in Buckinghamshire near the villages of Wing and Cublington, which had recently been threatened by plans for the third London airport. I had followed the anti-airport campaigning of the villagers with special interest, since I was then living in Harlow, Essex, under the flight-path of another airport site at Stansted. Edward described with great relish the achievements and set-backs of the campaign at Cublington and told me a book about it was planned, to be penned by a well-known television journalist. I thought no more about it until a month later when with a long face Edward said the TV man had withdrawn, leaving a great story for which a publisher – the Bodley Head – had already been signed up but without an author. Would I by any chance be interested? I discussed the matter with Jenny, my wife, and decided I was interested: certainly the advance being offered by the Bodley Head would come in handy after the birth of our third daughter, Alice. So I set to work, reading up on the background from the Bush House cuttings library and making my first visits to Cublington with a BBC tape recorder and introductions from Edward Ashcroft.

Mr Justice Roskill with other members of the Commission on the Third London Airport – the 'dissident' member, Professor Colin Buchanan, is on the far right.

The decision-making on where to locate London's third airport, after Heathrow and Gatwick, was one of the most protracted, expensive and unedifying examples of muddled government thinking in Britain in modern times. It began in the 1950s and went round the houses more than once before arriving back where it had first started, 25 years later. I was going to write that it was '*the* most protracted, expensive and unedifying example' but the subsequent Brexit debate about withdrawing from the European Community would have challenged any such judgement. The starting point for the third London airport was, of course, Stansted in Essex with its 10,000 foot Second World War runway built by the United States Air Force, and that indeed is where the international airport was eventually sited and opened by the Queen in 1991. But in the intervening years, a new form of public inquiry and the resistance to it in the villages of Buckinghamshire made a thoroughly good story, and that was the subject of my book.

The new inquiry was the Roskill Commission, headed by Sir Eustace Roskill, a High Court judge. The main quality he brought to the inquiry was a strong desire to dispense justice and to be seen to be doing so, in a way that earlier decisions had clearly failed to do. Mr Justice Roskill gathered together a team of economists, well versed in the new economic tool of *cost/benefit analysis*, as well as a professor of aircraft design and two planners. The Commission's terms of reference had been set by the government in the main and so the first major task was to produce a short-list of sites. Eventually in February 1969, the short list of four was published – Cublington, Nuthamstead, Thurleigh in Bedfordshire and Foulness – but not including Stansted. The Press seized upon the omission as proof Roskill was radically different from everything that had gone before, but the Commission's rejoinder was that Stansted simply did not make the grade.

I knew that in the book I would have to look critically at the work of the Roskill Commission. I knew also that I would have to describe as fully as possible the resistance to the third London airport at Cublington, including the formation and operation of WARA (the Wing Airport Resistance Association). But what struck me most forcefully, as soon as I had visited the area and got to know some of the activists, was the intense and perhaps unique sense of community there. This sense of community was strong in all the villages but strongest in Stewkley, the largest village, and in Drayton Parslow. My guides – soon to become friends – were Geoffrey Ginn, Ernie Keen, David Stubbs, Mrs Susan Forsyth and Jeremy and Isabel Smith-Cresswell. Of great significance to the anti-airport campaign was a survey commissioned by the Roskill Commission from three sociologists at the University of Essex, which sought information about friends and where they lived: at Cublington, 62 per cent of the people surveyed said that all or most of their friends lived in the same parish as themselves and 84 per cent said that all or most of their friends lived in the local area (as against 56 per cent and 79 per cent at Nuthampstead, and 53 per cent and 72 per cent at Thurleigh). The university survey found that Cublington people felt closer to the land than at the other sites.

There was also a historical dimension to this sense of community. In the Middle Ages, Stewkley did not have a Lord of the Manor, resident or otherwise; its enclosure award in 1814 – later than in neighbouring parishes because the enclosure notices were torn down – showed land ownership more evenly spread; and the break-up of farms for smallholding was well established by 1892. A similar move towards smallholding took place in Drayton Parslow, where the owner of the largest estate – Lord Carrington, who had been in charge of agriculture in the 1905 Liberal government – handed over much of his land in the parish to small holders in 40-, 50- and 60-acre lots.

At Stewkley, as we have seen, the smallholding movement was already in progress. In the 1920s it reached Wing. The last owner of the large estate once held by the Earl of Chesterfield was Lady Wantage, widow of the soldier-politician, Lord Wantage, who had sat in the Commons as Colonel Loyd-Lindsay VC. She directed in her will that her tenants should be offered their farms at a price proportionate to their rents – an acre rented at 5s. being offered at £5. The vice-chairman of WARA, Bill Manning, remembers his grandfather standing surety for neighbours who were trying to buy their land under Lady Wantage's will.

* * * * *

From the beginning, the Roskill Commission created its own research. It was a policy designed to distance the Commission from the political assumptions and untested opinions which had informed earlier decisions about the third London airport. The Community Disruption Study by the sociologists from Essex University was one such piece of research. The most controversial research, however, was that carried out in the name of cost/benefit analysis. This was an economists' tool for public decision making, brought from America and largely unknown in this country until it was used in the planning of the Victoria Line for London Underground. For Roskill it had a three-fold attraction: it was the best check available on the public funds to be spent on what was surely Britain's biggest planned development; it was also a thoroughly objective way of assessing the merits of the four airport sites; and in any case the government had already drawn up an outline of cost/benefit analysis for use in large public schemes.

All well and good. But in trying to be comprehensive, the Commission and its researchers assigned a monetary value to almost every aspect of airport planning. When the cost/benefit analysis was published in January 1970, it rejected any idea that there could be two separate balance sheets – one for the benefits and costs that could be measured in money terms, and another for values that were more subjective. But critics were not persuaded. Instead they asked: into what cash terms would the Research Team translate such disparate items as the destruction of a Norman church, the effect on wild life, the loss of a quiet rural existence or savings in travel terms for both a company director going on business from Manchester to Tokyo as against a Bermondsey dustman taking his wife and children on a package holiday to Majorca? These were not left as arguable points of debate but, instead, incorporated in the final so-called 'passenger-user costs' which put the four airport sites in a sort of league table. For Foulness, out on the coast of Essex, the 'passenger-user costs' were calculated at £1,041 million, for Cublington £887 million, for Thurleigh £889 million and for Nuthampstead £863 million. The only comparable figures produced by the Roskill Commission were the costs of construction which in the case of Foulness on the North Sea coast heavily outweighed all the other sites.

* * * * *

But the decision-making about the third London airport was not made from actual costs and notional valuations. It was played out in public opinion and the media and, ultimately, in the political arena of Parliament. The village activists in WARA sensed this all along. Thus, while the organisation's leaders concentrated on raising money to pay the lawyers – who at a cost of £50,000 it has to be said did a good job, beside and parallel to many more lawyers acting for the two county councils and other public bodies – the activists put their time and energy into capturing the attention of the public. In this they were phenomenally successful, even to the extent of reviving public interest when it was sagging more than once.

The Roskill Commission's report, recommending Cublington as the site for London's third airport, was announced by the Secretary for Trade and Industry, Mr John Davies, in the House of Commons on Friday 18 December 1970. It was the last day before Parliament rose for Christmas. The Press that weekend was overwhelmingly hostile to Roskill and many of the newspapers featured photographs of demonstrations and posters in the villages. At Stewkley, where the congregation trooped out of the Norman church on the Sunday to sing around a bonfire while a band played, they also burned Mr Justice Roskill in effigy. The only bright note that weekend was the minority

The Cublington Tractor Rollout in December 1970

report by the Roskill commissioner, Professor Colin Buchanan of Imperial College, London, who rejected not only the choice of Cublington for the airport but the whole process of cost/benefit analysis on which it was based.

But it was winter and Christmas would soon divert attention away from Cublington – more effort was needed to win back the initiative. And so on 3 January, in freezing fog, 300 tractors and other country vehicles turned out to drive the 28 miles around the perimeter of Roskill's proposed airport: it was sent off by Bill Manning who claimed it was 'the biggest roll-on of agricultural ever put on the road'. The following weekend there was a rally held in the Equestrian Centre at Wing, attended by 8,000 to 20,000 people – depending on which newspaper you read. There were speeches from six MPs – two Labour and four Conservative

The people of Cublington had won and that was the climax and message of my book, published on 31 May 1972. But the people and Brent geese of Foulness had not lost after all. A few years later Stansted was back in the running and that is where – after yet another long and expensive inquiry – the third London airport was eventually built.

Cublington: a Blueprint for Resistance received a good press. The local Bucks newspapers all reviewed it in the first week of publication or soon afterwards, as did my former employers, the *Oxford Mail* and *Oxford Times*. In the following weeks there were reviews in the *Daily Telegraph, Sunday Telegraph, Birmingham Post, Times Educational Supplement, Times Literary Supplement, South Wales Argus* and *The Tablet*. A review in *New Society* pointed out that the government would have rejected Cublington and chosen Foulness even without the local campaign – 'and the author is intelligent and honest enough to admit that'. Overseas there were reviews in the *National Times* in Sydney, Australia, and in *Morgenposten*, a review in Danish. I was interviewed about the book on local radio which was all to the good, but on BBC Television's *Nationwide*, chaired by Sue Lawley, I faced and was brow-beaten by Derrick Wood, chairman of the Friends of Essex and a doughty defender of Foulness and its Brent geese.

The only real criticism of the book came from the barrister, Desmond Fennell, who was the chair of WARA. He objected to my chapter headed 'WARA's Disreputable Brother' in which I described the plans and activities of a 'Home Defence Group' who intended to stay put and resist construction of the airport should the Roskill

Commission's decision be implemented, and also of other instances of direct action. The homes of Sir Eustace Roskill and Peter Masefield, chairman of the British Airports Authority, were daubed with paint and placarded by activists, who were pledged not to inflict lasting damage. However, I did not include in the book a more hair-brained scheme by Edward Ashcroft and his neighbour, the novelist Geoffrey Household, to store explosives with a plan to blow up conduits under the roads, if construction vehicles arrived at Cublington. Most courteously, Desmond Fennell made his views known to me in person rather than in print.

* * * * *

Cublington was not my only book while working in Bush House. It had evidently done well in the shops as well as the reviews, and my publisher, Barney Blackley of Bodley Head, offered me an advance for another title. As he had learned of my theological college past and he worshipped in Berkhamsted, we settled on a book about contemporary church-going in Britain and some of the issues it encountered. *Change and the Churches* was a reasonable piece of extended journalism, but it chronicled a particularly fallow period of Christianity in Britain. It was written and published in 1977 before there was any real discussion or appreciation of the ordination of women as priests and bishops or the non-judgemental acceptance of homosexual believers – let alone gay vicars or other manifestations of LGBT – and certainly before the shocking revelation of sexual abuse (and its concealment) among the leaders of the Anglican, Roman Catholic and other churches. Instead the major theme of *Change and the Churches* was how the various denominations raised, invested and spent their money, and for this it got good reviews but not I think massive sales.

4.
The World Today

In November 1972, I left Current Affairs Talks to become a producer. My new department was called Talks and Features World Service and it produced two daily current affairs programmes – *The World Today*, a 15-minute single-subject feature, and *Twenty-Four Hours*, a 30-minute magazine – as well as a lighter, more cultural 30-minute magazine *Outlook*. All of these were repeated at different times during twenty-four hours to serve different time zones and the availability of different transmitters, short wave and in a few cases medium wave. FN broadcasts came later. In addition, there were special features on political or general topics, made by producers who had been released from the daily grind of scheduled programmes.

T&F (WS) was headed by an upright but rather shy journalist, Robert Milne-Tyte: he had worked on the old *News Chronicle* and before that on the *Oxford Mail*, where he was known as 'Bob Tite'. His deputy was someone I had met before – at the pre-interview in the pub garden – Michael Sumner. He was very much a BBC Club man, usually surrounded by junior producers and studio managers from whom he seldom refused a drink. I liked Michael and got on well with him most of the time, but our paths did not often cross. He was mainly responsible for *Outlook* while Robert managed the current affairs programmes.

The World Today was the main programme I worked on in 1972-73. We had a team of three producers, supported by three secretaries. One producer-cum-secretary would be working on the current day's programme – recording last-minute interviews, editing them for length, composing and typing the linking script, and then recording the programme in a studio, with an announcer voicing the scripted links (at one time it was an actor, until budgets were squeezed) and with a studio manager expertly controlling the microphones and tape machines. A second producer-cum-secretary would be working on the *World Today* for the following day – arranging interviews, booking studios, and so on. The third producer-cum-secretary would be taking it easier – doing the contracts and other documentation of the previous day's *World Today* and researching and possibly making contacts for a later programme. We had an office on the sixth floor of the Centre Block with windows overlooking Kingsway and Aldwych. I was promoted to Senior Producer in September 1973 and had a small partitioned-off area within the office. It was about this time that the ITN newsreader, Trevor MacDonald (now *Sir* Trevor MacDonald), began his broadcasting career as a *World Today* producer.

* * * * *

My first overseas *World Today* was made in Italy. The occasion was the 'Historic Compromise' (*Compromesso storico*) in May 1973 between the ruling Christian Democrats and the Communist Party (PCI). The initiative had come from the PCI leader, Enrico Berlinguer, for whom the overthrow of the left-wing Allende government in Chile showed that Marxist parties could not hope to govern in democratic counties unless they established alliances with more moderate forces. The initiative was well received by the Christian Democrats under their party president, Aldo Moro, a former Prime Minister, and in due course led to an historic alliance between the two major parties at the expense of any existing ties with other parties of the left or the right. It also meant that the PCI began to distance itself from the Soviet Union in a form of 'Eurocommunism' which also found favour among Spanish and French Communists.

I was fortunate in getting an interview with Aldo Moro – thanks to the veteran BBC correspondent David Willey, who the previous year had moved to Rome from being the Diplomatic Correspondent and quickly established good relations with all the political parties. Aldo Moro was an enthusiast for working with the Communists so long as they remained independent from Moscow and embraced the values and aspirations of the Italian public at large. It helped him that the Vatican had given its tacit consent to working with the left-wing atheists – Aldo Moro was, of course, better known for being kidnapped by the anarchist Red Brigade in 1978 and eventually murdered.

It proved more difficult to get an interview with the PCI leader, Enrico Berlinguer, in the time available so David Willey found me a worthy substitute. He was Renato Zangheri, the famous 'Red Mayor' of Bologna, and I interviewed him in his office in the Renaissance palazzo which served as the headquarters of the provincial government of Emilia-Romagna.

The main opposition to the *Compromesso storico* came from the Left, but the parties of the Centre were also unhappy with the new alignment – partly because they could see themselves losing influence with the Christian Democrats who, after all, had governed Italy since the end of the Second World War. I interviewed Ugo La Malta, leader of the Republican Party (PRI) whose argument was that the Communists could not be trusted and the Christian Democrats were in danger of losing touch with the majority of Italian voters. But the most vigorous critique of the new policy was voiced by the Union of Italian Communists (Marxist-Leninist) which had been moving further to the Left since its foundation in 1968 and, after a split, had also left Rome for Milan.

And so for my final interview I travelled to Italy's commercial capital, Milan, the main city of Lombardy, to interview Enzo Todeschini, the university professor who was one of the quadrumvirate leading the Marxist-Leninist party. He worked from the banking district and in his outer office I found a slim Scandinavian blonde secretary trying to type a document without damaging her long painted red nails. *'Ah, I see you have met the Principessa,'* said Prof. Todeschini when at last he arrived: he explained that his Swedish secretary was the wife of the chairman of the merchant bank which owned the building. Both the Princess and her husband were keen supporters of the Marxist-Leninists. The professor's argument against the Historic Compromise was far less interesting than his office setup, but I managed to get a suitable quote for *The World Today*.

* * * * *

In October 1973 I went to Turkey to cover the celebrations for the 50th anniversary of the foundation of the Turkish Republic by Mustafa Kemal Atatürk. The BBC's Foreign Travel booked my flights and hotels and I duly arrived in the capital, Ankara, and booked in at the Bulvar Palas Hotel, a splendid but old-fashioned hostelry which had been recommended to me by the Turkish Programme Organiser, Andrew Mango. No sooner had I unpacked than there was a message that someone was waiting for me at reception. I went down and a small, anxious-looking woman told me that I was in the wrong hotel – foreign journalists covering the anniversary celebrations were staying at the newly-opened Büyük

David and the belly-dancer in Istanbul

(Grand) Hotel as guests of the Turkish government. I explained that – with due respect – I could not be a guest of the Turkish government since the BBC always paid its own way. The woman looked even more worried and went away.

An hour or so later, I was again informed that there was someone asking for me at reception. I went down and found a tall, well-dressed woman who introduced herself to me as 'Yildiz Uztürk, a senior attaché at the Turkish foreign ministry'. I had created all sorts of problems, she said, by my independent attitude with the result that I had got her instead of a junior member of the department – throughout my stay in Turkey she and I would have to get separate bills for every drink, meal or taxi. She said all this with a broad smile, so clearly she welcomed the prospect of accompanying me and asking for separate bills.

My stay in Ankara was pleasant but not culturally exciting – it is not the most beautiful city in Turkey. There was a government reception and a visit to a museum display telling the history of the republic. There was also a visit to a night club, where I was photographed being hugged by a belly-dancer, much to the amusement of John Dickie, Diplomatic Correspondent of the *Daily Mail*, sitting opposite.

For more serious business, Yildiz arranged interviews for me with the leaders of the two main political parties – Süleyman Demirel of the Justice Party and Bülent Ecevit of the Republican People's Party. At the time Turkey had an interim government, following a *coup d'état* two years earlier when the Army overthrew an administration headed by Mr Demirel. Turkey had had a series of military coups at that time, including one in 1960 which led to the execution of the Prime Minister, Adnan Menderes. I found my interview with Mr Demirel disappointing: for obvious reasons he was rather muted in his comments about the Turkish military. The interview with Bülent Ecevit, on the other hand, was pure joy – he had worked in London at the Turkish Embassy, studied Bengali and Sanskrit at SOAS (the School of Oriental and African Studies), spoke excellent English and knew many of the people currently working in Bush House. Some years later, when I was working in the Greek Section, I met Ecevit again and he recited for me in Greek poems by Cavafy and Ritsos.

At the beginning of my last week in Turkey, Yildiz said that, although I refused to be a guest of the Turkish government, they were determined to show me their hospitality. As a result we were given a car and driver and went to Kuşadasi on the Aegean coast. We stayed in the Öküz Mehmed Pasha Caravanserai, a seventeen-century Ottoman guesthouse. Finally, we came back to Istanbul before my flight to London. I was staying in the old Park Hotel, a rambling building in wide gardens beside the Bosporus, and I was joined for supper by Yildiz and her Swiss husband – she was not asking for a separate bill on that occasion. Turkey at that time was a thoroughly cosmopolitan state with a sizeable Jewish minority in Istanbul, and all the waiters in the Park Hotel appeared to be Jewish. The dining room was empty apart from our party and we sat by the windows, far from the door. At Yildiz's suggestion, I ordered a bottle of the local Istanbul wine, Kavaklidere red, and one of the waiters brought it for me to taste. 'If you don't like it, send it back,' said Yildiz, which I did. She then told me of the custom that bottles which have been opened and sent back became drinks for the staff. Accordingly, I rejected the next five bottles of the Kavaklidere wine and the waiters formed a line to the door, passing the bottles to and fro. It was a memorable last night in Turkey, thoroughly enjoyed by me, Yildiz Uztürk and her husband – and half a dozen grinning waiters.

'Europe: the people will decide'

1974 in Britain was a year of confrontation and confusion. It began with a national coalminers' strike and the imposition of a 'three-day week' to conserve the use of electricity. This was an anomalous policy with all sorts of oddities and contradictions. The two national broadcasts – the BBC and ITV – were told to stop broadcasting at 10.30 pm but, when that caused a nationwide rush to the kitchen and a power surge, they were then told to stagger the shutdown. In Bush House, the canteen closed early and the BBC Club (like nearly all pubs) did not open at all; non-programme staff were sent home early with the result that we all had to work twice as hard to stockpile programmes. The three-day week left a lasting impression in people's memories, but it did not last long. The Conservative government was struggling and in desperation Prime Minister Edward Heath called a general election for 28 February – for which all restrictions on television were immediately lifted. The election resulted in a hung parliament with no majority for any party. Heath attempted to put together a coalition with the Liberal Party under Jeremy Thorpe. When this failed, a minority Labour government was sworn in, headed by Harold Wilson. He called a second election on 11 October which gave Labour a narrow working majority in the House of Commons.

For the Labour Party, a major issue at both elections was Britain's membership of the European Economic Community or Common Market. The party felt that Heath had conceded too much in his negotiations with the EEC and, in any case, had not put the issue of membership before the voters. Consequently at both elections in 1974, Labour promised in its manifesto to let the people make the final decision 'through the ballot box'. This form of words pointed not to another general election – that would have been the third in less than two years – but to a referendum which Labour brought into law by a Referendum Bill. It was a startling break with tradition and prompted some serious questioning. On the one hand, a referendum appeared to undermine the principle of parliamentary sovereignty.

Would the referendum result be legally binding on the House of Commons, or could it be overturned by a majority vote? And once referendums were introduced, where would it all end? Was Britain going the way of Switzerland which in the years 1972 and 1973 respectively held seven and eight national referendums, none of which attracted more than a 37% turnout?

The left wing in Britain had long been sceptical of the European Community – Bill Pickles had articulated this scepticism in his Fabian Society pamphlet *(right)* back in 1961. Harold Wilson was a nervous leader of the Parliamentary Labour Party, only too conscious of the anti-EEC feeling of MPs like Tony Benn, Michael Foot and Peter Shore, as well as others who owed their seats to trade unions. He therefore decided to suspend the usual rules of cabinet responsibility and allow ministers to campaign according to their conscience, provided they did not contradict government policy in parliament – only the left-wing Eric Heffer broke ranks and he was sacked.

At the heart of Harold Wilson's approach was his belief that he could negotiate a better deal than Edward Heath. As a result, Britain went into the negotiations with a long list of desired changes, not only changes to Britain's relations with the EEC but also changes to the way the Community itself was structured. In the event, only two of Wilson's main objectives were achieved – a budget correction for assessing Britain's contribution to the Community budget, and arrangements to allow New Zealand dairy produce to enter the Community. On other issues – including regional policy, capital movements and economic and monetary union – as Wilson told the House of Commons later, the negotiations had gone as far as they could go. The crucial stages in the negotiations were a summit meeting in Paris in December 1974 and a two-day summit in Dublin in March 1975 which I covered for *The World Today*.

I flew to Dublin on 9 March – the day before the summit – with a two-fold brief: to get a statement from the Prime Minister on the outcome of the negotiations and to get interviews with other Community leaders to see how they viewed the British negotiating stance. The BBC had booked me a room in the Shelbourne Hotel on St Stephen's Green, a splendidly large hostelry where most of the press and broadcasters were gathered. On the principle of 'You scratch my back and I'll scratch yours', a lot of drinking and networking was done that evening to make sure we got access to as many leaders as possible. By that means, at the end of the summit I joined the media scrum in Dublin Castle and managed to get interviews with the prime ministers of the Netherlands and Ireland – another new member along with Denmark and Britain.

But getting Harold Wilson was more difficult since Britain's renegotiation had been the major issue of the summit and there was a queue of interviewers from television first and then radio. Before me in the queue was a man from Independent Radio News (IRN) who did his interview and then rushed out to phone it over to London. I introduced myself to Wilson and was just 'taking level', when the door burst open and the IRN man reappeared:

"Prime Minister, Prime Minister" – he whined in a shaky voice *– "I'm awfully sorry but there's nothing on my tape. Can we do it again?"*
"Only if you let this BBC man help you", said Wilson.

Eventually I got my interview with Harold and pressed him as hard as I could on whether in the coming referendum he would recommend to the voters that Britain remained a member of the Community. But Harold was cagey – even more so than usual:

The Foreign and Commonwealth Secretary [Jim Callaghan] *and I will go back from Dublin tomorrow and make a brief report to Parliament on what has been discussed. Then the Cabinet in the very near future will get a report from us, not merely on Dublin but on the whole renegotiation – our assessment on how far we have been able to meet the requirements set out in the manifesto to be put to the British people and we shall get their reaction. And then we shall make our recommendation to the Cabinet and to the people and that will be voted on through the ballot box in a free vote of the British people – whether we should stay in on the terms we have been able to renegotiate or whether they want us to come out.*

The interview done, I returned to the hotel, got my flight to London and began making editing notes about the interviews in the taxi from Heathrow to Bush House. The next morning – since the World Service was always nervous about interviews with the Prime Minister for which it had certain procedures – I played my tapes to the head of Current Affairs, Bob Milne-Tyte, then wrote the linking script and took it to the studio for a live transmission of *The World Today*. I began the programme by saying that the summit had gone well with a good atmosphere – indeed one of its highlights had been the presentation of a birthday cake to Harold Wilson when he celebrated his fifty-ninth birthday on the first morning. The first interview was with the Irish Prime Minister, Liam Cosgrave, who said the negotiations had been long but successful. Then came Harold Wilson talking about the agreements to modify Britain's contribution to the Community budget and to admit New Zealand dairy produce – *because of our relationship with New Zealand and our kinship with so many British families there, we want to keep these life lines open.* Then came my interview with the Dutch Prime Minister, Johannes den Uijl, who said his country would have to make real sacrifices to accommodate Britain's reduced contribution to the Community budget, but

> "*there are very rational political reasons and economic reasons for that. Europe can't afford to let Britain out and Europe can't act as a real strong economic and political union in the world without Britain.*"

I closed the programme with an interview with my old friend from *The Observer*, David Howarth, who had been in Dublin for the *International Herald Tribune*. David gave his assessment on the negotiations and predicted that Wilson would recommend the outcome in the coming referendum, which would result in Britain remaining a member of the European Community on a low turnout.

David Howarth was right. Wilson recommended the outcome of Dublin to the electorate in a pamphlet entitled 'The New Deal' which stated that 'in or out, we would still have been hit by the oil crisis, by rocketing world prices for food and raw materials. But we will be in a much stronger position to face the future if we stay inside the Market than if we try to go it alone.' The referendum was held on 5 June 1975: there was a 64% turnout and the result was 67% to stay in the Common Market against 33% to leave. All the national newspapers had campaigned for Remain, with the exception of the Communist *Daily Worker*. There was no campaigning on social media, of course. The Labour Party was divided but the Conservatives and the Liberals had been solidly in favour of Remain. The general feeling was that the referendum result settled the question of Britain's membership of the European Community for all time. But then came divisions in Britain over the Maastricht Treaty of 1992, which transformed the European Community into the more integrated European Union. And then came the referendum of 2016 in which the British electorate voted 51.9% to leave the European Union, against 48.1% to remain, in a higher turnout of 78.2%.

5.
World Service features

In 1975 I was given two series of feature programmes, unconnected to politics or international relations. What bliss, being able to leave the newspapers to one side! I imagine it was Robert Milne-Tyte who thought of the feature subjects since it was he who briefed me on them.

The first series was just four programmes with the title *Marriage 75*. The idea was to get couples to speak about their relationships, traditional or otherwise, and discuss how far they were accepted by the society in which they lived. The first in the series was an arranged marriage for which I travelled to South Harrow to interview Kailash Boodwa – who was actually Programme Organiser of the Hindi Section in Bush House – and his wife. They were a charming and eloquent couple with teenage children. They described how, in their part of India, arranged marriages were the rule rather than the exception; they were second cousins in any case. They thought me strange to believe an arranged marriage could not include love – "love comes in its own time," said Mrs Boodwa. But they would not be arranging the marriage of their teenage daughter. I was reminded of the 1965 film, *Shenandoah*, in which James Stewart tells his future son-in-law that love is not enough: "I liked Martha – I liked her an awful lot – but it wasn't till later that I discovered I loved her".

For the second programme I travelled to Hove to interview a couple who both originated in Africa. Prisca, who was a college friend of my wife's sister, came from Zimbabwe, while her husband, Gabriel, originated in Nigeria. Both were Christians and they had had a Christian wedding but only after some cultural difficulties had been sorted out. As Priska explained, in Zimbabwe a bride price had to be paid by the groom before the marriage could be considered valid by the bride's family. On the other hand, said Gabriel, my family in Nigeria did not understand the concept of the bride price but did expect the bride to bring a dowry. An animated and very broadcastable discussion ensued, before Priska and Gabriel then explained that the threat of getting wed in London rather than Harare had brought both sets of parents to their senses. But was the dowry or bride price paid? Only as nominal sums, it seems.

The remaining programmes in the series were less dramatic. Dorothy and Julian, whom I interviewed in Dorset, were to have a traditional English village wedding; they had known each other since childhood and their families lived in nearby villages. The 'banns' had already been read and Dorothy's parish church booked for after Easter. Sarah and Fred, on the other hand, were not having a marriage ceremony but intended to live together 'in sin' as they put it and have children without benefit of clergy or registry office. We had an interesting discussion about the idea of 'Common Law marriage' which Sarah, who was a lawyer, explained had no foundation in English law – but should have.

Houses and their Times

The other features series was more ambitious. *Houses and their Times* was six programmes of visits to historic country houses and interviews with their owners or residents, followed by a studio discussion with an architectural historian about the period and its social context. For this role, I was fortunate to have Mark Girouard, an expert on the country house who had just moved on from *Country Life* magazine to a professorship.

The first programme was about Berkeley Castle in Gloucestershire, a house with a unique place in English history, since it had been the home of one family since the twelfth century and was, of course, the place where King Edward II was cruelly murdered. The Berkeley family were abroad when I called and so my guide – and interviewee – was their steward. Understandably he wished to gloss over details of the royal murder and concentrate on the castle's attractions for the modern visitor. However back in London an historian filled in all the background about Edward's disastrous reign and the war waged against him by his wife, Isabella of France.

The subject of the second programme was Ightham Mote near Sevenoaks in Kent – a real jewel of a house which I did not know about before. Described by one architectural historian as 'the most complete small medieval manor house in the county', Ightham was built around a courtyard and surrounded on all sides by a moat, crossed by three bridges. Both the guide from the National Trust and Mark Girouard stressed that there would have been many more small

Ightham Mote in Kent, the second house visited for the series 'Houses and their Times'.

Below: Dodington Park in Gloucestershire, built with money compensating the owner for freeing the slaves on his plantations in the West Indies.

manors like this, but others were changed to suit the fashion of looking outwards on to the owner's estate and gardens.

Compton Wynyates in Warwickshire – subject of the third programme – was also built around a courtyard and like Berkeley Castle has been in the ownership of one family for 800 years. The present Tudor brick and half-timbered building was visited by every monarch until the Civil War in the 1640s. One of the Compton family told me how the Cromwellian custodian took such a fancy to the bed in which kings and queens had slept that he took it away with him. When I visited, the head of the family was the 6th Marquess of Northampton, who liked to spend a few months there each year, though his principal home was Castle Ashby in Northamptonshire. This marquess opened Compton Wynyates to the public, but under his successors it has been closed to visitors.

For the fourth programme I visited Dodington Park in Gloucestershire. It was designed by James Wyatt in the Roman classical style in the early years of the nineteenth century; the gardens were laid out by Capability Brown. But the architecture of Dodington is less interesting than the source of its finance. The Codrington family owned vast cane sugar plantations in the West Indies, all worked by slaves. When slavery was abolished in the United Kingdom in 1833, the government compensated the slave-owners for the loss of their 'property'. So Sir Christopher Bethell-Codrington of Dodington Park received £29,863 (equivalent to £21m in today's money) for 1,916 slaves – that put the average value of each slave at just under £16! In 2003, the 300 acre estate was bought by the businessman Sir James Dyson for a reported £20m.

For the fifth programme I went to a house in Charlotte Square in Edinburgh. It is a square built around a garden and named after Queen Charlotte, wife of George III. It was the last part of the initial phase of the Edinburgh 'New Town' – the development of the Scottish capital on the opposite side of the valley from the medieval 'Old Town', financed by the new Scottish banks against the security of farmland. Charlotte Square was part of the original design by Robert Adam, who died in 1792, and was not completed until 1820. The lady who showed me over her house said you could tell the doors on the first floor were constructed during the Napoleonic wars, from the fact that one had inferior timber from its neighbour – best quality oak was reserved for Nelson's Royal Navy.

The final house in the series was Cragside near Rothbury in Northumberland. Built in 1863 by William Armstrong, founder of the armaments company Armstrong Whitworth, it incorporated many of his scientific innovations – it was the first house in the world to be lit by hydroelectric power. Set in acres of gardens, famous for their rhododendrons, Cragside was a magnificent example of the High Victorian stately home. In fact, Mark Girouard had just completed a report for the National Trust recommending that they acquire Cragside and preserve it – which they did in 1977.

My main recollection of Cragside is not architectural. In 1976 when I visited, it was still owned by the family and in residence was Lady Armstrong – Zaida Cecile Watson-Armstrong, widow of the 2nd Baron Armstrong. She greeted me warmly, on the recommendation of Mark Girouard, and said she had cooked some scones for our tea.

> *"Come with me,"* she said, leading me from the splendid entrance hall to a hydraulic lift, which took us down to a cavernous kitchen with row upon row of stoves. Without gloves or a rag, she pulled open an oven door.
> *"Let me help,"* I said.
> *"Not a bit of it,"* she replied. *"Men do not have asbestos fingers – we women do".*

Over the scones – which were delicious – she told me about the first Lord Armstrong, his wife who created the gardens and the visits by Queen Victoria and other royalty. She also explained the tortuous family history by which her late husband's father had inherited Cragside from his great uncle, but not his title. Lady Armstrong died two years later, aged 81 years.

6.
Twenty-four Hours

The other current affairs programme broadcast by Talks and Features World Service was *Twenty Four Hours*. It was a 30-minute magazine containing five or six different items – either scripted talks or interviews. When I joined the production team, there were two editions of *Twenty-four Hours*, one broadcast in our British morning to be heard in the prime-time evening slot in Asia, and the other broadcast in our evening, mainly for listeners in Africa and Europe. Later, two dawn editions were added for the benefit of listeners in the United States and the Western Hemisphere – more about them later. The team for *Twenty-four Hours* consisted of an editor (usually a senior producer) and two to three producers, who might include staff on attachment or trainees.

I joined *Twenty-four Hours* as editor and in September 1974 was promoted to Acting Executive Producer, a rank which I thought would give me fairly free reign in the choice of topics to be covered. I had reckoned without the presenter of the morning edition. John Tusa – now Sir John Tusa and a very public figure in journalism and arts administration – had been a BBC news trainee and senior producer, before resigning from the staff to give himself greater journalistic freedom. He was a great colleague to work with, but not a person to get into an argument with. That was what I found on joining *Twenty-four Hours*. I commuted from Ware in Hertfordshire and with luck and punctual trains would arrive in Bush House at 7.30 am. But by then the London-dwelling Tusa had not only decided on the main items for the programme but arranged a few interviews as well. "Oh, hello, David. I've set up a line to Kota Kinabalu for half past ten to find out what's going on in Sabah." I soon decided there was no point in arguing.

I had a different problem with the presenter of the evening edition of *Twenty-four Hours*. He was Nigel Rees, later to make a name for himself as a lexicographer and inventor of the popular Radio 4 programme, *Quote Unquote*. But in the 1970s Nigel was still making his mark in various broadcasting outlets at Broadcasting House as well as Bush. For some reason I cannot now remember – perhaps my wife had come to town and left a daughter with me – I had nine-year old Lucy Perman with me in the *Twenty-four Hours* office and Nigel

Rees said he would like to interview her. Lucy said she did not mind and nor did I so the interview went ahead and was intended for the *You and Yours* programme on the following day. As an experienced broadcaster, I should have monitored the interview more closely and quizzed Nigel on its actual purpose. But, No! The next day to my horror, I head my daughter being asked if she and her sisters were allowed into their parents' bedroom when they woke: 'No', she replied, 'we have to wait in our room until they fetch us.' Then the presenter – the well-known family psychologist Dr Wendy Greengross – declaimed in horror that it was disgusting, since every child needed to know the moment it woke that its parents were still alive and loved them. Fortunately, the young interviewee was identified only as 'Lucy'.

The ingrained distrust of interviews in the BBC External Services was vindicated in 1972 when I did my first spell as editor of *Twenty-four Hours*. In Uganda, General Idin Amin had been in power for almost a year after overthrowing the elected government of Milton Obote: that had made headlines but not for long – military *coups* were not uncommon in Africa. But in 1972 he surprised the world by expelling all of Uganda's Indian and Pakistani citizens. We decided we would cover the news in the evening edition aimed at Africa. I duly called up a stringer on one of the newspapers who had spent some time in Kampala: would he come in to be interviewed about Idi Amin – who he was and what else he had done besides being an army officer. The journalist – whose name I cannot now remember (just as well!) – said he could only come for a live interview with the presenter. To that I agreed since the journalist was often used by Bush House and, as I had been on duty since 7.30 am, I went home leaving one of the producers in charge. I came in the next morning to stern faces and a summons to see the Duty Editor in the Newsroom. The British High Commissioner in Kampala (the equivalent of an ambassador) had been called to the presidential palace and then imprisoned for the night: news agencies were reporting that it was as the result of a BBC interview! I rushed back to my office to find a recording of the previous night's *Twenty-four Hours*. The offending interview had said that Idi Amin was the illegitimate child of a well-known female sorcerer, and the father had died mysteriously soon after the birth, which enhanced young Idi's mother's reputation as a witch doctor no end. It continued in the same vein. I imagined the worst – a major diplomatic row and me sacked or demoted to a copy messenger. But the High Commissioner was released soon afterwards and the BBC interview dismissed as a very old canard. It seemed that Idi Amin was tickled pink by the attention of the BBC's *World Today*.

However, three years later when the true character of President Idi Amin was well known, the Foreign Office intervened to prevent a planned interview with the journalist David Martin, about a highly critical book he had written about the president. It was feared that Amin might target British citizens in Uganda if the interview went ahead. The BBC agreed to delay the interview, but held an internal review of the decision. The conclusion was that any immediate risk had passed and three weeks later the interview went ahead. There was no reaction inside Uganda.

Reopening the Suez Canal

In 1975, I was given a two-week duty tour to Egypt. The occasion was the reopening of the Suez Canal which had been closed for eight years. The canal had been at the centre of Middle East politics since the Second World War. Built in 1869 by the French-owned Suez Canal Company, it was nationalized in 1956 by President Gamal Abdel Nasser, giving rise to the 'Suez Crisis' – the ill-fated invasion of Egypt by Britain, France and Israel. In 1967 Egypt was again at war with Israel, with Jordan and Syria also involved, but the fighting was over in six days and resulted in Israel occupying the whole of the Sinai Peninsular up to the banks of the Suez Canal, which was consequently closed to shipping. In 1973 Egypt and its allies launched the so-called Yom Kippur War with the object of retaking the Sinai – and also the Golan Heights of Syria. The Arabs failed in both objectives but international pressure and shuttle diplomacy led to a partial Israeli withdrawal in Sinai which allowed Egypt to arrange for the British and United States navies to begin clearing the waterway of sunken ships and unexploded ordinance.

I duly indented for a Uher tape recorder from the Bush House Facilities department and asked Foreign Travel to book a hotel room in Cairo. I flew to Cairo and spent a very uncomfortable first night in the hotel the BBC had booked. I reported this the next day to the BBC correspondent, Jim Muir, who told me the said hotel was actually a low-class brothel. Jim then arranged for me to stay in the Yacht Club, a famous and comfortable relic of British occupation. After the move I observed the Yacht Club's Nubian staff shaking my clothes out of the window of my room, presumably to remove anything I had brought from the hotel. There were two days before I was due to travel to the headquarters of the Suez Canal at Ismailia, north-east of Cairo. One day I spent sightseeing – astonished by the crush of so many human beings, especially on the buses and trains, which I had been warned to avoid; I did my sightseeing on foot and somehow managed to visit the old cemetery, where people lived in the tombs, and also to walk through the district where camels were being slaughtered as food.

The second day I spent in the company of an intriguing diplomat – or maybe spy – named Hugh Leach *(pictured above)*. The introduction had come through a former secretary in the World Service, Angela Hind, whose father had been the colonel of a tank regiment during the Suez campaign of 1956. Hugh Leach was one of her father's tank commanders: indeed, as soon as we met, he suggested that at my meeting with the Suez Canal Authority I might return the company flag he had stolen in 1956 from the office in Port Said. After the Army, Hugh had joined the Foreign Office which sent him to learn Arabic at MECAS (the Middle East Centre for Arab Studies) at Shemlan in Lebanon. He then worked mainly in the

Middle East, partly – although he did not tell me this – for MI6. How a tall Englishman with fair hair could be a spy in the Arab world puzzled me. One interesting assignment that he shared with me was touring the remoter parts of Yemen and photographing the Jewish families who had remained after others had migrated to Israel. He said that having a few Jewish residents provided a village with a safety valve from the strict rules of Islam, and he showed me photographs of Yemeni boys with characteristic ringlets. I later learned that Hugh had taken the writer Freya Stark on a tour of Yemen. Although I was a stranger – and with him for only a day – he was remarkably open and generous with his experiences and his time. He drove me out to the Pyramids at Giza, saying that he often came there at night to sleep under the stars – the Egyptian police knew not to disturb him. He told me about the circus of which he was part owner, and how he had brought it to Giza for a successful visit. Before driving me back to the Yacht Club, he gave me detailed advice on my trip later in the week to Upper Egypt and the ancient sites of Thebes and Karnak. It had been a memorable day in the company of what one of his obituaries described as 'the last of a dying breed, the great British eccentric' [*The Daily Telegraph*, 25 November 2015].

* * * * *

The drive to Ismailia – head office of the Suez Canal Authority, formerly the British Army's base for the Canal Zone – was in a taxi, booked on my first day in Egypt. Sharing the taxi with me was a French newspaper journalist. The road north out of Cairo was busy but, when we turned off towards the canal, it was straight and empty through scrub woodland. We arrived at the canal headquarters and the driver demanded his fare, saying he had to be back in Cairo for a funeral. Backed by the Frenchman, I said that the contract had been for the return journey and he would be paid when we were safely back in Cairo.

Engineer Mashhour Ahmed Mashhour, chairman of the Suez Canal Authority, was an impressive man in achievements, contacts and attitude. A former soldier and friend of President Anwar Sadat, he had been in charge of the canal for ten crucial years including 1973 when the Egyptian army launched a massive assault on the Israelis across the canal. Before we went in to greet him, his secretary told us his nickname was 'the man of difficult missions' – and 1973 must have been one of them. But he was in an optimistic mood for our visit. He described the clearing of the canal of wrecks and explosives by the Royal Navy, added with a grin that it had been necessary to shoot a few local fishermen who had been throwing the bombs back into the water to kill fish. He spoke with great enthusiasm about his vision for the canal's future, of deepening it for larger ships and providing a bypass canal to enable more vessels to pass. I later wrote up Engineer Mashhour's vision for the British journal, *New Civil Engineer*, edited by Sidney Lenson, a former neighbour of ours in Harlow. Mashhour's vision of a deeper, more capacious canal did come about in 2015, but he had died seven years earlier at the grand age of 91.

Our interviews done, the French journalist and I had to wait some time for our taxi to return. By the time it arrived it was getting dark, and soon we could see why the driver had wished to avoid taking us back to Cairo. His vehicle had defective lights or battery or both: we could barely see the road in front of the cab. Fortunately the road was straight, but this was soon offset by a convoy of the Egyptian army coming in the opposite direction – with no lights at all! I have never embarked on a conversation in French with such undivided attention as I did with the other passenger.

Before returning to London I had the chance to see something of Upper Egypt and the famous tombs of the Pharaohs. I flew from Cairo to Luxor by EgyptAir which at that time on domestic routes used both the de Havilland DH 106 Comet and the Tupolev Tu-154 narrow-wing jet airliner. I was hoping to fly by Comet – the world's first commercial jet airliner – but unfortunately it was a Tupolev for that flight: we boarded, took our seats, took off and were then told to go to the rear of the aircraft while it gained height. Luxor at that time was a tourist destination but not the massive hub it is today. I was booked into the Winter Palace Hotel, which had a recently opened modern wing. I booked in and was directed to one of the new suites but – acting on the advice of Hugh Leach – I insisted on a room in the old building. With a show of reluctance, the staff agreed to my wish and I was directed to a side door in the reception area, which gave on to a darkened wide corridor and my splendid high-ceilinged chamber of Edwardian comfort.

The following morning I went early to the ferry station on the Nile. I could see various vessels of different sizes and decided to take the larger tourist ferry, rather than the smaller boat recommended by Hugh Leach. As I stood in the queue, a larger group of middle-aged Chinese men arrived. I got chatting to one of them and discovered they were a visiting official delegation from the Parliament of Singapore:

> *"What a coincidence,"* I said to him. *"I'm from the BBC World Service and last week we interviewed your Prime Minister, Mr Lee Kuan Yew."*
> *"Listen, everybody,"* shouted the parliamentarian with great excitement. *"Here's a man from the BBC who's interviewed LKY."*

I was ushered to the front of the queue to meet the Speaker of their parliament – not daring to admit it was actually John Tusa who did the interview. And for the next few hours I maintained that position, standing next to the Speaker, while we visited the tombs in the Valley of the Kings. I read somewhere that up to 5,000 visitors a day now pass through the Tomb of Tutankhamun – in single file and told to keep moving. My visit with the Singapore parliamentarians was nowhere near so hurried. We stood for some time before the treasures and artifacts, while the guide told us at length of Howard Carter's excavations culminating in 1923 in the discovery of the famous Mask of King Tut. I had seen the mask earlier in the Egyptian museum in Cairo

The following day, before flying back to Cairo, I had the chance to visit the imposing temples and towers of Karnak on the east bank of the Nile. *Karnak* was the name of the cruise ship in Agatha Christi's *Death on the Nile* and one of the television adaptations had Hercule Poirot clambering around the ruins of ancient Karnak in search of a murderer.

* * * * *

In September 1975 I was again promoted to Acting Executive Producer for the launch of the dawn editions of *Twenty-four Hours*. We had a week of trial editions before the actual launch. The new programmes went out live at 5.00 and 7.00 GMT, aimed at listeners in North America and the Caribbean who would have been listening in their prime time evenings. Since this was the World Service, the programmes were broadcast on both Medium and Short Wave as well as being rebroadcast by local radio stations. It was an exciting time to be editing a current affairs programme with an assured audience.

Preparations for the two dawn editions began the evening before, with the dawn team taking over from the team broadcasting the evening edition of *Twenty-four Hours*. Only rarely did we repeat an item from the evening show; whenever possible we liked to get a fresh angle on any running story. My team consisted of two producers plus one or two trainees or attachments from other parts of Bush House: the attachments were very welcome and useful, since they brought fresh insights and contacts. Unlike the daytime editions, the presenter of the dawn editions was a staff newsreader rather than an outside contributor, like John Tusa or Gordon Clough. This meant that any interviews had to be done by the production team, and also that the script had to be written by one of the team, usually the editor. By midnight, we aimed to have a provisional running-order for the 5.00 am edition. Some recorded pieces and interviews would have been done already, and others lined up for the early hours of the next day. The presenter would arrive half an hour before transmission with the script and running-order already typed up ready for him or her.

From the very beginning the two dawn editions did not have to go begging for current affairs topics to fill their 30 minute slots. World news was still dominated by the end of the Vietnam war – the North Vietnamese army and the Vietcong had attacked the southern capital, Saigon, in April leading to the panic evacuation of Americans and thousands of their Vietnamese dependents and supporters. In Britain the year-old Labour government was struggling to deal with the rise in the international oil price and record unemployment, while the Conservative Party had replaced its leader, the former Prime Minister Edward Heath, with the former Education Secretary, Mrs Margaret Thatcher – about whom very little was known in the world at large. It was an exciting time to be broadcasting.

It was also an interesting time to be working in that part of London. On the other side of Aldwych from Bush House was Covent Garden, now an aria of tourist restaurants but then still the site of London's traditional fruit, vegetable and flower market. As in Alfred

Hitchcock's 1972 thriller *Frenzy*, in which Barry Foster (the murderer, it turns out) played a market manager, Covent Garden was a riot of traders rushing here and there and of heavily laden trucks and wheelbarrows – there may even have been one or two porters with fruit baskets piled on their heads. Under an old law the pubs of Covent Garden stayed open all night, including the 'Nell of Old Drury' pub which featured in the film. We could have had a pint at 5.45 am but it was not a sensible thing to do with another World Service programme due to go out at 7.00 am.

Broadcasting at Dawn

In December 1975, while I was working as one of the editors on *Twenty-four Hours*, a strike was called by the National Union of Journalists. It was not in fact about the World Service, but concerned a dispute with BBC management over expenses for production assistants in television. But the NUJ leadership had made it an 'everybody-out' dispute – a common feature of strikes at that time of trade union militancy. I was of course sympathetic to the production assistants, and I had 'form' as a former Father of the Chapel at *The Observer*, but I was the editor of a current affairs programme going out to listeners with no knowledge whatsoever of British trade union negotiations. So in common with some of the editors in the Newsroom, I decided to cross the picket lines and work. At the time I was editing the mid-morning edition of *Twenty-four Hours*; I told the producers on the programme to safeguard their union membership and stay at home, while I produced the morning and the evening editions with the Assistant Head, Mike Sumner, as presenter. We were scrupulous in telling oversea correspondents we wished to interview that there was a strike on, and invariably we met with the response: *"Sorry, didn't catch that – it's a terribly bad line"*.

In due course, I received a note from the Bush House Father of the Chapel, saying: *'It has been reported that you are alleged to have been seen working on the day of the official NUJ strike'*. I met him in the Club and ribbed him for his un-journalistic turn of phrase. Almost a year after the strike, I received a letter from NUJ headquarters, telling me that the National Executive Committee had decided that a fine of £50 should be imposed in my case, but as my union membership had since lapsed no further action would be taken.

* * * * *

Bush House was always awash with freelances – 'Outside Contributors' as they were officially known – as well as people dropping in from other parts of the BBC. One of the latter was Richard Somerset-Ward who had been a major figure in Outside Broadcasts but for some reason had become a 'resettlement case'. He was resettled for a year or so as an editor in *Twenty-four Hours* where he regaled us with stories of World Cups and the *obiter dicta* of Cabinet Ministers and BBC bosses. He moved on to succeed Humphrey Burton as BBC TV's Head of Music and Arts, wrote books about music and then became the BBC's Representative in the United States. The son of a Church of England canon, he was last heard of in New Jersey where he was running a church choir.

It was during a spell as a senior producer on the other magazine programme, *Outlook,* that I got to know another refugee from the domestic media, named Richard. Richard Dingley, a submariner during the closing years of the Second World War, had worked for Light Entertainment in Broadcasting House, where he was one of the main producer/interviewers of *In Town Tonight* – *"Once more we stop the mighty roar of London's traffic and, from the great crowds, we bring you some of the interesting people who have come by land, sea and air to be In Town Tonight"* went the announcement after an excerpt from the *Knightsbridge March* of Eric Coates. Richard Dingley was another who regaled us with tales of the Great and the Good, although in his case they were not always good. On *In Town Tonight* he had interviewed many actresses, including in 1956 famously Kim Novak, and claimed that relations with most of them had continued long after the microphone was turned off. He came to Bush House when *In Town Today* – successor to the Light Programme's *In Town Tonight* – was axed in 1965 and was rather a fish out of water. Commuting to Bush House from Moreton-in-Marsh in the Cotswolds, he found it difficult to keep to the schedules of an ordinary producer of *Outlook*. But the management did their best for him by way of loosely scheduled feature programmes. On one occasion, he was due to fly to Orkney for a feature but first stopped off in the BBC Club; as my shift ended, I was just going home when

Richard appeared and begged me to raid the *Outlook* float to replace the expenses he had drunk downstairs.

It was remarkable how far Outside Contributors would travel to secure a spot on the World Service programme schedules. Casey Lord was another long-distance commuter – from Bognor Regis – although he claimed to be a more adventurous traveller, including to Sweden where he said he had conducted the national symphony orchestra. But eventually travel paid off for Casey who became a regular contributor on *New Ideas* and *Business Matters,* produced by Bob Finnigan who had worked with me on *Commentary* back in 1961.

* * * * *

In 1976 Robert Milne-Tyte went on sabbatical leave. He was a boss I respected immensely. When he died in 2010, one obituary said of him: *'at work, he seemed to his staff – especially the younger staff – a very private person. He was tall, dressed well, laconic in speech and always the model of a certain sort of BBC, or perhaps FCO, mandarin.'* He was also a great current affairs journalist, indeed the person who founded the programme I was working on, *Twenty-four Hours*. In his absence, the department was headed by Michael Sumner, a very different sort of broadcaster, more skilled at general and 'human interest' features. Clearly Michael would need a politically inclined deputy, of which Talks and Features WS had a good number, myself included – or so we thought. Instead Michael brought in one of his old chums, a former editor of *Outlook*, who had actually left the BBC to run an environmental charity. How he was allowed to do this was never explained. It certainly did not go down well among those of us who had been made Acting Executive Producers. One colleague, Mary Rutter – an accomplished current affairs producer, who for reference purposes always carried the previous week's editions of *The Times* with her in a carrier bag – immediately applied for a job in the Newsroom. I too began to look around for other opportunities.

7.
Becoming a Civil Servant

This episode in my career is so bizarre it deserves a chapter to itself, however brief. My thoughts were directed towards the Home Civil Service – that is its proper name to differentiate it from the Diplomatic Service – by a colleague who, fed-up with the lack of promotion in Bush House, applied to join the Civil Service by direct entry as a Principal. I was one of those who was interviewed during his 'vetting'. Anyway, David Williams was accepted and the last I had heard of him he was in the Northern Ireland Department, liaising with the military. That seemed to me a thoroughly worthwhile occupation, more useful perhaps than interviewing other journalists about some incident elsewhere in the world. I was interested in Northern Ireland, having reported from there for *Presbyterian Life*; I was also interested in other domestic issues such as prison reform. So I found out how to apply and sent in my application.

In due course, I was invited for an interview and written examination, which was all about general knowledge and current affairs – very much up my street. When taking the exam I noticed that among the other candidates were Army and Royal Navy officers in uniform. It seemed that I had passed, for I was then invited for interview with a psychologist, a friendly man of about my age with whom I got on well. He told me that I stood a better chance than the military men, because I did not *need* a job in the Civil Service and perhaps did not really *want* one. That all went without hitch and a few weeks later I was invited for an interview with someone from the Civil Service Department in offices in the Mall, next to Admiralty Arch. Here I was informed that I had passed all the tests for direct entry into the Home Civil Service as a Principal, and had done really very well. I was the sort of candidate who could well become a 'high flyer', I was told, moving from the first department of state where I would be on probation, learning how to be a Civil Servant, on to the Cabinet Office perhaps or the Treasury on the 'strategic reserve'. Very soon I would be invited to the department for my first job as a Civil Servant. Feeling rather pleased with myself, I went back to

Bush House to tender my resignation from the BBC and await the call to my first position in the Civil Service.

It was a good four weeks before I received an invitation to meet an Establishment Officer – as they called Personnel – in a government building on the south side of Lambeth Bridge. *"Welcome to the Department of the Environment,"* he said, *"although we don't know what reorganisation the government has in mind"*. This was a reference, I assumed, to the fact that the DoE had been set up by the Conservatives under Edward Heath and now we had a Labour government.

> *"I am going to take you across to Marsham Street, where you'll meet the Principal you are taking over from. It's the section in charge of Speed Limits."*
>
> "But I thought Speed Limits were a local authority responsibility," I said.
>
> *"You're very well informed. It's actually more about the philosophy and policy of Speed Limits."*

And with that we set off across the bridge to the Department of the Environment in Marsham Street, where he introduced me to the Principal i/c Speed Limits, and then left, saying we should talk later.

The Principal was a pleasant man, a few years older than myself, who explained that he headed a fairly large department of two Senior Executive Officers (SEO), six Higher Executive Officers (HEO) and Executive Officers (EO) and ten Clerical Officers of various grades. Since Speed Limits had become a hot issue – particularly during the oil crisis and the imposition of a 50 mph limit in 1973 – their main activity was framing answers to Parliamentary Questions (PQs) and Ministerial Questions (MQs). I found all this incredible and asked him why so many people were needed for a few PQs. He said his team was also engaged on motorway regulations and were preparing for the metrification of Speed Limits, from miles-per-hour (mph) to kilometres-per-hour (km/h). That was in 1976 so perhaps they are still preparing. When I asked if he ever got over to Brussels or Paris to see how Europeans were controlling traffic speeds, he said that was the responsibility of the Foreign Office – and besides, he had a gammy leg and didn't get out at all.

The Marsham Street towers, demolished in 2002-2003

I went back across Lambeth Bridge and told the Establishment Officer that I was not impressed by Speed Limits, and did not think I wanted the job. He replied that it was most unusual for someone to turn down their first job in the Civil Service, but he thought they might find me an alternative. I said I would have to think about it and might look for another post in the BBC instead. I asked if he or I should inform the Civil Service Department which puzzled him – "*but they simply look after recruitment.*" I said I had been told I was on the 'strategic reserve' which made him throw up his hands in horror – "*Oh, God. Nobody tells anybody anything these days!*"

Back at Bush House, they said that I had had a lucky escape from working for the 'Ministry of Marmalade', as Lance Thirkell, Controller of Administration, put it.

8.
Arabic Programme Organiser

It was a surprise to many people that I should apply to be Arabic Programme Organiser. My father-in-law, Harry Hyams (*not* the Harry Hyams who built Centre Point in Oxford Street) was brought up as a non-religious Jew and he saw my possible association with Arabs as odd and rather unwelcome. After all, I had no real knowledge of the Arab or Islamic world, apart from a ten-day duty tour of Egypt. Did I really know what I was letting myself in for? And Christopher Child – a former World Service producer who had spent four years as Arabic Programme Organiser before leaving to run a radio station in Abu Dhabi – said that I might regret getting the job, if in fact I did. But it was a position being advertised at exactly the right time, after my flirtation with the Civil Service. It was also a step up into BBC management, and I saw it as a challenge: I certainly did not see myself solving the Israeli/Palestinian problem, but I suppose I felt at the time that I could contribute in a small way towards a solution.

The job was advertised in Bush House and also in the Press in April 1976. It was a very full advertisement – I know because I asked Personnel for a copy of it at a crucial later stage.

ARABIC PROGRAMME ORGANISER
OVERSEAS SERVICES, EXTERNAL BROADCASTING
Grade MP5 Max. £6,657 p.a. (including MP LIFT)
Plus Managerial Lead
Plus MPAI Allowance £234 p.a.

<u>Duties</u>: The Arabic Service is on the air for nine hours a day and broadcasts a full range of programmes. Arabic Programme Organiser is responsible to Head of Arabic Service for planning, co-ordinating, control and supervision of all output. Duties include planning output from London and supply of programme material for the Cairo office; controlling programme expenditure; and directing work of a large number of Arab and British staff.

<u>Essential</u>: Familiarity with modern broadcasting techniques; mature editorial judgement and ability to work quickly under pressure; experience in the field of current affairs; ability to provide

creative leadership for and to coordinate the work of a number of specialist production units – e.g. Current Affairs, Music, Drama; experience of working with nationals of other countries; skill in economic use of resources.

<u>*Desirable*</u>*: First-hand knowledge of Middle East affairs and knowledge of Arabic. Selected candidate with no knowledge of Arabic would be expected to study the language.*

<u>*Based*</u>*: Bush House*

In late May I was called to an interview. The Head of the Arabic Service, Hamilton Duckworth, was accompanied by his boss, R.E. (Bob) Gregson, Controller of Overseas Services, and Alec Stevens, Senior Personnel Officer. It was a fairly predictable interview – going over my career in the BBC and whether I felt able and qualified to deal with the various problems and personalities of the Arabic Service. There were also two unexpected questions from Duckworth: he noticed from my application that my wife's maiden name was Jewish, and he asked if they were practising Jews; he also noticed that I had studied religion at theological college in Cambridge and asked if I would ever consider becoming a Muslim.

* * * * *

The Arabic Service was the BBC's oldest foreign language service, launched in 1938 to counter broadcasts by Mussolini's Italy aimed at North Africa and the British Mandate in Palestine. It had an interesting history. During the Second World War it was managed and edited by a German-born Jew, Sigmar Hillelson. His appointment was challenged in the House of Commons but defended by Brendan Bracken MP, Minister of Information, who said that Hillelson had been a British subject since 1908 and a distinguished member of the Sudan Civil Service from 1911 to 1933, and that high tributes had been paid to his work in Sudan by a succession of Governors General. [*A Jewish Scholar in a Muslim Community: The Sudan's Life and Writings of Sigmar Hillelson (1911-1933)* by Alhaj Salim Mustafa, *American International Journal of Social History*, Vol.2 No.3, May 2013]. He might have added that Hillelson was an outstanding scholar of both written and spoken Arabic and had studied at Baliol College, Oxford, and University College London.

After the war, the Arabic Service increased the frequency of its news bulletins but it was not thought to be an important way of reaching the Arabic-speaking public. This was particularly the case during the Suez Crisis of 1956, when British and French troops landed in Egypt in support of Israel after President Nasser had nationalised the Suez Canal. To give Arab listeners the view from Britain, Brigadier Bernard Fergusson, in charge of military intelligence, decided to use the Sharq al-Adna radio station (Near East Broadcasting Station) which was secretly funded by the British government – with disastrous results, for the station's management and staff were on the side of the Egyptians, and said so on air. The manager of Sharq al-Adna was arrested by soldiers with fixed bayonets, new staff were brought in and the station began broadcasting military messages as the *Voice of Britain.* After the Emergency the station was closed down, its medium wave transmitter was handed over to the BBC and the output of the BBC Arabic Service increased to nine hours a day.

Nine hours of broadcasts each day required a large staff. When I joined in 1976, the BBC Staff List showed 52 members of the Arabic Service, not counting secretaries, and it occupied the whole of the Fourth Floor of the Centre Block of Bush House, on both sides of the stairs and lifts. On the north side facing Kingsway, were the offices of the Head of the Arabic Service, the Assistant Head, the manager of the monthly magazine *Huna London* ('This is London') which was printed in Cairo, plus the heads of the production units for music and drama. On the south side of the lifts were the offices of the two senior staff in charge of News Bulletins – one Arab, the other British – the general offices occupied by up to thirty translators and newsreaders, the offices of the unit head of Current Affairs and the two British Talks Writers, a general office for the Facilities organiser and secretaries (including my secretary) and, finally, the office of the Arabic Programme Organiser. Thus my office was as far away as possible from that of my boss, Hamilton Duckworth.

My closest neighbours were the Facilities organiser, a charming and hard-working woman named Celia, and the two men who shared responsibility for the News Bulletins – at least in theory. So as not to disturb their ghosts, I will refer to them as Tweedle-Dum and Tweedle-Dee for they were constantly complaining about each other. Tweedle-Dum was a Lebanese Christian with an enormous chip on his shoulder; his main responsibility was to monitor the Arabic translation of News Bulletins and report any infelicities to his immediate superior – yours truly. Tweedle-Dee was an older man, an upright and fairly muscular Englishman who lived in Kent; it was his job to see that the News and Current Affairs had the requisite number of translators and news readers and ran smoothly to time. T-Dee was a great juggler of rotas, favours, promises and black marks.

* * * * *

On my first morning as APO, I attended the assembly in Hamilton Duckworth's office. Every department of the BBC had a morning assembly, rather like a school's morning prayers, when the Head heard about the output of the previous day and planned the day ahead with his team. But that in the Arabic Service was different. For one thing, there were more people present than I would have expected: the Head, the Assistant Head, myself as APO, the Senior Assistant Current Affairs, one of the Talks Writers and Tweedle-Dum, representing News. The procedure was for the Head to read out the main News Bulletin of the previous evening in English, while T-Dum followed the Arabic translation and the rest of us tried to look wise and tried not to catch someone else's eye. After the reading, the Head would discuss the Current Affairs output for the day with the Senior Assistant – a knowledgeable man named Amin Abdul-Hafiz, who I think was a Saudi or at least had worked for Aramco, the Saudi Arabian oil company – and then discuss a possible Talk with the Senior Talks Writer. The Head would then go off to the Controller's assembly where each of the Overseas Services would tell Bob Gregson what they were planning.

On my fourth day attending the Arabic assembly, I took T-Dum aside afterwards and asked him why one of the items in the previous evening's News had not been translated.

"What do you mean?"
"One of the items in the Bulletin wasn't translated, was it? I think it was the one about Israel."
"David, how do you know? You don't speak Arabic."
"No, but I can count. Hamilton read out nine items in the News, but you only had eight sheets to read in Arabic."

"Oh, David. Please don't. You are new here and don't understand the Arabic Service."

I mentioned the matter later to T-Dum's colleague, T-Dee, who looked up the identity of the translator and said he was an Iraqi with a well-known animosity towards Israel – rather like his compatriot, President Sadam Hussein. T-Dee explained to me that the translators were recruited for their knowledge of both English and 'Literary Arabic', the international language of diplomacy and journalism; Iraqis and Egyptians were good translators but would be hopeless as broadcasters because of their accents. The best broadcasters were Palestinians or Lebanese from the central countries of the Levant.

I did not let the matter drop but encouraged T-Dum to report to me missed items and mistranslations. He did make an effort in October and November 1976. The mistranslations included 'terrorists' who had attacked a Damascus hotel being translated as 'freedom fighters' and when they were captured by the Syrian authorities and 'hanged', that was translated as 'they hanged them by their necks'. I mentioned the mistranslations and untranslated item to Hamilton Duckworth who shrugged and said that these things happened. I also listened to one of the News Bulletins in the company of a reluctant T-Dum. What struck me was the pronunciation of the name Israel as *Ees-raay-eeel* with an elongation of the final syllable which sounded like an insult. But T-Dum said that was how the name was always pronounced and I was exaggerating. It also struck me as odd that the BBC Arabic Service transmission opened with an Āyah or verse from the Qur'an, but I let that pass.

* * * * *

Being Arabic Programme Organiser brought with it certain management privileges or openings. One day in Hamilton's absence, I represented the service at the Controller's Meeting and afterwards was invited with other senior staff to step into a side office 'to read telegrams'. These were situation reports from ambassadors in our area – usually classified as 'Restricted' – which I was told we could read on condition that we did not use the information in any broadcast. That struck me as an interesting form of censorship. On another day I was told that there was someone at Centre Block

Reception who wished to see me. He was a man in a suit, who gave me his name but not who he represented. After congratulating me on my appointment as APO, he said that 'we' were interested in one or two of my Arab staff and would be grateful if we could keep in touch. I assumed he was Special Branch or MI5, and said that BBC policy was that any approach by security bodies had to be channelled through Personnel, and could not come to programme staff.

One of my responsibilities as APO was to chair a fortnightly programme planning meeting with the unit heads. They were a diverse group of men in every respect – from nationality and political attitudes through to motivation and competence. At the top end were the organisers of Topical Programmes, Amin Abdul-Hafiz, and that of Drama, a Palestinian named Yacoub Musallam. I will not name those I regarded as representing the bottom, but they included the Egyptian in charge of Arab Music, who had been on a six months attachment to the Cairo office where he was reported to have done 'sod all'. In between were unit heads with various degrees of success at producing programmes on time and within budget – but all of them displayed enlarged egos, especially when sitting together in meetings such as the one I chaired. What made matters worse was that I had to write an annual report on each of them – or at least *draft* a report, for Hamilton Duckworth would invariably require me to tone down any criticisms.

A crucial meeting was held in July 1977 to discuss how we would celebrate the 40th anniversary of the Arabic Service the following year. Some decisions had already been agreed with Duckworth – there was to be a gala concert in the Sadlers Wells Theatre, produced by Yacoub Musallam under my general direction, and each unit head was to contribute to the concert as well as producing special, retrospective programmes in their own field. I said that Musallam would need other senior producers working with him and suggested Mohamad Badawi, a Sudanese translator. There was a hush in the room and Badawi stood up and flounced out. I caught him later and asked why he had walked out; he replied that Musallam had insulted him some years earlier and he, Badawi, had vowed to kill him but under pressure from colleagues had mitigated his vow to never speaking to Musallam again – not ever! At another planning meeting, after discussing how the Arabic Service would cover the Jubilee of Queen Elizabeth II in 1978, I mentioned that King Hussein had been on the throne of Jordan for exactly the same 25 years – should we not have a special programme for Hussein's Jubilee? The response was universal and vitriolic and taught me that memories of the Black September conflict between the king and the Palestinian Liberation Organisation (PLO) in 1971 lived on in Bush House as strongly as in the Middle East.

* * * * *

There was a steady flow of distinguished visitors to the Arabic Service and I was expected to play a role in their entertainment. The form was that they would be taken first to the Head's office, where Assistant Head, myself, Chief Talks Writer and probably Amin Abdul-Hafiz would sit in a circle with the guest, while the Head made some fairly formal remarks about the Arabic Service; then he would inevitably say: *"Now Mr Perman will take you to meet members of the service"* and I would have to take the VIP to my office for another circle of chat. Among the VIPs that I recall were Prince Abdullah ibn Faisal, eldest son of the late King of Saudi Arabia, the Saudi president of the International Fund for Agricultural Development (IFAD), Dr Al-Shaikhly, the Iraqi head of the Arab States bureau at the United Nations Development Programme (UNDP), Mohammed Beneissa, a Moroccan MP and former head of public relations at the United Nations Food and Agriculture Organisation (FAO), and Dr Radwan Mawlawi, chief information adviser to the Prime Minister of Lebanon. They were all good Muslims, of course, but many an Arab visitor would tell me he knew of the BBC Club and suggest we go there for its renowned single-malt whisky. After the second or third glass, the visitor would inevitably say that good Muslims were allowed to break the rules when they were travelling.

On his tour of Arabic Service offices, a VIP would often be accompanied by an aide who would distribute gifts. I was shown gold watches, jewelled trinkets and large denomination US dollar bills by beneficiaries of this largesse. Indeed, gifts were an important part of the culture. Members of the service would often return from a duty tour and leave a gift on my desk. I found that embarrassing as well as contrary to all BBC practice – until I devised a way of stopping it. I put the accumulating supply of gifts in a drawer from which I would give a recycled item to any member of staff I wished to praise. It worked: they stopped leaving trinkets on my desk and I was praised for *'behaving like an Arab'*.

As well as Middle East royalty, there was also the British Royal Family to deal with. In 1977, as President of the World Wildlife Fund, Prince Philip, Duke of Edinburgh, was due to visit Saudi Arabia and Afghanistan (then still ruled by its king), and I was sent by the Arabic and Eastern services to interview him at Windsor Castle. I duly Indented for a Uher tape recorder, took the train to Windsor and presented myself at the castle. The Duke was friendly enough until I asked him whether measures to protect wildlife did not sometimes interfere with the rights of the local human population. He said that was *"a damned stupid question"* and so I asked him something else. As the interview progressed, we came back to the conflict between the rights of animals and farmers, and he suddenly said: *"I suppose that question of yours earlier wasn't so stupid after all."* Back in Bush House, the interview was transcribed in English, translated into Arabic and Pashto and broadcast by the two services. It also featured in an edition of the Arabic Service magazine, *Huna London*, and I was told that it featured prominently in the Saudi newspapers. I was amused to read that, while in Saudi Arabia, the Duke went hunting with members of their royal family – so much for the World Wildlife Fund.

In the advertisement for my job, it had said a successful candidate with no knowledge of Arabic would be expected to study the language, but the BBC was slow in helping me do so. Eventually, more than 15 months after my appointment, I was sent on a five-day residential course of intensive Arabic study at SOAS (the London University School of Oriental and African Studies) in Bloomsbury. I was joined by nine British businessmen and a German engineer; our tutor was the splendid Dr Muhammad Haleem, educated at Cairo University and Cambridge and later made an OBE. It was a well-run course, using the Arabic language from the very beginning, and aiming to give us 500 key words with which we could engage in basic conversations. Inspired by the course, I asked Hamilton Duckworth if I could have a morning free each week to continue my study of Arabic, but this was refused. However, I did carry on with revision of the course papers and attempts to converse with some of the Arabs in the service. I learned at least the basic greetings in Arabic: *mahaba* (hello), *sabah el kheer* (good morning), *shukran* (thank you), *as-*

salaam-aleikum (peace be upon you). I also learned an Egyptian joke (Egyptians are well known for their jokes): *Who actually runs this country?* Answer: *IBM – Inshallah* (perhaps, if God wills) *Bokra* (tomorrow) *Malesh* (it doesn't matter anyway).

* * * * *

In May 1977 I received a memo from the Head of the Arabic Service about a complaint by T-Dum:

I have received from Mr [T-Dum] a formal complaint against you in which he alleges that during an interview in your office on the 10th of May you, as he puts it, subjected him to a most contemptuous and painful experience; in that you flew into a rage, shouted at him and ordered him out of your office and told him not to return. I should be glad to have your report on this incident.

In reply I sent a two-and-half page memo to Hamilton, beginning: '*I am saddened, though frankly not surprised, that T-Dum should have made our conversation of 10th May the subject of a formal complaint*'. I said that it had been clear to me and his colleagues for some time that T-Dum had been trying to precipitate a crisis in his position within the Arabic Service, either by means of a medical certificate (following his absence with migraine and chest complaints) or by means of a disciplinary issue. I said I appreciated T-Dum's personal difficulties – his health problems, the sickness of his son, his sensitivity as a Lebanese Christian in a largely Muslim service – especially given the sharp polarisation caused by the Lebanese civil war between Maronite Christians backed by Israel and the Palestine Liberation Organisation. I had therefore made it my duty to show friendship towards T-Dum, and try to build up his confidence. '*I made a special point of drawing him into meetings with his senior colleagues and of backing his authority in dealing with junior staff.*' But it soon became apparent that T-Dum was using our personal relationship as an opportunity for '*flouting his disenchantment with his present job*'. He admitted that he seldom listened to the afternoon Arabic Service transmissions, even though he was supposed to be monitoring the News output, and – after an initial period when he did report errors to me – he had lately refused to talk about the transmissions.

I told the Head that I had taken T-Dum out to lunch on one occasion and he had told me the friendship I showed him was not ultimately in his best interests. What he desired was a confrontation over not fulfilling his duties, and indeed that is what he had been trying to bring about with my predecessor and with the last Head of the Arabic Service, Charles McLellan. I warned him that to pursue that course of action could lead to his dismissal; to which he replied that he would then take the BBC to a tribunal and get compensation which was his right after he had been unwillingly transferred from the BBC office in Beirut and cheated out of his proper salary grade.

On the 9th May, in the absence of T-Dee on a course, T-Dum had been producing the programme *The World at Six* which contained a report on the important meeting in Geneva between President Carter and President Assad of Syria. The programme included a discussion about the meeting which I asked T-Dum to chair, but he begged me to excuse him. He then left the building at 5.15 pm and, when Radio Newsreel rang to say they had actuality of President Assad in Arabic, I had to see it into the programme, and consequently did not get away home until 8 pm.

On 10th May T-Dum was again meant to be producing *The World at Six* in the absence of T-Dee at a training seminar, and in the afternoon he asked if he could have a few words with me. I invited him into my office, where he said he did not intend to produce the programme again unless T-Dee was on proper leave. I said he could not refuse to do the programme and mentioned that he had left the office early the night before. I asked him if that was the action of a responsible radio journalist, but he did not answer. Instead he launched into a long tirade about his loss of status since leaving the Beirut office and his being subordinated to T-Dee. To put a stop to this, I told Hamilton Duckworth, I did raise my voice but the allegation that I flew into a rage was nonsense – and that could be corroborated by my secretary.

Hamilton said he accepted my version of what happened. But that was not the end of the matter by any means.

9.
A Tour of Arab capitals

In October 1977 I was given a month's Duty Tour of the Middle East. Officially, I was to have visited five capitals – Cairo, Damascus, Beirut, Baghdad and Amman – but, at the urging of the British ambassador to Jordan, I made it six by taking three days' leave and crossing the River Jordan to visit Jerusalem in Israeli-occupied Palestine.

It was an interesting time to be in the Middle East as a journalist. There was a lull in the Lebanese civil war, although Israeli jets continued to bomb PLO positions in Southern Lebanon. Throughout the summer, the United States – in the person of Cyrus Vance, President Jimmy Carter's Secretary of State – was trying to convene a peace conference in Geneva to tie up the loose ends after the end of the 1973 Yom Kippur War between Israel and its Arab neighbours. There were bilateral meetings and foreign ministers' meetings, but the peace conference seemed elusive, when out of the blue Prime Minister Menachem Begin of Israel issued an invitation to President Anwar Sadat of Egypt. On 19 November - a fortnight after the end of my Duty Tour – President Sadat flew to Israel and peace was suddenly back on the agenda of the Middle East.

Cairo

I began my tour in Cairo where I had a happier experience of hotels than on my earlier visit. I was staying in the upmarket suburb of Zamalek, although my business was in Central Cairo at the BBC office and the newspaper *Al-Ahram*, which printed the Arabic Service magazine *Huna London*. A new studio had been inaugurated at the BBC office but it had yet to send any recordings to London; the problem was partly technical and partly the result of confusion over the fees payable to Egyptian contributors. I had come with a mandate to change the fee structure. I was interested to see if the studio could be used for small drama productions as well as recording talks. I also visited Radio Cairo where I found the staff in an up-beat frame of mind, since radio had gained from a decline in television viewing in Egypt and from the restrictions the Sadat government had imposed on newspapers.

Cairo itself was still as chaotic as I had found it two years earlier – if not more so. The roads were congested almost to stand-still and public transport was unable to cope, even with large numbers of passengers riding on the outside of buses. Egyptian life is always like a cauldron, always threatening to boil over. I learned about some of the tensions from contacts at the British Embassy and Egyptian radio. President Sadat's visit to Jerusalem would certainly add to those tensions. But as one of my contacts put it: *"Egyptians are more concerned about where the next meal is coming from than about a homeland for the Palestinians"*.

Beirut

I flew from Cairo to Beirut to find Lebanon enjoying a lull in its civil war, which had begun two years earlier with fighting between the dominant Maronite Christians and the Palestine Liberation Organisation (PLO), but had gradually sucked in other communities. The lull, I was told, was an echo of the 'good days' when the various communities coexisted and Lebanon was the luxury playground of the Middle East. The lull was short-lived and before the civil war ended in 1990 many other forces had become involved, including Israel and Syria.

In 1977 central Beirut, the commercial centre running down from the hills to the sea and known as *Ras Beirut*, bore all the signs of war damage. But it was all too easy to escape the damaged buildings and find oases of calm, like the Bristol Hotel which seemed to be the gathering point for all the foreign correspondents in the Middle East. My guide was the Arabic Service's representative, Eric Bowman, a fairly laidback guy who later (in 1981) succeeded Duckworth as Head of the Arabic Service. Eric arranged for me to meet the Prime Mister, Selim Ahmed Hoss, a Sunni Muslim, who was accompanied by the Director General of the Lebanese Information Ministry. My main business in Beirut was to visit Radio Lebanon, just getting on its feet after the civil war in which it lost some of its staff and most of its listeners. Its main rival was the Voice of Lebanon (*Sawt Lebnan* or *Voix du Liban* or *VDL*), owned by the right-wing Christian Phalangist Party. VDL had no truck with Lebanese government censorship and had far better pop music programmes. Radio Lebanon, therefore, was desperate for outside help, including from the BBC, a request I passed on to the Transcription Services on my return to London.

Damascus

From Beirut, Eric Bowman drove me into the hills, across the Bekaa Valley and into Syria. Just over the border, our route took us to Maaloula, a pretty village built into the rugged mountainside and well known as one of the three remaining villages in Syria where Aramaic is spoken. The language is claimed to be the one spoken by Jesus, although the history of the survival of Aramaic after the Muslim conquest is complex. Many of the villagers were Christian – Catholic or Orthodox – but some were Muslim and they too spoke Aramaic as their mother tongue. Eric and I stopped in Maaloula for lunch, looked at the monasteries and saw the statue of the Virgin Mary, the patron saint of Maaloula – the statue was one of the casualties of the Syrian war when Islamic State forces occupied the village and destroyed most of its Christian artifacts. The churches and the statue of Mary have now been restored. We then drove down into Damascus where Eric left me to return to Beirut.

Syria in 1977 was ruled by the Arab Socialist Ba'ath Party under its leader, President Hafez al-Assad – father of the later president, Bashar al-Assad. During my tour it was the only country where the armed forces were much in evidence – apart from a military parade in Cairo to commemorate the October war with Israel. The streets of Damascus were awash with military vehicles, driven at great speed past held-back civilian traffic; according to my informant, this was a show of strength by the President's brother, Rifaat Ali al-Assad, who wished to have a greater role in the government. Damascus was noisy and dirty and in the process of being torn apart and rebuilt as the result of an economic boom, which was already past its peak. The one place of calm that I visited was the courtyard in front of the great Umayyad Mosque, built so it was said on the site of a church dedicated to John the Baptist. The mosque is impressive in its size and antiquity, and justifies its place as the fourth holiest site of Islam; it has also remarkably survived undamaged from the Syrian civil war – unlike its fellow, the Umayyad Mosque of Aleppo. I was also impressed by

The Great Umayyad Mosque of Damascus which, unlike its fellow in Aleppo, survived the Syrian Civil War.

the mausoleum across the courtyard containing the tomb of the Saracen general, Ayyubid Sultan Saladin.

It was difficult to get anyone to speak about the political situation in Syria. The Assad government appeared to be sitting on a pile of foreign policy mines, any of which could have exploded at any time. There was Lebanon, from which Syrian troops had withdrawn, probably soon to return; there was tension with Israel which still occupied the Golan Heights and parts of Southern Lebanon; there was the rivalry with the other Arab Ba'ath regime, Iraq; there were difficult relations with the United States and Saudi Arabia. And there was the domestic situation: the Ba'ath government was drawn from the minority Alawite community who followed a form of Shiite Islam, while the majority of the population were Sunni Muslims.

Baghdad

My flight to Baghdad was not straight forward. I did not realise that with some Arab airlines flights had to be confirmed on the day: so arriving at Damascus airport, I was told that I could not board the plane, even though I had a valid ticket with a seat reservation. There was no other flight to Baghdad that day, so I flew to Amman and there took a flight to Baghdad, arriving eight hours later than I had intended. Surprisingly I was met at the airport by an official of the Iraqi Ministry of Information, who said he would have had to wait for the next day's flight from Damascus if necessary. The Ministry of Information was much in evidence during my stay in Iraq and was effectively a part of the security services. Wherever I went in Iraq, I was accompanied by an official from the Ministry of Information.

Iraq is very different from its Arab neighbours. Other Arabs consider Iraqis to be rough and easily provoked: in the taxi from the airport I saw a fight in the street. And the Iraqi form of Arabic is markedly different from the language spoken in Lebanon or Saudi Arabia. In the Arabic Service we employed Iraqis as translators or producers, never as broadcasters. When I visited, Iraq was the mirrored opposite of Syria: a Ba'athist government drawn from a Sunni minority – the Tikriti clan – ruling a nation which was overwhelmingly Shia. The president was Saddam Hussein Abd al-Majid al-Tikriti – Sadam Hussein, for short. Using Iraq's oil wealth, Saddam had promoted himself as the friend and patron of the Palestinians. Indeed, just before leaving on the tour, I had had to deal with a Palestinian member of the Arabic Service telephoning from Baghdad and asking us to set up a line to receive an interview he had done with the Foreign Secretary; so as not to embarrass the man, who was telephoning from the minister's office, I did set up a line but the interview was full of insults against Syria, and therefore unusable.

On my second day in Baghdad I was taken to a gala banquet in honour of a visiting delegation from Fidel Castro's Cuba. It was held in a very large marquee in one of the city's parks. There were thirty or so tables set up, each with a dozen bottles of Iraqi beer – a strong but palatable beverage – and imitation Scots whisky, rather strange I thought for a Muslim country. The delegation arrived with a large number of Iraqis and I found myself sitting next to a Cuban journalist, who introduced himself as a member of the Politburo of the Cuban Communist Party. We conversed over a large meal and he told me he listened to the BBC World Service, mainly to find out what was happening in the United States. Then the cabaret began with a mixture of Iraqi musicians and dancers and Western singers. My left-wing companion looked disgruntled: *"Nowhere near as good as the Crazy Horse in Las Vegas"*, he said.

While in Iraq, on the recommendation of the Arabic Service's drama specialist, Yacoub Musallam, I went to meet Jabra Ibrahim Jabra, acclaimed as the world's finest translator of Shakespeare into Arabic. He lived with his wife in one of the smarter suburbs of Baghdad and when we arrived – after the usual pleasantries required in Arab conversations – his wife took my Ministry of Information minder aside so that I could have a private conversation with Jabra. We chatted about mutual acquaintances in Bush House and talked about the London theatre, which he knew from listening to the BBC World Service. I asked him about his translations of the Shakespeare canon and how far he had got. He replied that he had done *Hamlet, Coriolanus, King Lear, Macbeth* and *Othello* and many of the sonnets, and was then working on *The Tempest*, which would probably be his last. *The Tempest* he found particularly tough because its intrinsic poetry was difficult to render in Arabic. Out of hearing of my minder, we also discussed the political situation in Iraq: he said there had been a series of shootings at night in his area of Baghdad, which the authorities said was to get rid of stray dogs – *"funny that we never saw any stray dogs during the daytime"*.

I was treated to two cultural experiences in Iraq. One was a day's drive south of Baghdad to view the Hanging Gardens of Babylon – one of the Seven Wonders of the Ancient World. Since there is no archaeological or other evidence of where the Hanging Gardens were, or indeed if they were not just a mythical idea, what my Ministry of Information guide showed me was part of the history of Saddam Hussein's rule. The president saw himself as a modern King Nebuchadnezzar, who had conquered the Assyrians and established Babylon as the centre of his empire – for Assyria substitute Iran or Persia which Saddam was later to attack. What I saw was an archaeological site, excavated by the Germans in the 1920s, with some wall carvings but no sign of the Hanging Gardens. The other experience was far more worthwhile. The Iraq Museum, before it was plundered and destroyed during the Gulf War in 2003, was one of the greatest archaeological museums in the world, comparable to the Cairo Museum. The artifacts on display included objects found at Babylon and also at the Assyrian capitals of Nimrud, Nineveh, Tall Brek and Ur. It was the Assyrian treasures which impressed me most – ranging from large monumental carvings like those in the British Museum to exquisite jewelry and domestic objects. Many of these disappeared in the looting which accompanied the Gulf War and may never reappear for public view.

Amman

After Baghdad I returned to the Jordanian capital, Amman, this time for much longer than when I had changed flights. After the militarism of Damascus and the security paranoia of Baghdad, Amman felt like a paradise of freedom. All I knew about Jordan before my visit was that it was a kingdom ruled by King Hussein and that it was not an oil producer. I had seen the film of *Lawrence of Arabia* and assumed I would see the indigenous people of Jordan, the Bedouin, in the streets of Amman, but most of the people I met appeared to be Palestinians.

I was fortunate to have two knowledgeable guides for my stay. One was Samir Mutawi, who had been a journalist in London and an Outside Contributor to the Arabic Service – he would go on to become King Hussein's Head of Information. Samir and his friends, Ahmed, took me to supper in one of Amman's fine restaurants, and Samir and his wife invited me to a fondue supper to which they invited a number of Jordanian and British friends.

A few days later, having ascertained that I was doing nothing else, Samir and Ahmed drove me out of Amman down the long desert road to Petra – *'a rose-red city half as old as time'*, as the Victorian explorer, John William Burgon, described it. Petra is now all too familiar from its appearance in films like *Indiana Jones and the Last Crusade* and *Transformers: Revenge of the Fallen*, but in 1977 for this little-travelled traveller it was a wonder. Samir, Ahmed and I were not the only tourists visiting that day, but there was not the crush of tourist buses and the hubbub that is apparently common today. We left the car near the entrance and hired horses – three rather mangy ponies – to take us down the narrow ravine, known as the Souk, into Petra itself. Emerging from the Souk we were confronted by the famous Al-Khazneh or Treasury, the pink temple carved in the Greek style and set in the sandstone rock which encloses the city. Petra was the capital of the Nabatean kingdom dating back to 300 BC: the wealth of the Nabateans came from the levies they exacted on traffic passing from the spice fields of Africa to the markets of the Middle East. We spent a few hours exploring the different temples, and Samir explained that there were people living in Petra, although the Jordanian authorities were set on evicting them. Another story was that Petra was a graduation challenge for Israeli Special Forces, who had to cross the desert frontier and take back a piece of pink rock without being captured by the Bedouin. As we emerged from the Souk, without the horses this time, I heard one of the most vivid of Arabic insults being shouted by one horseman at another: *"Ya wahid kalb"* (you singular dog, you).

The hotel where I was staying was the delightful Hotel Jordan Intercontinental, where in the foyer waiters in Bedouin dress would constantly replenish your cardamon-scented tea unless you turn the cup upside down. It was there that I met my other guide, Nuha Batchone, who owned an art gallery and shop in the hotel. Like Samir Mutawi, Nuha was a devoted listener to the BBC World Service and said she wished to show her gratitude by showing me some of the historic sites of Jordan. Since I had already seen Petra, she said she would show me something of Jordan's Byzantine history. And so she drove me to Madaba, a town to the south-west of Amman. Here in the Greek Orthodox Church of St. George, we saw the famous mosaic map of the Middle East – 'the known world' as it would have been – with Jerusalem at its centre. I have long been fascinated by old maps – like the Mappa Mundi in Hereford Cathedral or the Gough Map at the Bodleian in Oxford – but this was older than either and far more pictorial. It was as if the monk laying the mosaic floor had said to a young apprentice: *"go up a mountain and sketch Jerusalem, making sure you include all the main buildings"*. That is probably what did happen and it would have been Mount Zion where the sketch or engraving was made, since Jerusalem is depicted from the west. The

Part of the Madaba mosaic map, with the walled city of Jerusalem at the centre. Below: the city of Jericho and, on the opposite bank of the Jordan, a gazelle being chased by a lion which has been obliterated.

map dates from the sixth century, for archaeologists say it includes the Church of Mary, the Mother of God (*Theotokos*), dedicated in 542 AD but does not show any building erected after 570. The map was probably made for the early Christian community in Madaba, which was the seat of a bishop.

The Madaba map is a wonder to behold and a wonder that it has survived. That part of the Byzantine empire was conquered by the Persians in the seventh century and by the Muslim Umayyad empire in the eighth century, when Madaba was largely destroyed in an earthquake and abandoned. It was resettled in the nineteenth century by Greek Orthodox Christians who built a new church. But it was only in 1964 that the mosaic map was revealed and saved from further damage – thanks to a grant of 90,000 Deutschmarks from the Volkswagen Foundation. During our visit, we saw German archaeologists still working on parts of the mosaic map, and on the mosaic floor of the demolished chapel of the Virgin Mary.

Nuha then took me to another Byzantine site at Mount Nebo. Here again were archaeologists at work on the mosaic floor of a demolished church, but the importance of this site was its location. Mount Nebo is the highest point on the mountains overlooking the Dead Sea and the Jordan Valley. It was here, according to the Book of Deuteronomy, that God allowed Moses a sight of the Land of Canaan and told him he would not be allowed to enter the Holy Land – according to legend, Moses is buried nearby. It was a clear, bright day for our visit. Nuha and I stood on the peak and looked west as Moses had done. I fancied that I could just see the golden dome of the Al-Aqsa Mosque in Jerusalem and Nuha – with a sigh – said how much she wished she could go back to the city of her birth. By that time I knew that I would be crossing the River Jordan to Jerusalem – and I felt a sense of guilt for what we, the British in particular, had done in this part of the Middle East. At that point, there was a sharp report, a sort of bang, and we could see a truck winding its way up from the edge of the Dead Sea. I had imagined it was a gunshot.

Jerusalem

I had gone to the British Embassy the day after I arrived in Amman. After a meeting with the First Secretary and the Press Officer, I was told that the ambassador wished to see me. The ambassador, Mr J.C. Moberly, asked whether I intended to go to the Israeli-occupied West Bank during my tour. I said *"No, it is not on my schedule"*, to which Mr Moberly said:

> *"Well, I think it should be. The Consul-General in Jerusalem tells me you have some very interested listeners in the West Bank. I think you ought to meet them."*

I went back to the hotel and sent a telex to Hamilton Duckworth, saying that the ambassador had suggested that I visit the West Bank – could I have permission to do so? The reply came a day later, not from Duckworth but Alec Stephens, Senior Personnel Officer:

> *'You may go to the West Bank only if you take leave. The trip will not be part of your Duty Tour.'*

On the advice of the embassy I registered with a tour company in Amman, who provided tickets for the bus down to the Allenby Bridge over the River Jordan and the bus from there to Jerusalem. I also booked a hotel in the city by fax and changed my flight back to London to Tel Aviv instead of Amman.

The Allenby Bridge (named after the British General who led the conquest of Palestine from the Ottoman Turks in 1918) was a temporary wooden truss-type structure, following the destruction of the proper bridge in the 1968 Six-Day War – but a modern paved bridge was erected alongside in 1994. I arrived in the bus and we all alighted and walked over the low water of the River Jordan. I was surprised – though I should not have been – to see that the Israeli soldiers manning the crossing were mainly young women. In due course, I reached the head of the queue at passport control where there was some consternation at the Syrian and Iraqi stamps in my passport. An officer was called and I carefully explained who I was and why I had visited Arab states. My explanation appeared to satisfy the officer, who directed that I could enter the West Bank without an Israeli stamp in my passport.

I stayed in the American Colony Hotel in East Jerusalem – rather expensive, particularly as the BBC was not paying, but then I was there for only three nights. It was convenient for the Old City and the Anglican St George's Cathedral, but also the Garden Tomb which some Christians believe is the site of the burial and resurrection of Jesus – rather than the later Church of the Holy Sepulchre. As soon as I arrived, I did what every tourist does and began to explore the Holy City on foot, going through the Damascus Gate into the Old City and down the Via Dolorosa towards the Temple Mount, but not joining the crowds at the Holy Sepulchre which would soon have been closing. It was a warm evening for late October and very pleasant.

The next morning, my first duty was to deliver a letter. It was from Peter Saleh, whom I had met at the Information Ministry in Amman, to his sister, Doris Saleh, who was head of the Palestinian YWCA in Jerusalem: it probably contained money, perhaps funds for the PLO, which may have been rash but I was travelling as a private citizen not a representative of the BBC.

Britain does not have an embassy in Jerusalem. When Israel was founded in 1947, after the first Israeli-Arab war, its temporary capital was Tel Aviv on the Mediterranean coast. The capital of Israel later moved to Jerusalem but, because of the dispute over the status of the city, most foreign embassies remained in or around Tel Aviv. Israeli governments have long campaigned for Western powers, like Britain, France, Germany and the United States, to recognise Jerusalem as the capital but it was only in 2018 that President Donald Trump acceded to that demand and moved the American embassy to Jerusalem. Thus, Britain has no embassy in Jerusalem – or does it? The British Consulate General is officially said to represent the UK government in Jerusalem, the West Bank and Gaza, and to provide consular services to British subjects in those areas. But it does more than that and is in some ways, an embassy to the Palestinians, independent of the official embassies in Tel Aviv and Amman, a sort of left-over from the days of the British Mandate from the League of Nations to govern Palestine.

On my first morning in Jerusalem – Monday 31 October – I went to the Consulate-General in the mainly Palestinian quarter of Sheikh Jarrah, and met the Consul-General, Michael Hannah. As his colleague in Amman had said, Mr Hannah had plenty to say about the BBC Arabic Service and the Palestinians. He emphasised the strong affection that many Palestinians had for the BBC, mainly the World Service to which educated Palestinians listened, but also the Arabic Service. Many Palestinians had grown up with the BBC and the Literary Arabic in which it broadcast was something many of them aspired to work and write in. However, in the past few years, its position had been challenged by a new Arabic language station, Radio Monte Carlo Doualiya (RMC), which was supposedly independent but was in fact funded by the French government. RMC had a strong signal from a Medium and Short Wave transmitter in Cyprus and its programmes were in many ways livelier than those of the BBC. That was something, said Mr Hannah, that the people in London ought to take note of. We discussed Palestinian politics and I told him that I was going to visit Birzeit University (BZU), on the recommendation of Doris Saleh of the YWCA – what were his thoughts on that? The Consul-General said that BZU had an interesting history: it had progressed from being an elementary school for girls to a teacher training college and then a university, and only the year before had become a full member of the Association of Arab Universities and was creating many new faculties. But it was controversial. The university's president – a member of the original founding Nasir family – had been exiled to Lebanon by the Israelis for being close to the Palestine Liberation Organisation. I should certainly go to Birzeit, said the Consul-General, and would meet all shades of Palestinian opinion there. At that time, the PLO was classed as a terrorist organisation by Israel and the United States because of its mission to liberate Palestine through armed struggle, but since the Oslo Accords of 1993-94 the PLO has repudiated war as its aim and been given observer status at the United Nations. Since then the PLO has been marginalised by the growth of Hamas in Gaza and Fatah in the West Bank.

Birzeit is a small town near Ramallah, about ten miles (17 km) north of Jerusalem. The university as I saw it was a collection of modern buildings around a series of courtyards. Incongruously, perhaps, when I arrived a rehearsal was in progress of Mendelssohn's oratorio *Elijah* and I waited in an ante-room, basking in the glorious music. Not all the faculty members who came to meet me were singers. Others had waited in their rooms for the music to stop. One of these was Hannan Ashrawi, Professor of English at Birzeit, and later an important figure in the First Intifada Palestinian uprising in 1988 and the follow-up to the signing of the Oslo Accords by Yasser Arafat and Prime Minister Yitzhak Rabin in the 1990s. Professor Ashrawi was a great friend and admirer of the Palestinian-American.

Two of the staff if Birzeit University – Dr Hanan Ashrawi and Dr Gabi Beramki.

scholar Edward Said. Also there were the political philosopher George Giacamon, the educationist Gabi Baramki and many faculty members. They wanted me and the BBC to know that education and academic thought were flourishing at Birzeit among Palestinians, who had stayed rather than going into exile. This was the real threat to the Zionist concept of the State of Israel, they said. They valued the BBC but asked that there should be more news about what was happening in the Middle East. They were particularly critical of the way that Palestinian affairs were ignored – there was far more attention to Israeli domestic politics than to the Palestinians. I came away from the meeting with many ideas to take back with me.

* * * * *

Before leaving Jerusalem, I went to see one of my oldest friends, Zvi Jagendorf. We had been together at school in Islington – the partial setting of his novel, *Wolfy and the Strudelbakers,* which was long-listed for the Booker Prize. We also overlapped for a year at Oxford. Zvi became an actor, appearing in plays for the Israeli Habbimah Theatre, including *The Dybbuk.* On Broadway he simultaneously translated from the Hebrew for Habbimah and in New York met his wife, Malkah. They moved to Israel and Zvi taught English and Theatre at the Hebrew University of Jerusalem. His 'Jerusalem Diary' – describing how he and Malkah read Jane Austin during the night bombing of the Six-Day War and the next morning compared notes with their Palestinian landlord about the different claims of Israeli and Jordanian radio – was published in the *London Review of Books* in 1991. He returned to the theme of Israel in the sixties in his second novel, *Coming Soon: The Flood*, published in 2018. Zvi had acted in the first ever performance of a medieval mystery play in the Holy Land, *The Flood,* at the Hebrew University – he of course was Noah.

* * * * *

Back in Britain, I spent some time with my family whom I had not seen for a month and in Bush House, when I returned to work, I found myself assaulted by all manner of distractions. The major one was the fortieth anniversary of the Arabic Service, on which everyone had been working in my absence. The main event was to be a concert in the Sadlers Wells Theatre for which the producer was Jacoub Musallam; my role was to fill the gaps in everyone else's preparations and to be on hand for advice and logistical support.

Consequently, it was three weeks before I had finished writing my Duty Tour Report, to be submitted to Bob Gregson, Controller Overseas Services, via the Head of the Arabic Service, Hamilton Duckworth. The report was in four sections: first a description of the political situation in the five countries I had visited; next a résumé of how radio was organised in the five states, including external broadcasting in languages other than Arabic; a small section covering the problems of the BBC's Cairo Office and its new recording studio;

finally, a longish section on 'Reactions to the Arabic Service'. Since this last section was criticised by the Controller, who asked me to omit it from wider circulation of the remainder of the report, I will summarise the main points it made:

1. The general image and reputation of the BBC is good, and the credibility of BBC News in English and in Arabic is high.
2. But BBC Arabic Service programmes appear remote from today's listeners and old-fashioned. BBC Arabic had lost listeners to Radio Monte Carlo Doualiya (RMC), and even to Voice of America.
3. BBC Arabic Service News is mostly a translation of the World Service News with little independent coverage of the Middle East. No other station broadcasting in Arabic devotes such little space to Middle East news.
4. BBC Arabic Service programmes could at least give greater prominence and more detail to Middle East stories already in the News.
5. BBC Arabic broadcasts seem second-hand; they should have more voice reports from the Middle East.
6. Voice of America in Arabic had recently extended its dawn transmission with more comment and analysis of Middle East affairs. BBC Arabic should do the same.
7. Apart from News and Current Affairs, much of the rest of the BBC Arabic Service output seemed old-fashioned and outmoded.
8. In the opinion of many people, the BBC Arabic Service had lost the younger generation to Radio Monte Carlo Doualiya and was in danger, because of its less dynamic approach to Middle East affairs, of losing older, professional listeners as well.

I submitted my report on 25 November and two weeks later received a memo from Bob Gregson, asking me to send him eight copies of the earlier part of the report *'which reflected the stimulating talk you gave to the Programme Liaison Meeting'*. But he added:

The Reactions section seems to me to be more of an integrated thesis than a collection of reactions and I found it most interesting though I think it ought to be collated with what Audience Research Dept. tell us. Some of the suggestions are obviously desirable in principle (despatches in voice in Arabic) but face difficulties of finance and reliability of journalists. Have you discussed them with H. Arabic S?

The phrase *'more of an integrated thesis than a collection of reactions'* made me see red, I am sorry to admit. I sent off a memo to Bob Gregson, asking if he was doubting my veracity, saying that I could show him notes made at the time – after meetings with Tahsin Basheer, Egyptian ambassador to the Arab League, Geoffrey Hancock, Minister at the British Embassy in Beirut, and Mohammed Sayseed, Under-secretary of Information in Amman – which all confirmed my summary of reactions. Besides a report just written by Raymond Micallef of the Audience Research Unit said much the same as I had done.

The Controller said he was sorry that I had written that note and asked to see me. At our meeting, he said that my summary of reactions in the Arab World to BBC Arabic Service programmes might not have been wrong, but it was unbalanced. The Audience Research report had balanced good and bad reactions, mine had not. He said he was disappointed in me: at one time he had seen me as a future Head of the Arabic Service.

10.
Sacked!

On my return to Bush House, I was thrown into preparations for the 40th Anniversary of the Arabic Service. All of the Arab unit heads were preparing programmes to celebrate forty years of broadcasts in their respective fields – drama, Arab music, international sport and so on. The culmination of the anniversary was a concert at the end of January, featuring artists from most parts of the Arab world and attended by ambassadors, BBC luminaries, academics and Arabic Service staff, past and present. It was staged in the old Sadler's Wells theatre in Islington, where in my teens I had seen the Sadler's Wells Opera (later the English National Opera) and the Sadler's Wells Ballet (later the Royal Ballet). But my memories of Bizet and Tchaikovsky were quickly blanked out by the sound of ouds and drums, singers scaling their half-tone chants and the hubbub of Arabic in a dozen accents and vocabularies.

My role was to sit in the control booth and do my best to smooth out any problems. It was a crowded booth containing the overall producer, Yacoub Musallam, his secretary with a stack of files, other unit heads coming and going as their acts took to the stage, a Sadler's Wells lighting guru and two BBC sound engineers, controlling levels for the live broadcast going out via Bush House to every part of the Arab world. I sat and marvelled as they modulated the output of a Lebanese pop group and then a male chorus from Morocco. The first half seemed to go well, followed by an interval during which World News in Arabic was to be broadcast back in Bush House. The two sound engineers left to find refreshments.

I looked at the programme and saw that an Egyptian singer was due to open the second half – she was not the internationally renowned Umm Kulthum, but a singer almost as famous for Egyptian audiences. I turned to Salah, in charge of music programmes, and said:

"*I hope she's ready.*"
"*Oh, no,*" he replied. "*She's waiting at the hotel and won't come until one of the English heads of the service goes to fetch her.*"

Not stopping to tell Salah what I thought of him, I hurried out of the theatre and hailed a taxi to the Waldorf-Astoria Hotel in Aldwych where I found the overdressed Egyptian *chanteuse* looking slighted and impatient at the lack of attention from the BBC. My apologies were profuse but it took some time for me to persuade her that the Director-General himself would have come, had he not been detained by Royalty. I ushered her to the waiting taxi and we arrived back at Sadler's Wells only 25 minutes behind schedule. Later I asked one of the sound engineers how they had filled the gap. "*Oh, they read the News in Arabic a second time,*" he said, "*but more slowly this time.*" A few days later, I attended a meeting in which Hamilton Duckworth praised Yacoub Musallam for the success of the concert without mentioning the contribution of others, including myself.

* * * * *

The anniversary concert overlapped with a sequence of happenings in which I was accused, tried, found guilty and then officially reprimanded for an incident which took place in December. It was a drawn-out process which left me hurt and rather puzzled. It began on 12 January when I received a memo from Hamilton Duckworth:

I have received a serious complaint against you by Mr Bishuty, a copy of which I attach. You will recall there was a complaint of a similar nature last year by [T-Dum]. Under the circumstances I have no alternative to pursuing this present complaint. Would you please let me have your written comments as soon as possible?

Musa Bishuty was the talented but rather touchy Palestinian who headed the features unit: the complaint was about a recording session for the 40th anniversary. Bishuty was in the studio with some outside contributors and I had interrupted the recording session because a contribution had just come in from Cairo, which I understood Bishuty wanted to include in the programme. He had certainly objected to my interrupting his recording, but I did not recall the sort of stand-up fight which he related in his two-page complaint, which he had dictated to Duckworth's secretary – so it said. That puzzled me. I was also puzzled by the reference to the scene with T-Dum about which I thought Duckworth fully accepted my explanation. I needed to collect my thoughts very carefully before replying – and in any case I was busy sorting out the contracts for the anniversary concert. On 20 January I received another memo from the Head:

Further to my memo of 12th January 1978 I should be glad to have your reply without further delay.

On 26 January he called me to his office and ticked me off for not replying. He then said he would record the interview, to which I objected that I should have been given notice of that. He said *'it was an investigative not a disciplinary interview and notice was not necessary'*. I explained why there had been a delay in my reply but he said (according to his record of the interview) *'I further said that I was not prepared to allow a management issue of such seriousness to remain unresolved and I required his written reply by 1200 on 27th January 1978'*.

I sat up late that night to put my case in a four-page memo and to meet his deadline. I explained the delay in my reply and my version of the events complained of. I also protested that Bishuty had told me that he wished to withdraw the complaint but Duckworth had told him *'the complaint had been made and cannot be withdrawn'*. I said that my relationship with the unit heads was good and I tried to be as supportive of them as possible:

'In conclusion, I feel that Mr Bishuty's complaint was the product of a talented but disorganised man who had sadly got himself into a terrible lather about a programme which he should have planned months ago. I was the poor Charlie who telephoned him when his Palestinian mettle was up. I am surprised that you have not appreciated this and that you have chosen to regard his complaint against me as "serious". I am also disappointed at your reluctance to allow this complaint to be dropped when Mr Bishuty requested it.'

* * * * *

That was not the end of the matter – not by any means. A week later I received another memo from Duckworth, asking me to attend for another recorded interview *'in connection with Mr Bishuty's complaint'* when the Head of Personnel, Chris Farmer, would also be in attendance. This was definitely going to be a disciplinary interview. The memo added that I could be 'accompanied by either an official Union Representative or a colleague on the staff of the BBC other than a practising lawyer'. I did not ask anyone to accompany me.

The interview took place on the 3 February and the record of it, written by Duckworth, ran to four pages. It was a devastating charge sheet complete with conviction. It again went over the complaint by Bishuty saying *'unfortunately this was not an isolated incident and I was bound to take account of others affecting myself and other members of the Service'*. He then outlined complaints against me by two of the unit heads, one of them being the News organiser, T-Dee, to which I replied that both incidents had resulted in apologies all round and that I was subsequently on good terms with both men. He accepted that, but then referred to Annual Reports he had written about me. In one Annual Report he had described me as *'contentious and quarrelsome'*. In another he had referred to my *'abrasive manner and tendency to get involved in altercations of which there had occurred a number with myself'*. This brought us to the heart of the interview, my relations with Hamilton Duckworth himself:

> *'I then reminded Mr Perman of two incidents affecting myself. On an occasion in December during the daily editorial meeting he had publicly referred to my editorial views as "nonsense". More recently, at an editorial meeting during the previous week he had suggested a talk about the situation in Tunisia. I had agreed that the suggestion was a good one, but said it would be premature to broadcast the talk immediately. It would be better to wait until the weekend or perhaps the beginning of the next week. Mr Perman had then commented audibly "or next month". This comment was either derisory of my editorial competence or sarcastic: either way it was entirely unacceptable to anyone in a managerial position such as mine.*
>
> *'There had been so many instances of Mr Perman's abrasive manner that I now had no option but to recommend that he should receive a formal reprimand. Regrettably he had now lost my confidence, and the incidents in which he had been involved called*

> *in question his fitness to work in a Service where tact and amicable relations were of supreme importance.'*

I was comprehensively condemned, and saw that arguments to the contrary would be pointless and self-defeating. I apologised for any personal offence I had caused to Duckworth and others.

* * * * *

Nor was that the end. In March, there was an attempt by the Assistant Head of the Arabic Service to embroil me in a discussion about refusing to take responsibility for editorial decisions. I side-stepped that and nothing further was said about it. Arabic Service affairs went on their way without any crises or altercations, at least in which I was involved. On 23 May, however, Lance Thirkell, the Controller for Administration, called me to his office and told me bluntly that Bob Gregson and Hamilton Duckworth had had enough: I was being removed from the post of Arabic Programme Organiser. Lance – the son of the novelist Angela Thirkell and, in happier days, a drinking companion in the BBC Club – then sent me a formal memo:

> *'I write with regret to inform you that you are being removed from the post of Arabic Programme Organiser forthwith because your relationships with your managerial colleagues have now become such as seriously to impair your effectiveness in the post.'*

He went on to say that an attachment had been arranged for me for three months with Central Current Affairs Talks – my old department, now headed by Leslie Stone – that my name would be placed on the resettlement list and every effort would be made to find me an alternative post, that efforts would also be made to safeguard my present salary though without the managerial lead, and finally that I had a right to appeal against the decision to remove me from my post. If I wished to take up that right, I was advised to discuss it with the Senior Personnel Officer, Alex Stevens.

The actual day of my departure from the Arabic Service was quite dramatic. I was told to go straight from Thirkell's office to Centre Block Reception, where my secretary was waiting with my brief case and some personal effects. I was told to go home to await a call from Alec Stevens. That call came five days later, when Alec outlined the procedure of appeal and agreed to accompany me to any appeal hearing in place of a Union representative, which I did not have. I was advised not to have any contact with the Arabic Service, but some of them contacted me. While I was still writing my appeal, a group of the Arab programme assistants – the rank and file, so to speak – invited me to the Club where we were joined by two or three of the unit heads. They had clubbed together to give me a leaving present, a pair of Egyptian brass plates decorated with Kufic calligraphy. Abdullah, a large Egyptian, had been deputed to present me with the plates; he put them on his chair while he went to the bar to buy me a drink. Forgetting where he had put them, he returned from the bar and sat on the plates. He bent them back into shape and they now hang on the wall in my sitting room.

My sacking as Arabic Programme Organiser was a shock, but not totally unexpected in view of the earlier recorded interviews and reprimand. Consequently, I had gathered together all the papers documenting my relationship with the service, and particularly with Hamilton Duckworth, and had taken them home. Since my earliest days in the External Services when Frank Barber destroyed all my Talks, I had been wary of my immediate bosses.

* * * * *

I set about preparing an appeal, having informed Alex Stevens of my intention to do so within the fourteen days laid down in BBC regulations, and submitted it on 14 June to MDXB – the Managing Director of External Broadcasting, Gerard Mansell. It was a lengthy document, running to nineteen foolscap pages, in which I argued that I had been summarily dismissed without any specific reason, that if the complaint of Bishuty was the reason then that was wrong since he had withdrawn the complaint, and then detailed over eight pages my achievements in two years as Arabic Programme Organiser. I wrote about the remoteness of Hamilton Duckworth, how for nine months he had sat on a request from one of the unit heads through me to appoint an outside contributor in Cairo, and how he had refused to discuss the recruitment crisis the Arabic Service was experiencing. I said that I believed the final straw for the Head of the Arabic Service had been my report on the Duty Tour to the Arab world, about which Hamilton Duckworth had said nothing to me at all. I mentioned my relationship with Duckworth and said that not once had he visited my office on the other side of the fourth floor of the Centre Block. I concluded the appeal with a plea for justice:

> *'I do believe ... that I can ask in all justice that both the disciplinary removal from my post and the previous, though connected, formal reprimand should be rescinded and that these decisions should be recorded on my personal file. I believe that, if it is conceded that my departure from the Arabic Service was necessary for managerial reasons but did not merit the disciplinary process that has been invoked, then I should be given either a simple transfer or voluntary attachment out of the Arabic Service and that efforts should be made to relocate me in a post of comparable responsibility and grade, while retaining my management lead on a standstill basis.'*

I discussed my dismissal and appeal with a number of friends. Their almost unanimous advice was that I should see what the appeal to Gerard Mansell produced, but should not then take the matter further – either by appealing to the Director General or, more seriously, by going to an industrial tribunal. If I did the latter then I could say good-bye to any further work in the media. But something curious happened in that regard. My wife's brother, Jonathan, was working in Personnel or Human Resources for a large industrial company and came across a barrister who was taking on unfair dismissal cases. Jonathan mentioned my case to him. A week later, the barrister was giving a presentation when he was approached by two Personnel officers from the BBC, who asked whether he was able to discuss a case for them. "*Oh, you mean the case of the Arabic Programme Organiser,*" the barrister replied. "*I know all about that.*"

* * * * *

Gerard Mansell gave his judgement on my appeal on 14 July 1978 – an auspicious date, I thought, since he was born in France. He began by dismissing my claim that I had been wrongly removed from the post of Arabic Programme Organiser, saying that my removal was not a disciplinary measure but the result of the Head of the Arabic Service losing confidence in my ability to do the job effectively. He said that my confrontational behaviour could not be excused by the frustrations I had experienced in the post, and added that he could not accede to my request that the formal reprimand I had been given should be rescinded or expunged. However, Gerry did agree with my claim that recent events should not obscure my professional competence as a journalist and current affairs man:

> *'I am happy to place on record that you are widely held to be a talented, versatile and imaginative current affairs and features producer, and that you have invariably shown yourself to be industrious and conscientious in the discharge of your duties. The latter also applies to your time as Arabic Programme Organiser, during which it is willingly recognised that you made laudable efforts to educate yourself for the job and worked hard to identify and seek to tackle the problems that faced you as Arabic P.O. However, you will recognise, I am sure, that in the latter capacity the wider managerial qualifications for the job do include the capacity to get on with those around you and to curb that side of your character which has led to the friction with them.*
>
> *'Every effort will be made to resettle you in an appropriate post, and I am sure that you will be treated on the merits of your performance. All will however depend on the success of your own efforts to correct the defects of which I know you are aware.'*

It was a fair judgement and I certainly did not expect the official recognition of my abilities as a journalist and current affairs producer – *'talented, versatile and imaginative'*. Wow! The tone of the judgement was positive and friendly, quite unlike the communications I had received from Hamilton Duckworth. And I certainly intended to follow the advice embodied in the final paragraph – to correct the defects of which I had been made aware in whatever job I was resettled. Two days after receiving Gerry's memo, I received another from Alex Stevens telling me I had the right to appeal further to the Director General. I had no intention of exercising that right and told Alex so.

* * * * *

Yet there were two aspects of my removal from the post of Arabic Programme Organiser, which were not apparent at the time and of which I became aware only very much later. One was that my removal was legitimised in terms of BBC Personnel rules as a *'redundancy'*. In other words, the post of Arabic Programme Organiser had been abolished. I learned of this five or six years later when someone asked me – in a confidential, it-doesn't-mean-anything sort of manner – whether I would ever consider going back to the Arabic Service. I then discovered that the new Head of the Arabic Service, Eric Bowman, wished to upgrade and rename the unit heads as *'organisers'*. But the word *'organiser'* was taboo unless and until I indicated that I had no intention of reclaiming my old job. I had a friendly chat with Eric and assured him that I was happy in my current job.

Just as interesting but more relevant was a second discovery, made much earlier. I was eventually resettled in the South European Service as Greek Programme Organiser, but it became clear to me that the Head, Andrew Mango, did not want me. He tried to get me to move back to the World Service as a current affairs producer. His persuasion was backed up with offers of various series of feature programmes, some of them involving extensive foreign travel and seemingly unlimited programme budgets. But where was the money coming from? Surely Andrew was not wasting his own department's resources on the whim of trying to get me to move on? Then someone in the know – I forget now who it was – told that the resources Mango was lashing out on feature series were not from his budget, but from the Arabic Service. Although the post of Arabic Programme Organiser had been abolished, it was still being charged to the Arabic Service budget and diverted to the South European Service. As a sweetener to persuade Mango to take me, he would receive the extra funds from the Arabic Service for two years.

11.
Interviewing the Ayatollah

I was at home in Ware in October 1978 when I received a phone call from Bush House, telling me that Mark Dodd, Head of the Eastern Service, wished to see me. I knew Mark – he lived in Broxbourne and we occasionally travelled up to Liverpool Street together. The Eastern Service was on the floor above the Arabic Service in Bush House, but I dismissed any idea that Mark might be offering me a resettlement job. He didn't, but the reason he had telephoned was intriguing.

During the summer – in another episode in the long-running feud between President Saddam Hussein of Iraq and his neighbour, Mohammad Reza Shah of Iran – Saddam Hussein had expelled from Iraq the Shah's bitterest critic, Ayatollah Ruhollah Mūsavi Khomeini. For fourteen years after the Shah had crushed a religious revolt against his rule, Khomeini had been living in one of Iraq's Shia holy cities and trying to rekindle an Iranian revolution while under virtual house arrest. Now he was let loose, living on a country estate in France and receiving his supporters and the media without hindrance. Mark Dodd told me all this and then said the BBC Persian Section thought they should interview Khomeini. After consulting throughout Bush House, he thought I was the person to do the interview – accompanied, of course, by a Farsi (Persian)-speaking colleague.

It was an intriguing assignment and a challenge. If I was to be resettled, following my sacking as Arabic Programme Organiser, then a high-profile interview with an Asian celebrity would do no harm. And so I began preparing for the interview. I knew only a little about Iran. At the *Observer Foreign News Service* I had commissioned a piece about Savak, the Shah's security police – doing so face-to-face with nothing in writing from a Tehran-based correspondent on leave, writing in London, and carefully not sending the piece to any newspaper in the Middle East – only to be told that the correspondent was arrested the day after we published it. I spent much time in the Persian Section, being briefed by a number of Iranians, especially by the Deputy Programme Organiser, Baqer Moin (pronounced *Mo-éen*). I also did a rapid study of the Shia branch of Islam, its origins in the disputed caliphate of Ali ibn Abi

Talib, the Prophet Muhammad's cousin and son-in-law, and also the beliefs and many distinctive ceremonies that separate it from the major Sunni branch.

I was fascinated by the ayatollahs or religious teachers of the Shia branch of Islam. Khomeini was not the only ayatollah, nor the most senior. As I read up about them, I wished I could instead be going to interview the Grand Ayatollah Hussein-Ali Montazeri, who advocated a liberal version of Islam. I was surprised to learn that at the University of Qom he taught classes on comparative religion, including Lutheranism. Montazeri was one of the leaders of the 1979 revolution and for a while was the designated successor to Khomeini before they fell out. But Khomeini was far from liberal, in religion or politics. The more I read about him the more I saw him as a revolutionary with a personal mission to overthrow the Shah and the existing order in Iran. I even wrote a poem about him, which was published in *The Listener*:

How the Name is Pronounced

Gin-and-tonic at the bar
to radio reporter from afar:
'You've met this ayatollah feller --
how d'you pronounce the name of the chap?
Is it Khó-many like a dry homily
or Kho-máiny -- as with a maniac?
Get my meaning?' said he with a slap.
'Neither. The stress is equal throughout:
Khó-méi-ní.' 'But that sounds
like a revolutionary shout.'
'Well, that's how the name is pronounced.'

Accompanying me to France for the interview was a member of the Persian Section, Ferydoon Jahed, the son of an imam but not, he told me, particularly religious himself. We travelled to Paris and had a meal together in a small restaurant on the Ile de la Cité, during which we got to know each other and swapped thoughts on the task ahead. In fact, it was tasks in the plural, since Fery had come armed with the addresses of other Iranian resistance leaders. So the following morning we toured the Paris suburbs by Metro, conducting short interviews with opponents of the Shah in a mixture of English and Farsi. The first was with Mehdi Bazargan, head of the Freedom Movement which advocated political and religious freedom of expression within the current constitution headed by the Shah. Another opposition figure was Shapour Bakhtiar of the National Front. At the apartments of both men, we were stopped, questioned and searched by armed supporters. Both men later played a brief role in Iranian politics – Bakhtiar as the Shah's last prime minister during the final days of the regime, and Bazargan as the first prime minister after the Islamic revolution, appointed by Khomeini but soon dismissed.

* * * * *

The next day – Thursday 9 November 1978 – the BBC's Paris correspondent, Stephen Jessel, drove us to the village of Neauphle-le-Château, west of Paris, where Khomeini's supporters had rented a house for him. It was a pleasant village without a chateau – nor had there ever been one, according to Stephen – and the house was a large one, on the main road. As we arrived, a red-haired woman was allowing her German Shephard dog to pee against the fence under the eyes of two uniformed gendarmes – a sign, perhaps, of local feeling about the Ayatollah. We parked the car and entered the courtyard, which was full of excited Iranians, many of them of student age. We were offered tea, to be drunk through sugar-lumps held between the teeth. There was a party atmosphere like a crowd before an inter-college football match or even a pop concert, quite different from the armed paranoia we had encountered in Paris the day before. Two older men greeted us – Ebrahim Yazdi, a pharmacologist who had flown over from America (later deputy prime minister and foreign minister under Khomeini, and then a leader in the liberal opposition), and Ayatollah Hujjat al-Islam Ishraqi, Khomeini's son-in-law (later also a member of the liberal opposition). At that early stage in what became known as the 'Islamic Revolution' it was the liberals and human rights campaigners who rallied to Khomeini; the hardliners and Islamic fundamentalists came later, after Khomeini had taken power.

The Ayatollah in the garden at Neauphle-
Le-Château – *photographed by a supporter.*

At a signal from Ebrahim Yazdi, Fery and I were ushered into the house and sat cross-legged before a crowd of Iranians, similarly seated. Fery pointed out to me Abolhassan Banisadr, a lecturer at the Sorbonne who was the BBC's contact with Khomeini, and later President of Iran under Khomeini. It was with Banisadr that the Persian Service had agreed four broad areas of questions I was going to put to the Ayatollah: did he want Iran to be ruled by Islamic laws, what was his main quarrel with the Shah, what was his attitude towards the United States and Britain, and how would he use Iran's oil wealth? What happened next is best told in words I recorded for a Radio 4 documentary in 2009:

"They showed us into this room and we sat cross-legged on the floor. Then he came in, sat down, squatted about two feet away, didn't look at us at all. A face of granite, no emotion whatsoever, no eye contact at all. The areas of questioning had been agreed in advance with the Ayatollah's people. The first question was about

Islam and I then assumed there was no place for the religious minorities, so I asked a question about the minorities. The Ayatollah answered it and then turned to his people. They all said to me: 'that was wrong, if you ask another question which is not in the script, we will stop this interview'. I said there is no script but they said yes there is, it's been agreed, there is a script."

It put me on the spot: to continue on those terms, with Khomeini just reading out his prepared answers from an exercise book, was not an interview as I understood it and certainly not an acceptable or broadcastable interview in BBC terms. On the other hand, to pack up and leave would have been discourteous and would certainly have antagonised Khomeini and his people. Besides we had come all that way to record what the Ayatollah had to say – better to get on with it and leave the issue of whether it was acceptable and broadcastable to others, back in Bush House. The producer of the Radio Four documentary, Mike Thomson, when he interviewed me said very firmly that I should have packed up immediately and left – though he did not include that point in the broadcast. In fact, I carried on with the interview, took it back to Bush where it was played and replayed, minus my English questions, and eventually broadcast to the angry consternation of the British Ambassador in Teheran, Sir Anthony Parsons, and Shah Mohammad Reza Pahlavi.

* * * * *

The Radio Four programme was in the 'Document' series, in which a producer looks again at a controversial issue in the light of newly released documents: the subtitle given to the programme was 'BBC Bias and the Iranian Revolution' – it can still be found online at *www.bbc.co.uk/programmes/b00j6lk*. The programme was followed by a study by academics, looking in greater detail at BBC and Foreign Office (FCO) papers in the National Archives and elsewhere [Massoumeh Torfeh and Annabelle Sreberny, *The BBC Persian Service and the Islamic Revolution of 1979*, I.B. Tauris & Co. London & New York, 2014]. From these sources I learned much more about the background to my interview with the Ayatollah than I could have done in the 1970s. I also learned some surprising judgements about my own involvement in the interview.

The sources revealed that the interview with the Ayatollah was not a hastily organised event that caught people by surprise; it was the sequel to a chain of events throughout 1978. During the summer anti-Shan demonstrations and strikes paralysed the country. By November, Iran was said to be *'within an ace of a total collapse of law and order'* and the military government had ordered that as a temporary measure the local media had to be brought under strict control. As a result the FCO was in constant communication with the BBC over the coverage of events by the Persian Service. The Shah's government mounted a campaign against the BBC which the British ambassador was only too happy to endorse; British supporters like Julian Amery MP and Lord George Brown attacked the BBC in print, claiming that young radicals had taken over the Persian Service and were calling for the overthrow of the Shah by force and his replacement by Khomeini. The Iranian ambassador in London made similar claims in a letter to Sir Michael Swann, chairman of the BBC Board of Governors. Gerard Mansell, Managing Director of the External Services, ordered an investigation which showed that all the claims by the Shah's people were ill-founded: from August to October 1978 the Persian Service had broadcast the words of Ayatollah Khomeini only twice and there had been no call for an armed uprising. The FCO knew that the BBC intended to interview Khomeini and, even though it tried to delay the interview until the situation in Iran was clearer, it did not try to stop it. On 14 December, the Foreign Secretary, David Owen MP, wrote to Sir Michael Swann:

> *I am a strong believer in the independence of the BBC and the value of the BBC's external broadcasts. I have therefore been scrupulous about defending your independence at all stages. I believe it would be gravely damaging to the long-term future of Britain's standing in the world if there were to be an attempt of Government interference. I have, however, to assure myself that you and your board are fully aware of the criticisms from foreign governments and I feel it is my responsibility to satisfy myself that you have given the representations of foreign governments full consideration.*

But by then our interview with Khomeini had gone out on the air to far greater effect than anyone had expected. In the Radio Four documentary Andrew Whitley, who was the BBC's correspondent in Iran, recalled the reaction: *"almost everyone in the country was talking about this, talking about what he had to say, the fact that he was interviewed at that time. People would stop each other in the streets, in the bazaars, saying: Did you hear him, he'd been finally allowed to talk? It had a huge impact."* Whitley was asked by Mark Thomson how he would answer the allegation that the BBC had fanned the flames of the Iranian revolution by broadcasting the interview:

> *I wouldn't use those words – fan the flames of the revolution – but the BBC did play a role and it was something that was uncomfortable for BBC management to admit openly – they didn't at the time. Yes, I would agree that the BBC made a difference. If it wasn't for the BBC's broadcasting to the country and the huge listenership, the revolution might not have proceeded as quickly as it did. ..... I think the BBC ought to be careful about overstepping the line between reporting and being seen as part and parcel of the opposition movement. I don't believe that the BBC as a foreign broadcasting organisation ought to be in a position of attempting to change the direction.*

Other commentators on Iran agreed that our interview with Khomeini made a difference and that we were used by the Ayatollah to put over his message without modification or supplementary questions. Mark Dodd, Head of the Eastern Service, admitted as much:

> *I think it's an unsatisfactory basis on which to conduct an interview. I have always thought so. You could argue that the man himself was the story. What you could get out of him was going to illuminate the character of the man. I think you can make a case for an interview of that kind. But I would have thought that our coverage was not as full as we would have wished, and there were undoubtedly gaps. I am not saying this was an impeccable service; there were occasions when we made mistakes. I am still sorry that we made those mistakes. They were infinitely less than our critics suggested.*

After our interview with Khomeini, events moved swiftly. The interview was broadcast later in November 1978; in December the Shah appointed a new prime minister, Shapour Bakhtiar, who carried out some reforms including the dismantling of the security service, Savak; on 17 January 1979 the Shah and his family left Iran; on 1 February Khomeini returned to Iran at the invitation of the government; on 1 April Khomeini declared an Islamic Republic after a referendum with only one question, Islamic Republic: Yes or No? Then later in 1979 came the so-called 'Iran hostage crisis' when 52 Americans were held hostage for fourteen months by student followers of Khomeini – a crisis which overshadowed the 1980 US Presidential Election in which Ronald Reagan defeated the incumbent President Jimmy Carter.

* * * * *

It is now widely accepted that the BBC and its Persian Service were used by Khomeini and his followers while he was in exile. But what of my personal responsibility for the interview – and even for the Islamic Revolution itself? Until 2009 and the Radio Four documentary, my role had been forgotten. My English questions had been cut from the interview with the Ayatollah Khomeini before it was broadcast so that Mike Thomson, producer/presenter of the documentary, could say that he had managed *"to track down"* the man who conducted the interview.

Both the Radio Four documentary and the academics' paper acknowledged that my role as the interviewer was limited, that the questions has been agreed in advance and formed the basis of the Khomeini's *'script'*. But not everyone agreed. Brian Alikhani PhD – an Iranian exile in America and a very busy blogger against Khomeini's Iran – argued that the BBC in collusion with the FCO was determined to bring down the Shah. Both Sir Anthony Parsons, the British Ambassador, and Andrew Whitley were involved, but their role was merely to prepare the ground.

The BBC's fatal blow to the Shah was delivered by David Perman who interviewed the mysterious Ayatollah in Paris in 1978. "Khomeini did what he wrote in his books," says Abbas Milani who is a visiting professor of Political Science and the director of the Iranian Studies program at Stanford University. We all know that all Perman had to do was to read the comic books of the Ayatollah to learn about his views about women, injustice, minorities, and other religions in Iran. "A responsible journalist should always read the books of the people they interview," says Milani. Perman, however, was determined to transform the granite face of the Ayatollah to a 'Gandhi-like figure.' BBC was indeed the microphone and the mouthpiece for the Ayatollah's dirty mouth.

I do not know how widely Alikhani's blog was read. And perhaps one should not take too seriously the views of a blogger who proclaimed that the letters B-B-C stood for the 'British Bragging Corporation'. But it is worth setting against that partisan attitude the way that the BBC reported the interview to the Prime Minister. Among the private papers of Margaret Thatcher is a note dated 29 October 1979 from Bob Gregson, Deputy Managing Director of the BBC External Services, about the interview with the Ayatollah:

Khomeini's voice was not heard [in BBC broadcasts to Iran] until two skilled interviewers from the Persian Service visited him in Paris. The austerity of their cross-examination revealed the thread-bare political ideas of the Ayatollah and his aides cut short the interview which was nevertheless broadcast.[1]

---

[1] 791101 James to MT (394-159).pdf

12.
Greek Programme Organiser

While the world digested the startling news from Iran, back in Bush House I was looking for another job. I was a resettlement case, in BBC terms a 'supernumerary', and had been warned that if I did not find another job that would be the end of my relationship with the Corporation. There was a vacancy in Broadcasting House for a Senior Producer with *Analysis*, the Radio 4 current affairs programme similar to *The World Today* on which I had worked in 1974. I applied and was short-listed for interview.

On 13 January 1979, I was given a recorded interview with JCH Farmer, Head of Personnel Language Services. I had known Chris Farmer in my freelancing days when he was Swahili Programme Organiser. He told me that I was to be given an attachment in the South European Service for six months as Acting Greek Programme Organiser; if my performance in that role was satisfactory, I would be appointed Greek PO substantive. I asked why a trial period was necessary; he replied it was because I had been removed from the position of Arabic Programme Organiser after an unhappy relationship with the Head. The vacancy in the Greek Section had resulted from the promotion of the previous Greek PO, Paul Nathanail, to Assistant Head of the South European Service following the death of Jim Nadler – formerly the Spanish PO and a good friend of mine. In fact, the attachment as Acting Greek PO lasted only two and a half months and I became the substantive Programme Organiser on 1 April 1979 – three days before the general election which brought Mrs Margaret Hilda Thatcher to power, as Britain's first female prime minister.

It was a good outcome, but unwittingly I had become the focus of a truly Byzantine *imbroglio* – involving the Istanbul-born Andrew Mango (whose brother, Cyril, was a professor of Byzantine Studies) and the question: who should control the Greeks? It was obvious that Mango did not want me and, if it had not been for the Arabic Service sweetener, would have dug in his heels to keep me out. For him I was damaged goods, a possible trouble-maker and, besides, he had already offered the job of Greek PO to someone else. That person was Richard Clogg, lecturer in history at King's College London whose *Short History of modern Greece* had been published in 1979.

In his later memoir, *Greek to Me* (I.B. Tauris, 2018), Richard said he was offered the position of Greek Programme Organiser having done it on a temporary basis while Paul Nathanail was covering for the sick Jim Nadler – taking 'scarcely five minutes' to finish his teaching in King's and cross the Strand to his office in Bush House. He wrote that when it was offered, he replied he did not wish to give up his academic job but was then told – in a spirit of generosity I found it difficult to reconcile with the Bush House management I knew – that there would be no trouble in keeping his teaching post while working full time for the BBC. Whatever the truth of that and whatever Andrew Mango's feelings about me, the clear winner of the whole episode was the financial inducement from the Arabic Service. Mango saw it as a win-win situation and intended to use the windfall to enrich the output of the South European Service, while at the same time hoping to persuade me to leave for a job in the World Service. Thus from 1979-81 I spent less time with the Greeks than I did making feature programmes in English, which were used in translation in Spanish, Italian, Turkish and Greek but were also broadcast as I had made them by the World Service. Andrew Mango was a wily character, a true Franco-Levantine, brought up in Turkey and formerly the Turkish Programme Organiser. He was fluent in a variety of European languages but spoke them with a guttural accent. He was a pipe smoker and had a terrible smoker's cough.

Two photographs of this period marked my transition from 'Acting' to substantive Greek Programme Organiser. The first was with a group of five Greek newspaper editors visiting Bush House; the photo also included Peter Fraenkel, Controller of European Services and a former Greek PO, Andrew Mango and Paul Nathanail. The other photo showed the 'newly-appointed BBC Greek Programme Organiser' with winners of the section's 40th anniversary essay competition, also with Paul Nathanail.

Before sending me off to spend the Arabic Service windfall on programmes, Mango was obliged to give me some experience of Greece. The opportunity was a promotional visit to Athens and northern Greece. In the capital a symposium was being held on the National Day (25 March) to celebrate the role of the BBC in two noteworthy events – the liberation from German occupation in 1945 and the end of the seven-year military dictatorship in 1974. A large

The newly-appointed Greek Programme Organiser (second left) with visiting Greek newspaper editors and Peter Fraenkel, Controller European Services (fourth left), Paul Nathanail, Assistant Head of the South European Service (fifth left), and Andrew Mango, Head of the South European Service (third right).

Below: saying my first public words in Greek at the symposium in Athens with Paul Nathanail.

lecture hall in the University of Athens was filled with veterans of both campaigns, seated in sombre ranks before a dais, and among the main speakers were Andrew Mango and Paul Nathanail, whose recent promotion had left the vacancy which I now filled. Paul coached me in a few words of Greek – 'I am honoured to be here where my countrymen gave their blood for your freedom'.

After the symposium, we took a ferry from Piraeus to Kavala, the principal port of the Province of East Macedonia and incidentally the centre of the Greek tobacco industry. It is an interesting city and we were booked into a hotel there, but our main business the following day was to travel to the village of Gallipolis to present the villagers with a bell. So the next morning, the four of us – Mango, Paul Nathanail, his wife Ketty who looked after Greek audience research, and I – piled into a taxi and headed into the hills of ancient Thrace. Gallipolis – not the site of the abortive Allied landing on the Turkish coast in 1915 but similarly named – was the home of a British Army veteran who had been elected mayor and had written to the BBC asking if we could help his village acquire a bell. Mango and Nathanail were excited by the publicity possibilities and sent a programme assistant to Portobello market to buy a second-hand bell. They alerted the Press in Athens and then arranged the trip to Gallipolis. The mayor, who was named Adonis, spoke excellent English but nobody had mentioned before that he was a Communist – not of the Euro-Communist KKEes but of KKE, the Marxist-Leninist party with unswerving allegiance to Moscow. So the ceremony, which was entirely secular and displayed no sign of the village priest or any if his supporters, included a rendering of the *Internationale* – all in front of reporters and photographers.

When the ceremony of hanging the bell was done and we had toasted the bell, the mayor and the village of Gallipolis in *tsipero* (the local spirit), a young child appeared and said the priest was inviting us to refreshments. We followed him to the far side of the village and a large house with a veranda where a portly cleric greeted us, surrounded by his family. He was clearly miffed that we had not greeted him first before consorting with the Communist mayor; that rebuke out of the way, the priest invited us to sit on the veranda while his wife served banana brandy and cakes. The priest said he was from Cyprus: when I said I had once interviewed President Makarios who had died in 1977, he said the late Archbishop was no better than the

Communist mayor of the village. There were clearly echoes of a *Don Camillo* dispute in Gallipolis.

* * * * *

In 1979 the South European Service moved from cramped offices in the South-East Wing of Bush House – on the same floor as the Talks department where I had first worked – to roomier offices in the North-East Wing. They were certainly roomier, but the Greek Programme Organiser's office was poky compared to the Centre Block room I had occupied exclusively as Arabic Programme Organiser. I shared my new office with a secretary, a gay Cypriot named Charalámbos Morphítis, known as 'Pámbos'. He was an efficient secretary, certainly, but he constantly complained of being victimised by the mainland Greeks. I soon understood that that was mainly for my benefit as his new boss; soon after I joined, the section held a party at the house in Tottenham which Pambos shared with his partner, a tall, kindly Irishman named Patrick, and it was obvious that the mainland Greeks liked and respected Pambos as much as they did each other – though some of them could not refrain from joking and pulling his leg. But he had a doughty defender in Kristina Koutsoudáki, a former actress who was always prepared to listen to Pambos's worries.

The South European Service moved to the North-East Wing, but there were fewer of us. Cuts in the Foreign Office Grant-in-Aid meant that the BBC External Services stopped broadcasting in Italian and in Spanish and Portuguese for Europe – broadcasts to Latin America in Spanish and Portuguese were unaffected. There were redundancies and an impassioned confrontation at a Service meeting, which Mango deflected by saying he and Gerard Mansell had done their best to get Whitehall to think again. One of those who had lost his job was Tony Menezes, the Goa-born Portuguese Programme Organiser. For a reason I cannot now remember, Menezes asked me if I had ever interviewed Tony Benn MP, who had been Secretary of State for Energy in the Labour government until April; if so, did I know him well enough to arrange a meeting? I did indeed know Tony Benn: he had been to the *Twenty-Four Hours* studio a number of times, always producing a pocket tape recorder so that he recorded what we were recording with no excuse for edits, and always finishing the interview in his own time – 'Well, you invited me for a four-minute interview and we've done four minutes – So Good-bye.' He had once been a producer in Bush House. So I telephoned Benn and took Menezes to meet him at his house in Holland Park. They got on well together – Menezes had revered Benn from his days as a student activist in Goa. As we were leaving, Benn turned to me and asked how we knew each other. I mentioned the interviews for *Twenty-Four Hours,* but added that I knew the elderly Communist couple who had lately caused his family such embarrassment. They were a Mr and Mrs Rowe, who had leased a cottage attached to my parents-in-law's house at Little Baddow, Essex, and then moved on to a property occupied by Benn's mother, Lady Stansgate, where – it was said – Tony would sit and read Karl Marx with them. They had recently been in the news because a neighbour was suing Lady Stansgate, claiming that Mr and Mrs Rowe were terrorising him by shouting slogans over the fence. I told Tony Benn of the connection and he got very excited – calling up the stair-well to his wife: 'Caroline, come down. There's a Mr Perman who knows Mr and Mrs Rowe and might give evidence for us.' I did not give evidence because the case was dropped to the relief of the whole Wedgewood Benn family.

Broadcasts from Bush House in Italian and Spanish and Portuguese for Europe had been curtailed but Andrew Mango managed to keep a residual service in those languages – the BBC would produce some feature programmes which would be dispatched to Rome, Madrid and Lisbon for broadcast by their domestic services. I was to be involved in the prototypes, a pair of interviews about the modern novel in Europe. Mango suggested Camilo José Cela, the Spanish novelist, poet and essayist who had recently been appointed a Royal Senator and member of the body drawing up a new Constitution after the death of General Franco; for the other, I suggested the exiled British novelist Anthony Burgess, who had fled Italy after an attempted kidnap of his wife and son.

I flew to Barcelona where I was met by Maria, a young woman from Spanish radio. She said she had come amid complaints from her daughter about going to Mallorca on holiday without her. We took the mid-morning ferry to Palma and walked from the port to Cela's house, which Maria had visited before. The poet understood some English but did not speak it, and so Maria translated my questions to

*Camilo Jose Cela and Anthony Burgess – two novelists
Interviewed for the BBC South European Service*

him and then translated his answers for me. It was a worthy, fairly anodyne interview – about his support as a young man for Franco, about his novels, short stories, essays and poetry, why some of his writing had been banned under Franco and his thoughts on present-day Spain and the novel in the 1970s. He was one of the greats of Spanish letters and was awarded the Nobel Prize in Literature in 1989, but there was also a controversial, naughty side to him which he did not show to the BBC – in 2007, in an interview for Spanish television, he boasted that he could absorb litres of water via his anus and offered to demonstrate it to the female interviewer.

To interview Anthony Burgess I flew to Nice and took the train to Monaco. I arrived at his house and he denied all knowledge of our appointment; in the background I could hear his son having a clarinet lesson. Then Burgess relented, saying that if I had any smokes – in fact I had some small cigars – he would supply whisky and we could talk. The interview covered a lot of ground. I expressed my admiration for the *Enderby* novels – there had been three at that stage, *Inside Mr Enderby* (1963), *Enderby Outside* (1968) and *The Clockwork Testament, or Enderby's End* (1974) – and asked if they were in any sense autobiogrsphical. He said they were and then told me of his feelings at being an exile, first to escape his critics and then the tax man. He had an ambivalent attitude towards Britain and things British. One thing he missed, he said, as a lapsed Catholic, was the hymns sung in the Protestant Church of England. He talked about the novel as a literary form – the subject of his 1967 book *The Novel Now* – and elaborated on the theme of 'dystopias' as used by Orwell in *Nineteen Eighty-Four*, Huxley in *Brave New World* and himself in *The Wanting Seed* and *A Clockwork Orange*. But then he said that he could not see a future for novels as expensive, time-consuming publications. He had met students who had photocopied their poems and were giving them away to passers-by and he thought novels would go the same way. We parted on good terms and his wife, Liana, took a careful note of my phone number which she used to chase up BBC contracts in the coming years.

* * * * *

In 1979 I realised that I had a 'guardian angel' in Bush House. He was a knowledgeable, influential, at times mischievous figure. His name was Austen Kark – at that time Controller of Engineering for the External Services but previously Head of the South European Service which embodied and extended his great love of Greece. I had first known him through the BBC Club, where he would stand at the middle of the bar with a glass of white wine and regale junior producers with tales of his earlier career as a journalist. He was married to the novelist, Nina Bawden, and they lived in a house backing on to the Regent's Canal in Noel Road, Islington, where my mother had gone to school. They each had children by earlier marriages and a daughter together, Perdita. They previously lived in the true-blue Surrey town of Woking and I recalled Austen's tale of delivering election leaflets for the Labour Party and sending little Perdita to push them through doors, while he and Nina hid behind a hedge. Austen later became Deputy Managing Director of External Broadcasting, under Douglas Muggeridge ('Doug the Mug'). It was then that he gave me an attachment to answer listeners' letters and write reports – such was Austen's sense of style and fun that he persuaded me wherever possible to include the phrase 'beyond a peradventure'.

The three-month attachment to Doug the Mug's office was informative and quite fascinating. The listeners' letters came from all over the world, including Britain which was not supposed to provide listeners to the World Service – that was the job of Radio 4

Austen Kark and his wife, Nina Bawden

and its sister stations 1, 2 and 3. However, at that time the World Service had a loyal and highly articulate audience in Britain. This was partly due to 'leakage' from the Medium Wave transmitter at Orford Ness on the Essex Coast, which beamed the World Service to Europe during daylight hours. It was also due to Radio 4 going off the air at 0100 and – because it would have been inconvenient and expensive to switch off its transmitters for just over four hours and then power them up again – switching to broadcasting the World Service. The National Anthem would be played to end Radio 4, then after a brief silence the World Service would be heard without any announcement or lead-in. At 0530, the World Service would be replaced by that splendid melody of patriotic tunes, beginning and ending with *Rule Britannia*, which went under the name of 'UK Themes' – composed by the Austrian-born Fritz Spiegl. There were sharp listener protests when 'UK Themes' was discontinued in 2006 as old-fashioned and replaced with something 'pacey'. At Bush House, I had to deal with letters asking why the World Service had to go off the air at 0530, what were the names of the anonymous newsreaders, where could listeners purchase a recording of *Lillibolero,* the signature tune for the News, so on and so forth.

It was through these night-time broadcasts that my father's long-lost cousin, Pat, an insomniac, made contact with me and then my parents. During the attachment, I was given the chance to visit the Long Wave transmitters at Daventry and Droitwich, in the company of Austen Kark, and there was an intriguing visit to the Monitoring Service at Caversham, near Reading, where a section devoted to traffic with the government's listening service, GCHQ, and the Americans, was emphatically declared off-limits to us.

Austen became Managing Director of External broadcasting in 1984 and was made CB. After his retirement, he and Nina bought a house in Nafplion in the Peloponnese but had to rebuild it after second-world-war Italian grenades were discovered in the roof. Austen was killed in the 2002 Potters Bar rail crash, in which Nina was seriously injured. I went with my partner, Danielle Hope, to the memorial service for Austen which was held in St Martin-in-the-fields and was full to overflowing; the mood of the service was one of hilarity, as friend after friend recalled incidents in Austen's life, especially the time when he had to have his claw toes straightened. The Potters Bar crash was caused by poor rail maintenance by the private contractor, Jarvis, and Nina Bawden wrote a furious indictment of the firm in her book, *Dear Austen,* which also included a poem by Danielle.

13.
Nafplion in the Peloponnese

It was probably through Austen that I got my job as Greek Programme Organiser. It was certainly through him that I was given a ten-week stay in Nafplion to learn Greek, starting in January 1980. He chose Nafplion on the assumption that there would not be many tourists there in winter to tempt me to speak English. He also arranged for a friend to be my fixer and guide – a splendidly hospitable Athens businessman named John Drossos. John held the Greek franchise for Ladybird children's books and conducted the business in such an un-Greek manner that one day he opened a newspaper to read that he was the biggest taxpayer in the country, i.e. the one who was most honest about his profits. John met me in Athens, drove me to Nafplion and arranged both my accommodation and my tutor in Modern Greek.

* * * * *

The Peloponnese is that region south of the Gulf of Corinth, containing many of the sites of Ancient Greece – Argos, Mycenae, Epidaurus and Sparta among them. The town of Nafplion is also ancient, but it is best known as a Venetian and Ottoman seaport which in 1821 became the first capital of the independent Hellenic Republic of Greece. Independence from Turkish rule was achieved with the aid of volunteers from all over Europe and there is a memorial in the town to these 'Philhellenes', including Lord Byron. Nafplion is at the top of the Argolic Gulf and the port is still active, including for cruise ships – unfortunately. In the harbour is the island of Bourtzi with a small Venetian castle, once used as a prison. When I was there I learned that it had inspired a children's skipping game: *'Ourtzi, Bourtzt, Fa, la, la'*. The town has many historic sites including a Turkish hamam or bathhouse and nearby the Church of St Spyridon, on the steps of which Count Ioannis Kapodístrias, the first president of independent Greece, was assassinated in 1831 by members of the Mavromichalis ('Black Michael') family. The house where Austen and Nina Kark lived was in the same area of the town. But the biggest and most visible feature from its history is the castle of Palamídi, built by the Venetians in 1686 but abandoned to the Turks in 1715. It overshadows the town from a 216-metre high hill. There are 913 steps up from the town, but a thousand to the very top, and a local challenge is to run all the way to the summit without stopping.

Nafplion is now a major tourist centre and hub. New hotels, fast food outlets and that bane of Greek heritage sites – glossy jewelry shops – have sprung up. When I went there to learn Greek, it was only five years after the fall of the Colonels. Greece had yet to apply to join the European Community and Nafplion was much as it had been at the end of the Second World War. Communications were quite primitive. A narrow-gauge railway from Corinth to Tripolis deeper in the Peloponnese ran through nearby Argos, but the only reliable public transport was the KTEL buses. The bus took two hours 20 minutes, with a stop near the Corinth Canal for toilets and souvlaki. Buses and cars had a long and tortuous journey through hamlets where it was said Heracles performed some of his legendary tasks. Now a European-financed motorway comes near Nafplion and the journey time for tourists is considerably shortened.

* * * * *

John Drossos had telephoned ahead to secure my accommodation. It was in the fishermen's quarter ('*Psariamachalás*'), up a steep hill or two flights of steps from the main street to a lane called *Zygomála*. I had a bedsit room in a large house, owned by Mrs Mastorákis, a woman with a large family who also gave bed room, Monday-to-Thursday nights, to girls from outlying villages attending the Nafplion *yimnásio*. The room was unheated but I was well provided with blankets. The rule of the house was that I was not allowed to use the bathroom, Tuesday-to-Friday mornings, until the girls had gone to school – fortunately there was a separate toilet. Kyría Mastoráki allowed me to use her electric cooker and fridge, but mostly I bought food from a single-room shop opposite the house. My lunch was usually a bread roll, feta cheese, olives in a twist of newspaper and a small bottle of local wine or retsina. I sent a description of the Mastorákis house back to the Greek Section and Pámbos, my secretary, replied that I made it sound like living in an Old People's home or orphanage. Another friend wrote that the lack of heating and poor weather made it sound like exile.

The castle of Palamidi seen from Nafplion harbour in 1980 before the cruise ships began arriving.

My Greek teacher was a schoolmaster from the *yimnásio* in Argos, who would come in by bus and begin our lesson in the bus station café. He spoke no English – or very little – and treated me as a three-year old, pointing at a house: *Aftá eenai éna spíti,* and asking how many windows the house had: *Pósa paráthira ekei to spíti?* I found this method of teaching slow and uninspiring and longed for the intensive language tuition I had had in Arabic with Dr Haleem of SOAS. During a shopping trip to Athens, I purchased a simple Greek grammar and phrase book and worked with those while continuing lessons with the schoolmaster. The language I was learning – or attempting to learn – was *Nea Eleeniká* (new Greek), a reformed version of *Dimotikí*, the Greek spoken by ordinary people. The 'cleaned-up' Greek of the nineteenth century, *Katharévousa*, was officially abandoned in 1976.

I arrived in Nafplion in January when the days were short and there were few tourists about. In a café by the harbour, a group of women – English and German or Scandinavian – who had married or dated Greek men at the height of summer, sat throughout the day looking deserted and resentful. There were a number of cafés and restaurants on the main street frequented by Greek families. By far the best was a fish restaurant on the harbour, known as *Savouras* – that was a Greek word for rubbish or the flotsam thrown overboard from a ship. The story was that the man who founded the restaurant was reluctant to hand it on to his son, whom he regarded as useless – 'rubbish'. But the son took it on, called it *Savouras* and made a success of it. It was a restaurant where customers were invited in to see the fish on offer: a chosen fish would be weighed and the price given before it was cooked. The speciality of *Savouras* was *sabouni,* red mullet.

Two doors away from *Savouras,* on the harbour, was the Yacht Club, a restaurant and bar run by two brothers. Yannis Psomadarkis did the cooking and Kostas Psomadarkis ran the bar, which he did with great flare. The cream of the Nafplion intelligentsia gathered in the Yacht Club which in the winter opened only in the evening. There was a doctor, the harbour master, two commercial travellers, the colonel in charge of the local police and few tourists who had forgotten to go home. Among these was Enrico Thorn Prikker, the Italian grandson of the Dutch-German artist Johan Thorn Prikker. Enrico had lived in Nafplion for two years. He was also a painter but his main interests were collecting tales about the traditional 'characters' of the Peloponnese. One of his stories was about an undertaker from a poor family who fell in love with the mayor's daughter, but was rejected by her and her family; later, when he had made a fortune from undertaking, he would follow the woman and whenever she ate in a restaurant he would go in afterwards and buy the cup, plate and cutlery she had used. Nafplion was full of *karaktires* like that, he said. It was Enrico who pointed out the townsmen with fair skins and blond hair – probably descended from the Austrians who in 1832 had arrived with Otto von Wittelsbach, the first king of modern Greece.

Kostas Psomadarkis became a great friend and offered to show me the antiquities of the Peloponnese and especially those near Nafplion. On a Monday in February, he drove me through Argos to Mycenae, the headquarters of Agamemnon who with his brother, Menelaus of Argos, started the Trojan war to bring back Helen, the errant wife of Menelaus. Mycenae is a hilltop citadel, entered through the impressive Lion Gate. New grass from the rain of November covered the site of the fortifications, looking down over the Plain of Argos; it is said Mycenae is at its best when spring flowers appear, but we were too early for them. Nearby is the Tomb of Clytemnestra, Agamemnon's queen and his murderer. The story of the Trojan war is told, of course, in the *Iliad* of Homer, but the tangled relationships of Agamemnon's family continued after the war and were the subject of the tragedies of Aeschylus, Sophocles and Euripides. From Mycenae, Kostas drove on to the great amphitheater of Epidaurus, where in the 4th century BC those tragedies would have been performed. The great theatre is a triumph of acoustics: it is said an actor in the centre of the stage can be heard at any of the seats above. There were few tourists on the day we visited but still there were people trying to be heard by friends high up on the terraces.

On another Monday – the day the Yacht Club was closed – Kostas and I took a ferry down the Argolic Gulf to Leonidhion, a fascinating port which was difficult to get to by road at that time. It sits in the cleft between the steep sides of two mountains. Because of its isolation, the port (also known as Plaka) became a favourite with Athenians who took the comparatively short sea journey from Piraeus. Among Greeks, Plaka is best known for its aubergines (*melitzána*): an aubergine festival is held every August, attracting chefs from all over Europe. One of the local sites is the Elona Monastery, clinging to the sheer cliffs just outside the town. Kostas and I had lunch in a small fish taverna beside the harbour and then took the ferry back to Nafplion – it was the same boat we had arrived on earlier, having in the meantime been to Monemvasia on the southern tip of the Peloponnese.

The closest of the antiquities, only three kilometres from Nafplion, was the 12th century nunnery of Ayia Moni. It was built next to a spring, dedicated to *Zoodochod Pigi*, the spring of life, and here it was said the goddess Hera came every year to renew her virginity. On a later visit, I told one of my daughters she should try it, but she was not amused. However, during our visit we saw hundreds of baby tortoises, each no bigger than a matchbox, and that was a real miracle.

David with Kostas Psomadarkis in the Yacht Club

The Yacht Club was a great asset for Nafplion, vividly remembered by generations of visitors. I took many friends there, as well as daughters and nephews, and they all remembered Kostas and the Yacht Club. Sadly, it is no more: Yannis Psomadarkis fell victim to an Athenian investment scam and the brothers were forced to sell.

* * * * *

I left Nafplion on 27 March 1980, in the week before Easter. Kostas and others urged me to stay for the festival which for Greeks is the greatest celebration of their year but, alas, my flight was booked long in advance. However, I did witness the National Day festivities with a colourful procession marching through the town, including girls from Kyria Myria's lodging house: they got a big cheer from the crowd, as did a detachment of the Greek Army, but the police were observed in silence. I left Greece having just begun my study of its language – I needed to do more studying back in Britain. But I left Greece with greater knowledge and very much greater respect for its people and its rich culture, of both the past and present.

14.
The True Cost of Sound Money

I arrived back in Bush House after Easter to take up the reins of Greek Programme Organiser. In my absence, the section had been run by Paul Nathanail – just as if I had never been appointed and nothing had changed in the past year. I expected a stressfree few months in which to renew good relations with the section and further my studies of the Greek language. I had another personal reason for wishing for a relatively quiet life. On my return from Nafplion, Jenny and I had agreed to separate. Since I acknowledged that the fault was on my side, I had moved out of the house in Ware and agreed to maintain the income of my wife and daughters. Important decisions would have to be taken – where to live and how to increase my income – so a period free of stress was highly desirable. I was certainly not prepared for another feature series, but Andrew Mango had other ideas. The extra funds from the Arabic Service were still there and so was his desire for me to move back to the World Service.

The subject of the features was to be 'monetarism', the belief or doctrine that strict control of a nation's supply of money is the chief method of stabilising the economy. It was certainly topical at that time but also controversial. In the United States, to control spiralling inflation in 1979 President Jimmy Carter had nominated Paul Volcker – known for his passionate belief in monetarism – to be chairman of the Federal Reserve. Volcker pursued a determinedly monetarist policy with the result that US inflation, which had peaked at 14.8 per cent in March 1980, fell below 3 per cent by 1983, but interest rates rose accordingly and so did unemployment. These policies were widely seen as major contributors to the recession which gripped the US and many other countries from 1980-82. In Britain there was a similar picture. Under the Labour government of James Callaghan, inflation had risen to more than 15% and the first task of Margaret Thatcher's government, elected in April 1979, was to bring inflation down. In this the Prime Minister was greatly influenced by Sir Keith Joseph MP, a strong advocate of monetarism and an admirer of Milton Friedman, who had won the Nobel Prize in Economics in 1974.

During April I worked on the feature series, reading up on the theories and jargon of monetarism – usually discussed, according to one commentator, 'in terms impenetrable to the public' – and identifying possible interviewees. Milton Friedman was in London and so it seemed essential to try to get an interview with the father of monetarism himself. It also seemed a good idea, since monetarism was now government policy, to try to include a minister. The Chancellor of the Exchequer, Geoffrey Howe, was not available, nor was his deputy, John Biffen, Chief Secretary to the Treasury, but the third man in the Treasury, Nigel Lawson, the Financial Secretary, was willing to talk about monetary policy for the BBC. After Keith Joseph, Lawson was the most ardent advocate of monetarism in the government. On the other side of the argument – those who believed with John Maynard Keynes that the business cycle could be regulated by government spending and taxation rather than regulation of the money supply – the principal figure was John Kenneth Galbraith. I had intended to go to Harvard University to interview him but found that Galbraith would be in Europe in May, staying in the Swiss resort of Gstaad. In Britain a stringent critic of monetarism and the so-called 'free market' was the former minister Shirley Williams MP, who with the Labour Party now in opposition was lecturing at Oxford University. But when I sought to interview her in Oxford, I found she had gone to Harvard. Such were the toings and froings of academics in those days. And that would have been my cast for the series – four interviewees, two for monetarism and two against, two economists and two politicians. But Andrew Mango had other ideas.

The BBC South European Service was still supplying feature programmes to domestic radio channels in Italy, Portugal and Spain and programmes about economic policy were top priority in all three countries, Mango told me. In Italy there had been a change of government and the all-important Budget portfolio was no longer held by a Christian Democrat, but now by Giorgio La Malta, of the Republican Party (RPI) – incidentally, the son of the PRI leader, Ugo La Malta, whom I had interviewed back 1973. Mango's contacts at Italian Radio (RAI-3) had assured him that the new minister was willing to take part in the programmes on monetarism – indeed he was said to be keen to do so. In order to make the interviewees an even number, I looked round for a sixth interviewee from southern Europe and Paul Nathanail suggested Adamantios Pepelasis, governor of the Agricultural Bank in Greece.

J.K. Galbraith

The first interview was with J.K. Galbraith in Gstaad. I flew to Geneva, a city I had not visited before, a beautiful location beside Lake Léman – it was difficult to understand how a faith as narrow in outlook as Calvinism could have begun in such fine surroundings. I took the train along the lake, passing Rolle, Morges, Lausanne and Vevey to Montreux, where I caught a glimpse of the Château de Chillon – the subject of Byron's poem about an imprisoned monk – before boarding the funicular to Gstaat. It was full of young Swiss in holiday mood.

At Gstaat no one had warned me there might be snow on the ground and I had come in a suit and flimsy shoes. All the same it was a warm, sunny day. I found the right chalet and the door was opened by an Asian woman. Galbraith was welcoming and the Asian woman brought us tea.

Galbraith spoke with feeling about monetarism, condemning it as another manifestation of conservative politics and essentially a reaction to the liberal economic consensus that had worked well in the United States, Britain and many other countries since Roosevelt's 'New Deal' in the Thirties. Of course, monetarists had a point, he said: control of the supply of money was important and lack of control was bad. But the unbending application of monetarist policies was indefensible. The idea that stable prices were dependent on what Friedman called the natural rate of unemployment could not be proved. It was there merely to defend a core proposition of capitalism: that free and unfettered markets are intrinsically stable, that the market cannot fail, but governments can fail and do. Yet monetarism had nothing to say about the abuses of capitalism – excessive bank charges, exploitative loans and so on. Government must have a role in managing the national economy, as in other spheres of life. If Friedman was wrong, said Galbraith, then the so-called 'monetary consensus' in Britain and America was even more wrong.

It was a good, rousing interview. The only drawback was that in the May sunshine the wooden walls of the chalet began to expand, leaving my recording with a series of background grunts and clicks to be edited out later.

Nigel Lawson MP

My next interview was with Nigel Lawson, who agreed to the interview on condition it was done at the Treasury in Whitehall. Accordingly, I went there with my tape recorder two days after interviewing J.K. Galbraith. The two interviews could not have been more different. Lawson had long been a propagandist for monetarist ideas and policies. In 1978 – the year before he was made Financial Secretary – he had written in *The Times* of the need for a new approach to economic policy in Britain, which would bring in a long-term programme to defeat inflation and provide a favourable climate for economic growth. 'At the head of such a programme must be a firm commitment to a steady and gradual reduction in the rate of growth of the money supply.' In our interview he spoke of the need for inflation to be 'wrung out of the system'. This could be done by returning to the old disciplines of reducing the Budget deficit and achieving a balanced Budget. The acid test of monetary policy, he said, was its record in reducing inflation. At a later stage, when he had become Chancellor of the Exchequer, Lawson toyed with the idea of getting rid of inflation altogether, but while he was able to bring in an economic boom his policies ultimately led to the old pattern of boom and bust.

Shirley Williams MP

In June I flew to Boston to interview Shirley Williams, the Labour MP and former minister, then teaching at Harvard University. Her main criticism of Milton Friedman and what she called 'the cult of the free market' was that society had many needs which the market was incapable of meeting – for clean water and clean air, for example, for public health, for a good transport system and so on. The market was geared, she said, to individual demands and the purse of the individual; it did not count social costs or social consequences. She went on to say that there were individual demands that could not be achieved because the individual could not afford to satisfy them. Typically, these would include treatment for serious illness, chronic invalidism, care in old age. The market was a system ill-adapted to the life-cycles of an individual, which moved from dependence through independence and back to dependence again. The same was true of the cycles of the economy. Monetarists attacked public spending and said it must be reduced in nearly all circumstances. However, in many European countries public expenditure amounted to 40 per cent or more of the gross national product, but who could say that Sweden, Denmark or Germany were less prosperous and less free than Spain or Argentina where a smaller proportion of GDP went into public expenditure? Monetarist policies were a failure. They survived only because they sustained and empowered a parasitical managerial class, who were able to influence governments to adopt monetarist policies. Shirley Williams incorporated many of these points in her book, *Politics Is For People,* published the year after our interview.

Adamantios Pepelasis

For the fourth interview I flew to Athens to interview Adamantios Pepelasis, governor of the Agricultural Bank, one of the leading commercial banks in Greece. During the military dictatorship of 1967-74, he had taught economics at universities in the United States.

I asked him first about the current state of the Greek economy, which I had read was going through a difficult period with rising inflation. Pepelasis said that, like many economies, Greece had enjoyed a golden age in the early sixties with low inflation and low unemployment, and investment growing at 12 per cent a year – the highest in Europe. But the oil crisis of 1973 had exposed the weakness of the Greek economy, exacerbated by the next oil crisis in 1979. The fall of the Colonels in 1974 had exposed the fundamental economic problems Greece faced – its complex and often quite arbitrary tax system and the unchecked growth of the public sector. He said that these problems had been there for some time but were hidden in the euphoria of the end of the Colonels and the new civilian government of Constantine Karamanlis. They could become very much worse, he said, if the opposition PASOK party, under Andreas Papandreou, were to win the legislature elections due for October

1981. His assessment of PASOK was all the more interesting since Pepelasis told me he and Papandreou had been close friends and colleagues earlier in their careers. He did say, however, that the main hope for the Greek economy was membership of the European Economic Community (EEC) due to begin in January 1981. He added that some control of the money supply was necessary in Greece, as in any economy, but the rigorous theories of monetarism were not the answer for Greece which faced more fundamental problems.

Sadly, Pepelasis proved to be only too accurate in his diagnosis of the Greek economy. Joining the EEC – which granted Greece membership for mainly political reasons, as a prop for the newly restored democracy – did stabilise the economy, particularly by attracting outside investment, but the fundamental problems of an unfair tax system and the top-heavy public sector and social welfare remained. I had learned about the tax system in talks with John Drossos, the friend of Austen Kark, and was astonished to learn that public sector pensions could be passed down from father to son or daughter. I encountered the wider scandal of the public sector on my first visit to Greek Radio and Television (ERT), where many employees seemed to sit around reading newspapers and where any decision took days to arrive and more days to implement. The Greek public sector was an oriental creation, I learned, a relic of the Ottoman Empire, riddled with clientelism and the culture of favours. Under the practice of *Rousfetia* (a Turko-Greek word), at election time representatives of both main parties would receive the backing of village heads or other community leaders in return for the promise of jobs in the public sector for the less employable, younger sons and daughters of the community. These were the ones I saw reading newspapers at ERT.

That was the Greece I knew in the early Eighties. In 2001 Greece entered the Eurozone and was among the first countries to issue euro notes and coins to replace the drachma. It was all very euphoric. In August 2004 the XXVIII Olympic Games were held in Greece, with the motto 'Welcome Home', and there was spectacular spending on the necessary infrastructure, including construction of the Athens Metro and preservation of the archaeological riches the construction revealed. Then came the economic crisis of 2007-8 and quite quickly the international banks lost all confidence in the Greek economy. The bailouts of 2010, 2012 and 2015 followed and by 2018 it was calculated that the Greek economy was 25% smaller than at the beginning of the crisis, with outstanding debts still amounting to €96.9 million (£85 million).

Pepelasis was a thoughtful and generous interviewee. After we had finished the recording, he said he had laid on a tour of Athens for me with a guide often used by the Agricultural Bank.

Milton Friedman

The fifth interview was with Milton Friedman himself who came into the studio in Bush House. Friedman was very much flavour-of-the-month at that time: a few months earlier, in January 1980, he had published with his wife Rose the best-seller, *Free to Choose: A Personal Statement*, which argued that the free market works for all members of society and can solve problems where other approaches have failed. *Free to Choose* was also made into a television series, shown in the United States and Britain. In our interview – because it was to be transcribed and translated into languages other than English – he restated the basic principles of his thinking on monetarism. If the national supply of money rises faster than the rate of growth of national income, he said, then the result will be inflation. Inflation is always a monetary phenomenon in the sense that it is produced by a more rapid rise in the quantity of money than in national output. He said that to increase the money supply for political purposes, such as to create employment, would always result in inflation; that was why the goal of full employment was a fallacy and would always result in inflation. There was a natural rate of unemployment and attempts to reduce or abolish that resulted not only in inflation, but also in lack of growth and economic stagnation.

La Malta – or Caravaggio

In late July, I flew to Rome to interview my sixth and final contributor, the Italian Minister of Treasury, Budget and Economics, Giorgio La Malta. I reported to the offices of RAI-3 from where one of the economics correspondents took me to the imposing Bank of Italy building in Via XX Settembre. We let them know we had arrived and waited in the outer office. The Minister was in conference. After half an hour or so, the door opened and Signor La Malta emerged. He shook my hand most cordially and asked if we could do the interview the following day, Tuesday. I agreed and went back to my hotel where I faxed Andrew Mango to tell him the good news.

The following morning, I went to the offices of RAI-3 and was told that the interview was postponed until the Wednesday. I faxed Mango in Bush House, asking whether I should stay on. He replied in the affirmative. So with a whole day to kill in Rome, I looked for a guide to the city's art treasures and at a street kiosk found a paperback of Rome altarpieces by Caravaggio. Michelangelo Merisi da Caravaggio had long fascinated me, partly because of his ground-breaking technique of extreme *chiaroscuro* shadow work – or 'tenebrism' – and the dramatic subject matter, but also of course because of his scandalous life-style. He would have stayed in Rome longer had he not been charged with murder. The guide said that the largest collection of Caravaggios was in the Galleria Borghese and so I made my way there. I was stunned by the seven Caravaggios – ranging from a touching but unorthodox *Madonna and Child with St. Anne* (*dei Palafrenieri*) to a debauched *Bacchus* and a realistic *David with the Head of Goliath*.

On Wednesday morning I again reported to the offices of RAI-3, only to be told that the Minister had been called to Brussels until Friday when – I was assured – the interview would take place. I returned to my hotel and faxed Andrew Mango, asking whether I should stay on in the hope of the interview taking place and, if so, asking for more funds to subsist on. Mango replied that I should stay on and arranged with RAI for extra funds. So another day with Caravaggio beckoned. This time it was the Contarelli Chapel of San Luigi dei Francesca with its three paintings depicting St. Matthew – the startled evangelist being dictated to by a cheeky angel in *The*

Caravaggio: The Rest on the Flight into Egypt

Inspiration of St Matthew hanging between paintings telling of the saint's *Calling* and *Martyrdom*.

On the Thursday, I visited the Doria Pamphilj Gallery in the palazzo of the same name. The collection is rich in old masters – Titian, Velasquez, Pieter Bruegel the Elder – and there are just two Caravaggios. But one of them is, to my mind, among his greatest and most intriguing works. *Rest on the Flight to Egypt* puts the virgin and child on one side while a bright angel in the centre plays a violin to music held up by a shadowy St Joseph. In the afternoon, I viewed another extraordinary Caravaggio – *The Conversion on the Way to Damascus* in the church of Santa Maria del Popolo: it shows a prostrate St Paul with a large horse standing over him, its rump towards the viewer. I loved the story in the church's guide: Caravaggio was asked why he had put the horse in the middle of the picture, to which he answered 'Because!' – 'So, is the horse meant to represent God?' 'No, but he stands in God's light!'

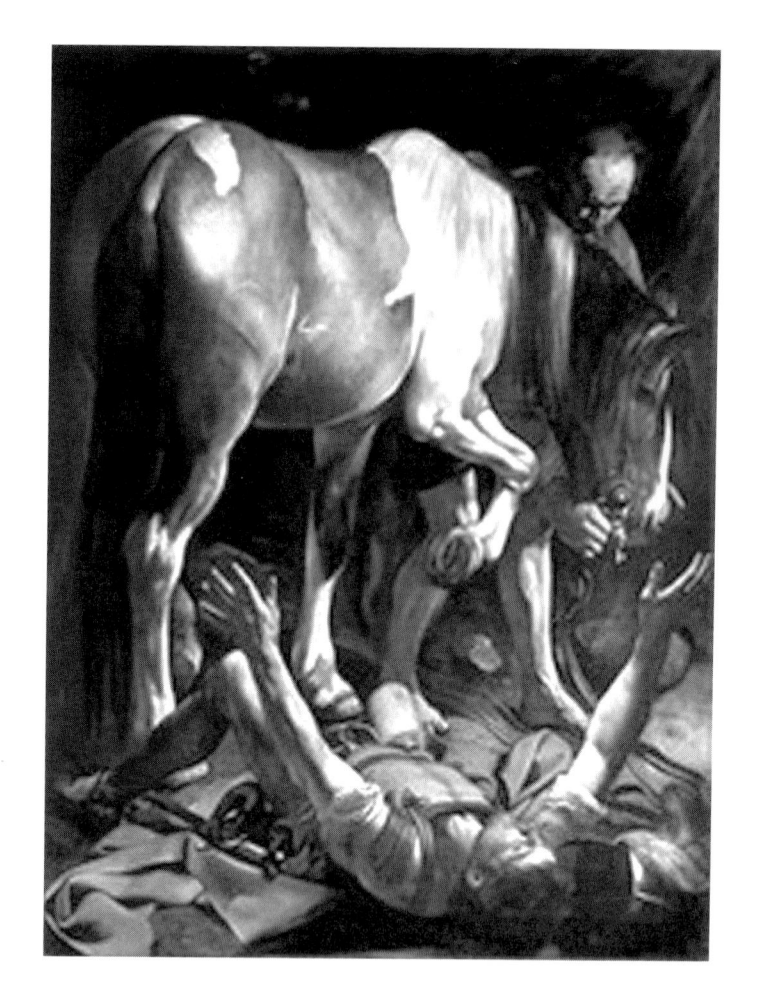

Caravaggio: The Conversion on the Way to Damascus

On the Friday, I was told that the Minister had flown to the United States and would not be back for a week. This time Andrew Mango agreed that I should return to London but, as the series was billed as having six interviews, he still insisted on having a contributor from Italy. He said I should ask RAI for the names of suitable Italian academics.

I countered with the name of someone I had interviewed previously for *The World Today* – Professor Sir Andrew Shonfield, currently teaching at the European University Institute in Florence.

Sir Andrew Shonfield

'Ackey Shonfield' – as he had been known in Fleet Street when he wrote for *The Financial Times* and *The Observer* – was most amenable to being interviewed by the BBC on the subject of monetarism. His famous book, *Modern Capitalism* (published in 1966), had become a textbook for the mixed economy, in which by means of economic planning a government could control and direct private enterprise without taking it over or nationalising it, as left-wing socialists wanted to do. He was close to the British Labour Party and the West German Social Democrats. As such, he rejected Milton Friedman's idea that all that was necessary to have a successful national economy was control of the money supply. In our interview, he characterised monetarism as a typical example of American right-wing reaction. He said that, if the United States represented Europe's future, 'I have seen the future and I reject it'.

I interview Shonfield at the Institute at Fiesole, the hill above Florence, but sadly did not have time to explore the art treasures of that city. My programme schedule was now tight. I worked on the six interviews at Bush House and they were broadcast in September – Friedman first, followed by Galbraith, then Lawson, Shirley Williams, Pepelasis and finally Andrew Shonfield.

Margaret Thatcher MP

There was to be one more interview before the year was out. In September 1980, Mrs Thatcher was due to fly to Athens – the first visit by a British Prime Minister since Harold Macmillan back in 1958. It was a long overdue visit in other respects also – President Constantine Karamanlis had visited London the year before as Prime Minister and in the same year had signed the Accession Treaty making Greece a member of the European Community on 1 January. Mrs Thatcher's two-day visit was intended to be a welcome and recognition of Greece becoming the Community's tenth member. She was to hold talks with the new Prime Minister, George Rallis, including questions of how the NATO alliance should react to the Soviet invasion of Afghanistan earlier in the year.

I went along with a tape recorder to the Cabinet Office in Whitehall, where I found the portly London correspondent of ERT – Greek TV and Radio – also waiting. Mrs Thatcher came in and sat facing us, when the TV man said that his cameraman wished to do some continuity shots. He then began to explain to the Prime Minister what continuity shots were, but she interrupted him:

I know perfectly well what continuity shots are. They are shots where we keep absolutely still and don't move a muscle – which is fine for me but it means that you cannot move that silly lock of hair hanging down the middle of your forehead.

There was indeed a lock of hair on his forehead and the Greek was sweating profusely. It was a hot day for the end of September.

I had met Margaret Thatcher before: she had been the guest at an NUJ lunch when she first became leader of the Conservative Party and on that occasion she had been thoroughly charming. I particularly admired her dress and hair and complexion. After the man from ERT had left, I did my interview, which was intended for both the World Service and the Greek Section. She spoke warmly of the historic bond between Britain and Greece and said that, on a personal note, she had always admired the 'Glory that is Greece' and acknowledged that the ideals she had always held dear had their origin in Greece.

* * * * *

At the end of 1980 I was living in London in a series of hotels and bedsits. It would be some time before I could find a house, preferably in Ware to be near my daughters. But at least I had found a way of augmenting my income. I had become the London correspondent of the *Jerusalem Star*, a newspaper published in Amman, Jordan – quite different, of course, from the better known *Jerusalem Post*, published in Israel. The appointment came through my old Jordanian friend, Samir Mutawi. It was not onerous work. Twice a week I would look through the British Press and recommend possible stories to the editors in Amman. I would then type them on to a telex tape in the little telex room, conveniently opposite my office in the North-East Wing of Bush House, and take the tape to the Western Union office near the Temple Tube Station for transmission to Jordan.

15.
America, Europe and the World

1980 was a busy year for me. I had spent ten satisfying weeks in Nafplion, learning Modern Greek and soaking up the culture of that delightful country. I had interviewed six eminent personalities about the pros and cons of monetarism and, incidentally, seen some fascinating altarpieces painted by Caravaggio. And I had resumed my duties as Greek Programme Organiser. But I was still interested in what was going on in Iran – indeed I could not have failed to be interested when relations between Iran and the United States were in the news every day.

On 4 November 1979, 55 US diplomats and ordinary citizens had been taken hostage in the US embassy in Tehran by a mob of students calling themselves the 'Muslim Student Followers of the Imam's Line' – in other words, followers of Khomeini. The hostage-taking was seen as punishing the United States for supporting the Shah and giving him asylum. It had widespread coverage in America and around the world and President Jimmy Carter said; '4 November 1979 is a date I will never forget'. As the crisis drifted over into 1980 there were attempts to secure the hostages' release by diplomatic means, but they made no progress. In April, President Carter ordered the US military to attempt a rescue, but it was a humiliating failure with the destruction of three helicopters and the deaths of eight American servicemen and an Iranian civilian. Inevitably, the hostage crisis became a major issue in campaigning for the US presidential election in November 1980. The Democratic candidate and incumbent, Jimmy Carter, a born-again Christian from Georgia, was being challenged by Ronald Reagan, a former B-movie actor who had been Governor of California, for the Republicans. There were accusations that the Reagan camp had managed to delay the release of the hostages to give their candidate an advantage. In the event, Reagan won by a landslide and the hostages were released the day after he was sworn in as President of the United States on 19 January 1981.

The 1980 presidential election was seen as a 'realignment election' – an election when consensus policies on the economy, human rights and foreign relations were fundamentally changed. Reagan – at 69, the oldest president to be elected – was greatly influenced by right-wing think tanks, like the Heritage Foundation, which advocated that the Cold War could be won decisively by the United States and Communism rolled back everywhere and forever. In domestic policy, the new president had declared his opposition to 'big government' and vowed to balance the budget, reduce tax rates and roll back government controls.

As the world waited to see who Reagan would include in his cabinet and how he would carry out his radical policies, Andrew Mango called me into his office and said that a feature series on US foreign policy was needed. Rather than going to the usual commentators and academics, I suggested that we should interview 'real people' – those who in any country made or implemented foreign policy. Such an ambitious project had to be sanctioned by the Controller, since interviewing government leaders could easily backfire on the BBC. But Peter Fraenkel and Austen Kark approved the idea and the funds for such a project were available anyway – from the Arabic Service. Thus *America, Europe and the World* was born. It was to be a series of thirteen half-hour programmes to be broadcast in the World Service from the beginning of May 1981 to the end of July. A lot of work was involved and a lot of travel, which would have to be carefully tailored to the statesmen or stateswomen who were available. This was especially difficult with members of the present and past administrations in the United States. While negotiations were going on with potential interviewees, I carried out three interviews in London.

Lord Carrington

For many practical and diplomatic reasons my first approach was to the Secretary of State for Foreign and Commonwealth Affairs, Lord Carrington – the ultimate paymaster of the BBC World Service. Peter Alexander Rupert Carington, 6th Baron Carrington, was one of the great figures in British political life. He had served in every Conservative government since that of Winston Churchill. He had been Defence Secretary before becoming Foreign Secretary and in February 1981 had accompanied Margaret Thatcher on a state visit to the United States, where he held talks with the US Secretary of State, Alexander Haig. He was a good friend of the BBC World Service and widely regarded as one of the most honourable people in politics. In 1982, when Argentina invaded the Falkland Islands, Lord Carrington took personal responsibility for this failure of diplomacy and resigned.

I interviewed the Foreign Secretary at the Foreign Office. He began by giving his take on the delay in Washington in announcing foreign policy decisions. 'I think that what the Americans very sensibly are trying to do at the moment – a new government, a new administration coming in – is to sort out their ideas, to get themselves really well-informed about the situation before they launch into discussions on which they are imperfectly briefed.' I asked him about the strong views of the Reagan administration on the Soviet Union, to which he replied:

> *I think over the last few years we have been rather worried about Soviet expansionism, in Afghanistan, in Africa, in South-east Asia, and President Reagan came to power determined to see that that expansionism should not go any further. And I think that is greatly welcomed by America's allies.*

However, said Lord Carrington, many international issues did not involve the Soviet Union. He pointed out that neither the Arab-Israeli conflict in the Middle East nor all the problems of Africa were fundamentally East-West issues. He said that he did not believe that the Reagan administration saw these issues in those terms, although, he said, perhaps some of Reagan's supporters in Congress might do so. He went on to give this warning:

> *I think we have got to be careful not to accept the proposition that everything in the world is East-West. We have got to be very careful that in our conduct and in our policies in those areas we don't make them become an East-West problem.*

Lord Carrington was due to take over the presidency of the European Community's Council of Ministers on 1 July and would therefore be playing a key role in the Community's initiative over the Israeli-Arab problem, the so-called Venice Declaration. The Venice Declaration embodied two principles: that the Arabs had got to recognise the right of the State of Israel to live in security within its boundaries, and equally that the Israelis had got to accept the rights of the Palestinians to self-determination. But the controversial phrase in the Declaration was that the 'Palestine Liberation Organisation must be associated with the negotiations'. Lord Carrington met American Jewish leaders in Washington earlier in the year and was criticised because of the European Community's Venice Declaration.

I was rather surprised when I went to America and spoke to six representatives of the various Jewish organisations, that it was quite clear to me that they hadn't actually read the Venice Declaration. And when I explained what it was and what it was about and how it was evenhanded, they were rather surprised that anybody could have objected to it as such.

He said there was naturally a nervousness about the PLO, because there is equally no doubt that there is a section of the PLO who were terrorists. Equally the PLO was not in itself terrorist and there were a great many members of the PLO who were not terrorists at all.

We then turned to southern Africa and what attitude the new American administration might take over Namibia. Namibia, also known as South-West Africa, had been controlled by white-governed South Africa under a League of Nations mandate but, after popular uprisings and demands for political representation by native African political activists, the United Nations had assumed direct responsibility over the territory. That move by the UN happened in 1966, but South Africa maintained *de facto* rule. How could that be resolved? Lord Carrington said he believed some modifications to the original UN plan were desirable.

The South Africans at the ill-fated meeting in Geneva, earlier this year, made it clear that they were not prepared to go along with it. I think probably what the Americans will seek to do is to try and get some constitutional safeguards for the minorities in Namibia.

At the present time, the United Nations' plan visualises really "a winner takes all" situation.

One solution being proposed was a roundtable conference, similar to the Lancaster House Conference which Lord Carrington had chaired the previous year, bringing to an end the Unilateral Declaration of Independence by white Rhodesia. This led to the creation of the Republic of Zimbabwe, with Robert Mugabe as prime minister. But there was one major problem about trying to repeat Lancaster House for Namibia: 'The Lancaster House conference was possible because there was one country responsible, Britain, and therefore we were charged with that responsibility. In Namibia, it's not so, because it's a United Nations mandate and I don't really believe that the United Nations could do a conference of that kind.'

Roy Jenkins

My next interviewee was the former Labour Party deputy leader, Roy Jenkins, very much in the news at the time for two reasons. One was that in January 1981 he was one of the 'Gang of Four' – with David Owen, Bill Rodgers and Shirley Williams – who left the Labour Party to form the Social Democratic Party (SDP); the other was that, until the end of December 1980, Jenkins had been President of the European Commission. It was in that second role that I interviewed him in his London home. This was the fine terraced house overlooking the gardens of Ladbroke Square, Notting Hill, where he received me with great warmth. We went to his study and he poured us both gin-and-tonics with ice, which I welcomed until I found that during the interview, when I asked my questions, he would shake his glass– creating audible *klinks* which later I had to edit out.

We began our interview with relations between the United States and Europe. Under the previous US administration of Jimmy Carter, tensions had appeared and it was feared that they would become worse with Ronald Reagan as president. Roy Jenkins said that one reason for areas of disagreement between the two wings of the Atlantic Alliance was the increased political co-operation then taking place within the European Community. Political co-operation, meaning moves towards a common European foreign policy, had increased greatly:

In my first two years as President of the European Commission, at meetings of foreign ministers and meetings of heads of government, political co-operation occupied 15-20 per cent, at the most a quarter of the time on the agenda. In the past year it has occupied something much more like 50 per cent of the time.

This had been an example of the members of the European Community trying to work out a common foreign policy position and also, in a year when Americans were pre-occupied with the presidential election and with the Iran hostages crisis, of Europe trying to fill some of the foreign policy vacuum left by the United States.

One particular area of disagreement was the Arab-Israeli issue. At the European Summit in Venice in June 1980, European Community leaders had launched what became known as the 'Middle East initiative' or 'Venice Declaration'. It had come in for some criticism in both the United States and Israel, but had increasingly found favour in the Arab world. Jenkins explained why the European leaders had gone ahead with their initiative, despite opposition from the Americans:

Obviously, the threat of war in the Middle East with its possible repercussions is extremely damaging for the whole world. We stand equal with America so far as that is concerned. But the second reason why the Middle East is of great importance is because it is the source of a great part of the oil of the world, but it is a source of a much greater part of European oil than it is of American oil. Therefore, it is not manifestly the case that America has a greater interest in the Middle East than does Europe.

Even so, there was clearly great reluctance among American leaders, in both the previous administration and the present one, to share control of the Middle East peace process with the Europeans. President Carter had warned that it could disrupt the Camp David peace process which had begun with negotiations in 1978 by the Egyptian President Anwar Sadat and Prime Minister Menachem Begin of Israel at the US president's country retreat, Camp David. These 'framework' negotiations included the future of the Palestinian territories but were written without the participation of the

Palestinians, and therefore condemned by the United Nations. The Venice Declaration had sought to redress the balance by calling for the Palestinians to be associated with future negotiations and represented by the PLO

George Ball

My third London interview was not with a Briton, but an American – George Ball who was in London on business. Between 1961 and 1966 he had served as Under Secretary of State in the administrations of Presidents Kennedy and Johnson, and was known as the major figure in the American government who opposed expansion of the Vietnam war.

We began the interview with the Reagan administration's attitude towards the Soviet Union, which George Ball described as 'the fundamental problem which we face in foreign policy, which broods over everything. We and the Soviet Union are the only two nations in the world that can destroy civilisation.' But he went on to say that America ought not 'to put so much emphasis on the Soviets' – constantly talking about the problem and in many cases trying to view every local situation in Cold War terms.

> *I would spare the rhetoric. I think the rhetoric that is coming out of the new administration up to this point is rather silly. I mean there is no point in calling the Russians names and returning to the kind of bad manners of the worst Cold War period.*

Under pressure from its European allies, particularly West Germany, the United States had agreed to try to open negotiations before the end of 1981 with the Russians on limiting what were called 'theatre nuclear weapons'. George Ball said the world had to keep 'looking for ways and means to get control of this insensate drive towards more and more sophisticated nuclear weapons'.

On relations between the Reagan administration and its European partners in the NATO alliance, Ball said he could see problems ahead.

> *There has been a vast re-distribution of wealth and income in the world, and the Western European nations, on a per capita basis,*

approach the same income as the United States. Japan has become a very powerful economic factor. And I think what is galling and in time what is likely to create problems is that there has been no commensurate re-distribution of responsibilities. And this is something I think which is going to have to be faced, or we are going to have some very abrasive problems within the Western Alliance.

Another area of concern was the Reagan administration's attitude towards human rights. The new president had explicitly criticised the Carter administration for putting human rights above security issues, but George Ball disagreed.

Obviously, we have to have a concern for human rights. I must say that I thought the Carter administration overdid it in the kind of presumption that went with making a report card for every nation around the world. We can't be God and we can't pass judgements in that public way. But I certainly think that the idea that we go in and help every 'jefe' in Latin America, who comes along, as they do traditionally in that part of the world, to repress the people is nonsense. I hope that we won't get ourselves in that position.

Günther van Well

For the next interview, I flew to Bonn to meet State Secretary Günther van Well, permanent head of the West German Foreign Ministry. It was not my first trip to what was then the West German capital. I had been to Bonn many times during National Service in Sennelager near Paderborn: while others took their local leave adventurously in Hamburg's notorious *Reeperbahn* or at Checkpoint Charlie in divided Berlin, I went with a group of friends to Bonn to see Beethoven's birthplace and then crossed the Rhine to the delightful area around Königswinter. Bonn of course ceased to be the German capital when the two halves of the country were reunited in 1990 with the capital in Berlin.

I was interviewing Günther van Well because he had much better English than any of the politicians on offer – he had an American wife and, when we met, had just been told of his appointment as the West German permanent representative at the United Nations in New

York. In view of the strong anti-Communist rhetoric coming from the new administration in Washington, I asked him about East-West relations in Europe and whether in view of recent actions by the Soviets the policy of *détente* was still viable. His reply was direct.

Indeed, we were disappointed about several aspects of Soviet policy which have undermined confidence in the possibilities of détente. One was the rapid military build-up on the part of the Soviet Union in the nuclear field, in the rocket field, in the maritime field, in the air transportation field. So we had a rapid increase of conventional, as well as nuclear capabilities on the part of the Soviet Union after the conclusion of the Final Act of Helsinki. Secondly, a very disappointing experience was the series of advances, of power political advances by the Soviet Union in the Third World from Angola up to Afghanistan, for extending their power and political influence there.

'The Final Act of Helsinki' was one of the agreements signed in the Finnish capital in 1975 by the Americans and Soviets to lower tension in Europe. They were a development of the East Policy (*Ostpolitik*) initiated by West Germany under Chancellor Willy Brandt in the 1960s to encourage greater cooperation and communication through the so-called 'Iron Curtain'. But despite the recent disappointments, West Germany's leaders felt it was important to maintain contact with the Russians and to go on talking to them. Günther van Well explained why, during the height of the Afghanistan crisis, Chancellor Helmut Schmidt had visited Moscow and why in the spring the West German Foreign Minister, Hans-Dietrich Genscher, had also gone to Moscow. 'We believe, that in particular in difficult times, it is important to maintain the dialogue. To present your position clearly, to give the other side the opportunity to really speak their mind and to try to avoid misunderstandings and miscalculations.'

West Germany's State Secretary for Foreign Affairs also outlined the two-track policy which his government was keen to follow over European security. 'It means that we have to pursue the parallel course of modernisation, of stationing these weapons [cruise and Pershing missiles] here in Western Europe, and at the same time negotiating limitations of these weapons, mutual and balanced limitations of these weapons.' There had been resistance in many parts of Western Europe to the stationing of American cruise and Pershing missiles, and this had given rise to a number of American warnings about the dangers of 'neutralism'. But Günther van Well was confident that West Germany would not be too greatly affected:

You have a certain segment of public opinion, which is entirely honourable – they are people who are in favour of disarmament, some who are unilateral disarmers, the environmentalists who have a basic aversion against nuclear power, whether it's for peaceful or for defence purposes – but the important thing is that the large majority, the overwhelming majority of the people, are for our common defence policy, for our participation in the NATO Alliance.

Zbigniew Brzezinski

I flew to the United States in late April, with firm assurances of three interviews and the possibility of a fourth. Opposition figures were not so much a problem: I had two of them lined up – Zbigniew Brzezinski, who was the National Security Adviser to President Carter, and Cyrus Vance, President Carter's Secretary of State. The big challenge was getting members of the Reagan administration. I was told that Mrs Jeane Kirkpatrick, Reagan's Ambassador to the United Nations, was 'almost certain' to be available and – the big prize – the new Secretary of State, General Alexander 'Al' Haig, would *probably* give me an interview.

The Polish-born Brzezinski or 'Zbig', as he was known, was a major figure in America's foreign relations, both during and after the presidency of Jimmy Carter. He was widely seen as 'hawkish' with a strong desire to roll back Soviet influence throughout the world. When the Soviet Union invaded Afghanistan in 1979, Zbig went to Pakistan to distribute money for arms purchases to the *mujahideen* guerrillas, opposed to the Soviets. Brzezinski's critics accused him of arming Osama bin Laden, the founder of the pan-Islamic militant (or terrorist) organisation al-Qaeda, but bin Laden was only one of the *mujahid* leaders the Americans supported.

The Carter Administration's 'hawk' and 'dove' on foreign policy – Zbigniew Brzezinski (left) and Cyrus Vance (right).

Zbig invited me to his house in Washington DC for our interview. I began by asking him about the strongly anti-Soviet rhetoric of the Reagan administration: did he as a strong critic himself of the Soviet Union agree with that sort of rhetoric?

What is important to recognise (he replied) *is that not all of foreign policy can be reduced to the confrontation with the Soviets, that also rhetoric, even tough rhetoric, is not a substitute for action, that there are areas in East West relations in which accommodation is needed and possible even while competition is going on – arms control, East-West relations, Eastern Europe and so forth – and that thirdly, the rest of the world is very important, that its difficulties and problems cannot be reduced to the American-Soviet confrontation, and that it has to be dealt with on its own terms, whether it is in Central America or the Middle East.*

During his time as National Security Adviser to President Carter, the United States had tried to sign the Strategic Arms Limitation Treaty (SALT2) with the Russians, but it had been thrown out by Congress. Now under pressure from its European allies, particularly West Germany, the United States had agreed to try to open negotiations with the Russians on limiting 'theatre nuclear weapons'.

I asked Brzezinski what he thought of that move. *'America has to compete with the Soviet Union',* he said, *'because competition between the two systems is a deeply-rooted one, and yet on the other hand one needs to co-operate if one is to avoid a war, a highly destructive confrontation.'* However, Brzezinski could foresee problems if the Europeans tried to hold too tightly to the gains of the *détente* policy with the Soviet Union to the detriment of playing their full role in the common Western defence system.

> *If that view were to become widespread, there is certainly something reminiscent between that view and the notion that somehow or other détente in Europe can be compartmentalised and thus kept separate from the wider international competition or tensions. In effect, what it implies is a posture of neutrality and that may not be compatible with the notion of an alliance, or even shared values.*

Cyrus Vance

If Zbigniew Brzezinski was the hawk in the Carter White House, Cyrus Vance was certainly the dove. Throughout his long career in public office culminating in his service as Secretary of State, he had consistently favoured negotiation over conflict and had worked hard to further the cause of peace through international treaties. The Camp David accords between Israel and Egypt were one successful result of his work. An unsuccessful outcome was the Strategic Arms Limitation Treaty (SALT2) with the Soviet Union, which the United States Senate refused to ratify. His most dramatic intervention in US foreign policy, however, was his last. In April 1980 when President Carter, on the advice of Brzezinski, tried to secure the release of the American hostages held in Iran by military means – rather than continuing to negotiate – Cyrus Vance resigned 'with a heavy heart' on principle.

I met him in Washington and began our interview by asking what he thought of the foreign policy of the Reagan White House.

> *At this point, I hear the rhetoric with respect to foreign policy issues, but I must confess that I find it difficult to ascertain what the policy is. I look at East-West relations and managing the relationship with the Soviet Union, and I hear very tough rhetoric*

but I don't see any policy. I look at the Middle East and again I see an absence of concrete policy. I look at Africa, particularly southern Africa, and again there is no policy clearly formulated and so it goes across the globe.

While welcoming the announcement about negotiations over 'theatre nuclear weapons', Vance warned that this could not be a substitute for Strategic Arms Limitations agreements or SALT. The United States had been fortunate in maintaining the strategic *status quo* up to that point in time, but they could not count on that continuing indefinitely. There were pressures – both within the Soviet Union and within the United States – which would eventually force actions to be taken which would make it impossible to continue to adhere to the treaty. Before he was elected, President Reagan said that he would try to renegotiate SALT-2, but Cyrus Vance was sceptical of any renegotiation.

I think that if they eventually get around to talking about the treaty again, and if they try to open up the substantive provisions of the treaty, they will find that it is impossible to renegotiate those without ending up with a treaty which is less advantageous from the stand-point of the United States, than is the treaty in its present form. I believe it is possible perhaps to get some cosmetic changes and if cosmetic changes would satisfy the Reagan administration – fine, as long as they get on with ratification of the substance of the treaty.

I then asked Vance about his involvement in the Camp David accords in 1978-79 between Israel and Egypt and what he thought of the stalemate that seemed to have overtaken all the parties involved since then. He replied that the agreement for Israel to withdraw from the Sinai was *'a major force for good in the region and in the world, because I believe that as long as Israel and Egypt remain at peace it will be extremely difficult for there to be an outbreak of a major war between Israel and the Arab nations.'* He added, however, that the Sinai withdrawal was an important building block and it was necessary to put the next block in place by resolving the Palestinian issue.

Asked about the role of the Israeli Prime Minister, Menachem

Begin, in the negotiations, Vance said Begin gave the leadership which was necessary to agree to full withdrawal from the Sinai – *'it would have been very difficult for a Labour government to have reached that. On the other hand, when one talks about the West Bank and Gaza, then there has to be more flexibility than I think Mr Begin has been willing to show up to the present time.'*

So did he agree with the view that the United States was too close to Israel and that other parties, such as the European Union, might be able to further peace in the Middle East through their Venice Declaration which would include the Palestinians. To that he replied:

I think it is really up to the parties that are involved in the negotiation, and they have to decide who is going to be included and who isn't going to be included. It has been their clear view that the parties should be limited as they were at Camp David. I think, however, it is important that the European Community discuss and make its views clearly known to the United States in the period between now and the resumption of the negotiations, so that each knows clearly where the other stands and can have the benefit of the thinking of the other.

* * * * *

It was in Washington, while staying at the Georgetown Inn, that a button came off my trousers – funny how little domestic problems feature so large in memories of foreign travel. I went to the Reception and asked where I could obtain a needle and cotton. The black clerk looked at me in horror and, in a sonorous indictment which turned quite a few heads, asked:

'Why do you require cotton?'
'To sew a button on my trousers,' I replied.
'Oh, you mean thread,' he said.

He then collapsed in laughter as he appreciated that this Englishman did not intend to open a cotton plantation in the South or restart the Civil War. Once he recovered his composure, he courteously wrang the hotel's Housekeeping for a needle and thread.

Jeane Kirkpatrick

I interviewed Mrs Jeane Kirkpatrick in her office at the United Nations in New York. It was rather disconcerting since she treated the interview as a contest and took the initiative from the start. As I sat down, she thrust a jar towards me and said: *'Take a jelly baby. Everyone interviewing anyone in the Reagan administration has to have a jelly baby.'* It was the in-joke of the year: Regan himself chewed jelly babies.

Jeane Kirkpatrick was an academic and a Democrat when she was chosen by Ronald Reagan to be his ambassador at the UN – but a very hardline Democrat. She became known for the 'Kirkpatrick Doctrine' which advocated US support for authoritarian regimes anywhere in the world if they subscribed to US policy. She made a big distinction between authoritarian regimes (good) and totalitarian regimes (bad). She was virulently anti-Communist and had a keen interest in Latin America. At that time the US supported the military regime in El Salvador and supplied its armed forces with weapons. When in December 1980 three nuns and a laywoman were raped and murdered, Mrs Kirkpatrick dismissed claims that any Salvadorean soldier was responsible and insisted that the nuns were leftist political activists. Earlier in 1980 Archbishop Oscar Romero had been murdered – again, it was claimed, by Salvadorean soldiers.

I began by asking her about Central America and about the news that the West German governing party, the Social Democrats, had offered support to the guerrillas in El Salvador. She replied that

> *West Germany's policies in Central America today are really quite unpalatable from the point of view of a good many of us. But that does not threaten the Alliance. Why? Because the Alliance is like a family in a sense. One does not have to agree with all members of one's family about all things in order to maintain those ties. It seems to me that for some time, our Western*

European allies have claimed quite a larger right to disagree with us than they had been willing to grant us to disagree with them.

Within weeks of coming to office, the Reagan administration announced increased military and diplomatic support for the government of El Salvador to counter what Washington called Soviet and Cuban-led infiltration. I asked her about this and about her government's lack of concern for the human rights of the Salvadorean people.

I think we do indeed have a genuine, authentic concern for the Salvadorean people, who by the way suffer a great deal. And I think that we would be very sorry to see the El Salvadorean people fall to a tyranny which would be even more repressive and oppressive than the miserable, bad government, under which they have traditionally suffered. I also think that we do not desire to see the transformation of El Salvador into another staging ground for a Soviet-Cuban offensive in the Western Hemisphere.

I then asked Mrs Kirkpatrick about the different emphasis on human rights by the Reagan administration. She replied that Nicaragua, which now had a left-wing government formed by the Sandanista National Liberation Front, had been an example of how the Carter administration's human rights policy had gone wrong.

In Nicaragua, it was expected that a moderate and liberal democratic regime would follow the deposition of [President Anastasio] *Somoza. The Carter administration's doctrine of human rights, when translated into policy, produced unexpected and undesirable results because it was based on bad theory. I believe that the approach was too abstract, that it was Utopian, that its application was too arbitrary, and that for these reasons it was unsuccessful.*

I asked her if the United States would consider invading Nicaragua to change its government. She replied – with a steely smile – that there were more ways to destabilise a regime than an invasion. It was revealed only later that the Reagan administration was already funding the Contra rebels to undermine the Sandanista government.

In the Middle East, the European Community had launched the Venice Declaration embodying the principles that the Arabs had to recognise the right of the State of Israel to live within secure borders and equally that the Israelis had to accept the rights of the Palestinians to self-determination. The controversial phrase in the Declaration was that the 'Palestine Liberation Organisation must be associated with the negotiations'. Mrs Kirkpatrick gave a straight answer to that:

We do not regard the PLO as a national liberation movement. We regard the PLO as a terrorist organisation, tied to the Soviet Union, and bent on in fact spreading terror in various parts of the world. And we do not do business with it. But neither did the Carter administration.

With the Reagan administration playing such an active role in Latin America, it was clear that I needed to get an opinion from south of the Rio Grande.

Jorge Castañeda y Álvarez de la Rosa

I flew to Mexico City by way of Miami to interview the Foreign Minister, Jorge Castañeda y Álvarez de la Rosa. Castañeda, a career diplomat – along with President José López Portillo – represented an assertively independent Mexico. New oil reserves had been discovered in the 1970s and Mexico no longer behaved as if it was subservient to the United States. Just before our interview, Castañeda had gone on record as saying that the US was the cornerstone of Mexico's foreign policy *'but that does not entail a passive or submissive acceptance of political, economic and cultural dependence'*. One example of the new stance was Mexico's recognition of the left-wing Sandanista government in Nicaragua, which had overthrown the 52-year-long dictatorship of the Somoza family backed by the United States. When I arrived in Mexico City, I witnessed a large rally in support of the Sandanistas, being addressed by their leader, Daniel Ortega, who later became the left-wing President of Nicaragua – and later still a right-wing President.

I began our interview by asking Castañeda about Central America and attitudes towards it by the new administration in Washington. He replied that El Salvador and other countries in Central America were experiencing violence because of their failure to reform themselves.

> *When we assess what is happening in Central America, we do see the need for authentic revolution in El Salvador and other countries, that are still suffering from quite old social structures, that are not adequate for a modern state. This is the main problem among our Central American neighbours – we don't see their problem as a sort of ideological dispute between East and West.*

During our interview Castañeda revealed that Mexico and Venezuela were trying to influence the two sides in the El Salvador conflict to come to the negotiating table. *'But our efforts to that end have to be taken with a certain caution. We have said that we will not try to impose these views, we would act as mediators only in the case that both sides would ask for it.'*

Robert Mugabe

While I was still editing the interviews recorded in the Americas, a message came from Salisbury, capital of newly independent Zimbabwe, that Prime Minister Robert Mugabe was willing – indeed keen – to take part in the series about US foreign policy. Mugabe was then 'one of the good guys', viewed quite differently from the dictator who was forced out of office in 2017. He had emerged from the Lancaster House Conference of December 1979 as the Prime Minister of a Commonwealth nation which acknowledged Queen Elizabeth II as Head of State. It was only in 1987, after the bloody repression of all opposition, that Zimbabwe became a republic with Mugabe as President.

I booked a direct flight to Salisbury (later renamed Harare) with British Airways. It was quite a small plane, filled mainly with white Zimbabweans returning from Europe and holding all-night parties in the aisle. I was booked into the famous Meikles Hotel for two nights, which meant that apart from interviewing the prime minister there was little time to see any of the country outside the capital – I regretted not being able to go to the Victoria Falls. The interview was in the Prime Minister's Residence – recently vacated by Ian Smith – and was clearly regarded as an important event. A photographer was in attendance and took a dozen photos of Perman extending his BBC

Perman in 1981 meeting and interviewing Robert Mugabe, then Prime Minister of newly independent Zimbabwe.

microphone towards Prime Minister Mugabe. I was also issued with a Press card, dated 2.6.81.

The big issue in southern Africa at the time was Namibia and whether the Reagan administration would back a United Nations plan for Namibia's independence. On this the Zimbabwean leader was being diplomatic:

> We don't want to judge the Reagan administration hastily. I think they have begun well, except that some of their pronouncements have given rise to apprehension on South Africa. We want to see them act positively, act in defence of democracy, the ideal of democracy, the principles that are enshrined in their own constitution. Those are the principles they must see established in our region.

The Reagan administration was seen as edging its way towards a policy in southern Africa, and particularly the question of the independence of Namibia. The administration had held meetings with white-ruled South Africa, with the members of the 'Contact Group' of European and North American states which tried to bring all the parties to the negotiating table in Geneva, and also with the leaders of black Africa. Dr Chester Crocker, President Reagan's Assistant Secretary of State for African Affairs, had twice visited southern Africa in 1980 and one of his stops was Salisbury.

> *We had Dr Crocker here, said Mr Mugabe, and he made known to us that the Americans were thinking of modifying the UN plan, under Resolution 435, and that the requirements were that there should be a kind of Lancaster House Conference to work out a constitution first. Well, we couldn't accept that procedure, or that modification, for two reasons. One, the UN plan hasn't been tried. What is required is really an implementation plan rather than a completely new plan. The plan has been agreed by the whole international community and the United Nations. And secondly there was no equivalent power to play the role that Britain had played at the Lancaster House conference on Rhodesian independence, because South Africa was not the colonial power in Namibia. It was the former trust power of a UN trust territory and the UN had voted to take the trust away from it.*

While agreeing that some reassurance for the whites of Namibia was desirable, Robert Mugabe did not see the need to grant them constitutional guarantees. 'The guarantees that the whites were given in our constitution were needless, we didn't have to have them, and in fact they militate against the whites because they tend to create out of the whites a separate community, deriving its existence from the past system.'

Abba Eban

The next two interviewees were key players in the Arab-Israeli confrontation. But my journey to the Middle East was beset with problems and I was on a tight schedule, anyway. My work plan for the series had been to record three to four interviews at a stretch, then book a studio – either with a 'studio manager' or a self-op – to top and tail the recordings and iron out any infelicities (such as noises off) and thus have the programmes ready for broadcasting six weeks before they were due to go out. The long time-lag was necessary because, as well as the direct broadcasts, the BBC World Service sent recorded programme tapes to its relay stations around the world, as an insurance against any interference to the short wave signal. In the first two weeks of May 1981, I was working on the recordings to be transmitted in July while the first two interviews – with George Ball and Lord Carrington – were already being broadcast. My schedule for the rest of May was to fly to Israel to interview the former Foreign Minister, Abba Eban; then to fly via Cairo to Amman to interview King Hussein; then to return to London with the two Middle East interviews before, two days later, flying to Moscow to interview Georgiy Arbatov, Director of the Institute of US and Canadian Studies. At that stage, I did not know what would happen about the final programme in the series, since the messages I was receiving indicated that Secretary of State Al Haig was unlikely to do the interview.

I arrived at Heathrow to fly to Israel in the midst of a civil service strike, which also involved air traffic controllers. Nevertheless, we boarded the British Airways aircraft which was very full because a TWA flight from New York to Tel Aviv had terminated at Heathrow and the passengers had transferred to our aircraft. We sat on the tarmac throughout the morning and early afternoon and were then informed by a steward that the crew had come to the end of their legally permitted shift and were leaving the aircraft. Since passengers were not allowed to remain on board in the absence of the crew, would the passengers kindly make their way to the exits in an orderly manner? There was uproar. The mainly Jewish passengers from Brooklyn refused to move, tempers became heated, security men were called. I was travelling business class and the man next to me, an urbane Israeli businessman, suggested we leave the aircraft in an orderly manner and find a British Airways Lounge – which we duly did.

The aircraft finally took off in the early hours of the following day and we arrived at Lod Airport (now known as Ben Gurion) fifteen hours late. Fortunately, there were taxis waiting and one driver told me that delays of more than eight hours for incoming flight were not uncommon. My interview with Aba Eban had been arranged for the previous evening, but I had telephoned from London and he agreed to see me that very evening at his home in Hertslyia, north of Tel Aviv – only twenty-four hours late in my recordings schedule.

Abba Eban was a remarkable man, as a politician and also as a scholar. Cambridge educated and a former officer in British Intelligence (when he was known as Aubrey Evans), he entered the Israeli parliament, the Knesset, as a Labour Party member in 1959 and was Foreign Minister from 1966 to 1973. During that time he had to defend Israel's actions in the Six Day War at the United Nations. He was not only fluent in Hebrew and Arabic – as well as English of course – he was a scholar, translator, teacher and author in those languages, winning praise from all who dealt with him, friends and enemies. I had not met anyone so linguistically gifted since my interview with Bülent Ecevit in 1973, but Abba Eban was fluent in ten languages not just three. In our interview in Hertslyia, he exhibited all the fluency of a skilled parliamentarian and I was glad I had studied his speeches and committed my questions to memory.

I began by asking him about something very unusual in Middle East politics – the United States condemning Israel for its raid on an Iraqi nuclear reactor near Baghdad:

The raid in Baghdad found the Reagan policy in a dilemma. Until that time, the Reagan administration had made great efforts to put more emphasis on its relations with Israel. But the raid on the Baghdad reactor was something different, because from the American point of view it fell outside the Middle Eastern context. This was the first physical attack on an atomic reactor, it was therefore the first exercise of the principle of pre-emption in the nuclear exaction: the practice of the nuclear age had been deterrence not pre-emption. The United States did not use its monopoly in nuclear power to prevent the Soviet Union from becoming a nuclear power in the four or five years in which that was possible. The Soviet Union and the United States had a capacity for preventing China from becoming a nuclear power – they did not use that capacity . . . Therefore, the Israeli action fell outside the particular Middle Eastern regional context and became an historic event of almost revolutionary importance. The United States was disconcerted by any lack of consultation, its lack of knowledge, the failure of its own intelligence, to be suddenly confronted by an intervention in its international strategy, produced by a country which it called its friend and ally – therefore the repercussions will I think go much deeper than in any other episode of American-Israeli relationship.

Most of the interview concerned the aftermath of the Camp David accords and of the Israeli-Egyptian peace treaty, following the historic visit to Israel by President Sadat in 1977. Was it possible to build on those events – I asked Abba Eban – to create a wider peace involving the Palestinians, and perhaps Jordan?

I do feel that unless there is further progress on the Palestine question, the Egyptian peace with Israel will become a very cold, formal thing; it will lack that confident dynamic, the human content, which would make the peace worthwhile from the Israeli point of view. And having lost Sinai, having made the renunciation of a tremendous bargaining asset with nothing to show but a flag flying over a rather under-populated embassy in Tel Aviv, it will be an anti-climax. Moreover, Egypt will not be able, even if it wishes, to carry the peace treaty into anything that can continue for long, if Egypt is believed by the Arab world simply to be serving its own interests and not contributing anything whatever to the alleviation of the condition of the Palestinians.

Two views of the Arab-Israeli issue from Abba Eban (left) and King Hussein of Jordan (right).

At that time there were signs that the right-wing government of Menachem Begin intended to use the Camp David accords for its own purposes of denying the Palestinians a role in any peace treaties.

> *It is true that under the Begin government, the treaty was seen as a corridor leading to nowhere – if anything, it was a corridor leading to annexation. Mr Begin falsely reading the text of the Camp David agreement thought that it left open the possibility of annexation of the West Bank and Gaza. But it doesn't because it says that the future status of the West Bank and Gaza including the situation of the boundaries will be decided by four parties, three of whom are Arab – Egypt, Israel, the Palestinians and Jordan.*

My interview with Abba Eban took place in 1981 but in the years following there was little progress on addressing the Palestinian issue. The Israeli Labour Party returned to power in 1992 under Yitzhak Rabin who held talks with the PLO leader Yasser Arafat in Oslo, but in 1995 Rabin was murdered by a right-wing fanatic. After that, the chances of a peace settlement involving the Palestinians went into rapid decline. More Israeli settlers built their settlements on disputed land in the West Bank, and in 2002 the government began to build the 7000 km barrier wall to protect Israelis from bomb attacks by Palestinians.

King Hussein of Jordan

The delay in leaving Heathrow had seriously disrupted my plans. I had intended to arrive in Israel on the Tuesday afternoon and interview Abba Eban the same evening. Then my intention was to fly to Amman, changing planes in Cairo, on Wednesday and interview King Hussein on Thursday afternoon. But I had not been able to interview Abba Eban until Wednesday evening and there were no connecting flights to Amman on Thursday morning. The only alternative was to go overland, crossing the River Jordan at the Allenby Bridge and hoping for the best. I consulted the BBC's correspondent in Israel – the wonderful gravel-voiced American Michael Elkins – who said that the Jordanians did not allow west-east crossings but he would make some enquiries on the assumption that it could be done. Elkins was good at his word and made what arrangements he could.

Before dawn on the Thursday, I took a taxi from Tel Aviv and arrived at the Allenby Bridge as the sun was rising above the Jordanian hills. There I made myself known to the Israeli guard commander, an Israeli Arab, whose name Elkins had given me. He told me I would have to take my life in my hands and walk from the Israeli immigration post and over the bridge: he refused to guess what the reaction of the Jordanians would be. And so, with the Uher tape recorder in one hand and my case in the other, I set off down the slope to the bridge. I managed to reach the far shore before I was challenged by two soldiers, pointing rifles at me. I stopped and an officer was called. He spoke to me in English:

Go back, Sir. You are not allowed to enter Jordan this way.
    But I have a visa, issued by your embassy in London.
That does not matter. You are not allowed to come this way.
    But I have an appointment in Amman for this afternoon which I must keep.
You must not come this way. Who is your contact in Amman?

I gave him the telephone number of the Royal Palace and everything changed in a matter of minutes. I was ushered into the guardhouse, given tea and very soon a car appeared to take me to Amman.

Hussein bin Talal, Monarch of the Hashemite Kingdom of Jordan, was the longest reigning leader in the Arab world. Since 1953 he had led his country through three wars with Israel and had been forced to expel thousands of Palestinians after the Black September attempt to take over the kingdom in 1970. When I met him, he still regarded himself as the ruler of the occupied West Bank – a claim he gave up in 1988 when the Palestine Liberation Organisation was internationally recognised as the sole representative of the Palestinian people. Hussein was regarded as a great survivor, successfully balancing pressure from Arab nationalists, the Soviet Union, Western countries and Israel, and gradually transforming Jordan into a modern state.

When I met King Hussein at the Basman Palace in Amman, he struck me as smaller than I had imagined but very friendly and a good interviewee. I offered to explain what my series was about, but he said that was not necessary – he had heard the first two programmes and liked them: he was known as a fan of the BBC as well being a dedicated radio ham. The King was decidedly gloomy about the prospects for further progress towards Arab-Israeli peace with Menachem Begin returned to power in Israel and Ronald Reagan in the White House. He was due to meet President Reagan later in the year, but had been quoted as saying the peace process was now a 'dead horse'. I asked him if that was still his opinion.

I believe it is a dead horse and I believe there is no hope of seeing any progress towards the establishment of a just and durable peace if the Camp David accords are frozen. The Egyptian-Israeli aspect of the problem was the least complicated of all. Israel is still in occupation of the entire area of Palestine and of territories belonging to other Arab states. And unfortunately, as far as the Americans are concerned, they give so much in terms of material help, moral help, military help for a time, for very little in return – not even a promise for withdrawal or the upholding of the principles which were incorporated in UN Security Council Resolution 242. And as a result, nothing has happened. The situation in the Occupied Territories is worse than ever. So much is heard the world over of Human Rights, but nothing really appears to shock this world into taking action in terms of the reality of conditions in the Occupied Territories, the denial of a people of their human rights in every way and respect and attempts to change that on the ground continuously in a manner that creates obstacles, real obstacles, to the achievement of peace in the long run. There has to be a new approach. And that is why we have welcomed all moves to bring the matter again before the world community; we have welcomed the initiative of our friends in Europe, even the Soviet suggestion recently in the same spirit that the matter should be dealt with by all concerned in the area, including the Palestinians themselves – after all, it is a Palestinian problem, with the PLO as the sole legitimate representative of the people of Palestine – and obviously the United States and the Soviet Union and possibly Europe and others, whoever wishes to make a contribution for the establishment of peace.

When I interviewed him in 1981, King Hussein was resolutely opposed to signing a peace treaty with Israel before there was real progress in recognising the rights of Palestinians in the Occupied Territories. But he did sign such a treaty in 1994 – and shook hands with the Israeli President Ezer Weizman – despite the total lack of progress on the Palestinian issue. Indeed, there had been a Palestinian uprising against Israeli rule in the First Intifadas from 1987-1991. What had changed was the invasion of Kuwait by Saddam Hussein of Iraq, followed by the Gulf War which brought American and British troops into the Middle East and which exposed the vulnerability of Jordan. Signing the treaty with Israel was the king's attempt to make Jordan again a player in Middle East affairs. King Hussein died in 1999 and was succeeded by his eldest son, Abdullah II.

Georgiy Arbatov

One of the salient features of the Reagan presidency – or at least of the rhetoric coming out of Washington – was its strongly anti-Soviet stance, the idea that the United States should 'roll back' the Soviet bloc and somehow end the Cold War. It seemed desirable, therefore, to have a Soviet voice in the series. The year was 1981 and the Soviet Union was still intact, although with multiple economic troubles and without, as yet, discoveries of oil or gas. Joseph Stalin was long dead and his reforming successor, Nikita Khrushchev, was also dead with his reforms gradually being reversed by Leonid Brezhnev, who was known to be in very poor health. So who could speak for the USSR? The best choice seemed to be Georgiy Arbatov, a member of the Central Committee of the Soviet Communist Party and Director of the Institute of US and Canadian Studies in Moscow, who had appeared on television in the US. He was said to have good English though with a strong accent. So I made contact with Comrade Arbatov through the Soviet Embassy in London and an appointment was made for me to meet him in Moscow the week after I returned from the Middle East. In fact the temperature in Moscow was higher than it had been in Jerusalem or Amman.

I flew Aeroflot to Moscow where Intourist had booked me into the National Hotel, just to the north of Red Square. It was a large, fairly basic hotel where many of the foreigners gathered. One disconcerting thing was that on my first morning a middle-aged Russian woman came and sat at my table at breakfast and again at lunch. I asked an Englishman I met in the bar if she could be a KGB spy: he said she was probably after British cigarettes or chocolate. At supper that day the woman spoke and asked if I had any Western fashion magazines.

Since I had completed the editing of the Middle East interviews, I had arranged to spend three days in Moscow which I had never visited before. There were few tourists at that time and I must have looked conspicuously non-Russian as I walked about the city. As I passed an exhibition of Picasso paintings, on loan from France, with a long queue outside, a young woman stopped me and asked if I was from the West: I said I was, whereupon she gave me her ticket and quickly walked away. I enjoyed the exhibition and went round smiling at the Russians I met. After all, there was a clear and important distinction to be made between Russia and Russians and the Soviet Communist system – a distinction, I felt, that many politicians in the West did not acknowledge. So in cheerful mood, I explored the residential area near the hotel with its *art nouveau* houses, including the house of the novelist and playwright Maxim

Gorky. And I discovered the fascinating Tretyakov Gallery of nineteenth-century Russian art.

I interviewed Georgiy Arbatov in his office at the Institute of US and Canadian Studies and asked him first about the stream of anti-Soviet rhetoric coming from the White House and other branches of the new Reagan administration in Washington. His answer was typically combative, yet laid back:

> *I think this is not only anti-Soviet rhetoric – this is anti- very much things. And this is dangerous. I have the feeling that many of these people at the top in the United States, they are really angry with the world, with the fact that it has become a little uncomfortable for the United States and does not love the United States as they think it should love the United States. They seem to display that gut feeling that they do want to punish the world – their allies and the Third World countries and us too.*

From then onwards, the interview became a tennis match, with the Soviet academic spokesman repulsing charges which had appeared in Western media as I lobbed them at him. I asked him about the failure of the SALT strategic weapons agreement to pass the United States Senate and the desire of the West Europeans for the Reagan administration to open talks with the Soviets on Theatre Nuclear Weapons: he replied that you could not pick out one set of weapons from the negotiations. As far as the Soviet Union was concerned, all American nuclear weapons were a threat to its security, the only difference between strategic and theatre weapons was their flying time! I asked him about the Soviets supplying arms to Third World countries like Angola; he replied that the United States had been doing the same in Ethiopia. I asked him about the Soviet military intervention in Afghanistan; he replied that Afghanistan was a neighbour of the Soviet Union with which it had enjoyed good relations for many years until civil war broke out in 1978. I asked him about the 'linkage' of their intervening in Afghanistan in December 1979 after the US Senate had rejected the SALT Treaty. *'I hate that ugly word'*, he replied but then went on to list the many events of that month which had worried the Soviet Union. I also asked him – as some Western commentators had suggested – whether the Soviet Union was already regretting its Afghan sortie in view of the almost universal international condemnation it had provoked. He did not answer that one.

But the repercussions of the Afghan civil war spread more widely and catastrophically for much longer than any of us imagined in 1981. The Soviets did indeed withdraw their troops when Gorbachev ordered a change of policy in 1989, but in the meantime the civil war had taken on a new and more frightening character. The nationalist and fiercely anti-Western Taliban had entered the fighting, but so too had elements of Pakistan's armed forces and the fundamentalist al-Qaeda under its Saudi-born leader, Osama bin Laden. A rolling international crisis had been set in motion which would not stop with the 9/11 outrages in the United States and the American-led invasion of Afghanistan in 2001.

Caspar Weinberger

Back in London in June, I learned that my interview with Secretary of State Al Haig was no longer possible. Instead I was offered the Defence Secretary, Casper Weinberger. It was a second-best with real benefits for Weinberger was a close friend and long-time associate of Ronald Reagan and had served in the Republican administrations of Presidents Nixon and Gerald Ford. But his key role in the administration was best seen in the spending power he controlled – a five-year programme of defence spending which was expected to total 1.5 trillion dollars ($1,500 billion), the biggest budget of any American Secretary of Defence in peacetime.

I met Mr Weinberger in his office at the Pentagon and asked him whether the assumption behind a rearmament programme of that magnitude was that in the past few years American foreign policy had been conducted from a position of weakness.

I think that's right – both with respect to the actual strength of the armed forces and, perhaps even more important, a weakening of the national resolution and the will to take some of the difficult measures that are necessary to enable the country to be sufficiently strong, so that its voice and its desires can be considered. We saw too many times a lack of resolution, a lack of will and consequently a lack of effectiveness in American foreign policy in the last few years.

The focus of this increase in defence spending was Soviet expansionism, which he said had threatened the freedom of the United States and its allies. It was not so much a policy of 'containment' of the Soviet Union, but rather of deterrence. The Soviets had used the era of *détente,* which had a particular appeal for people in Europe, to increase their defence spending – *'the important point is that neither during the détente period, nor during the SALT period, was any restraint exercised by the Soviets – the only country that was restrained by SALT or détente was the United States.'* Interestingly, on the question of whether the United States could afford the massive increase in defence spending, he had this to say:

Well, we are certainly looking for any way in which we can to save money, to illuminate any waste or unnecessary expenditure, and the resources that we have sought for defence – the seven per cent real growth – are of course a very large amount. But we have to bear in mind that we have had a number of years of neglect. We didn't do any modernisation or strengthening after the drawdown caused by the Vietnam war, and we have had a long period in which we have not kept up the strength of conventional or strategic forces. So a great deal has had to be done all at once. It is a very large expenditure, but I don't think this is anything which the American economy cannot afford. The key to the whole thing is to ensure that total governmental spending remains down and that is the intention. There's no doubt at all that pressures will grow from various constituencies that are thought to be more popular than defence spending. But we have here a President who is not nearly as worried about his re-election as he is about doing the right thing. And the right thing from his point of view is to maintain a policy which will not cause inflation by government overspending and at the same time to strengthen America's defences.

It was a fair summary of President Reagan's defence policy, and an appropriate quote to end my series of interviews. Later in the Eighties, Weinberger became embroiled in two negative aspects of that policy – one was the Star Wars anti-missiles system and the other was the Iran-Contra affair, in which the United States was found to be secretly and illegally supplying military hardware to Iran so that by a roundabout route the Contra rebels in Nicaragua could be given weapons to try to overthrow the left-wing government. Weinberger became a controversial figure but he was also an Anglophile – indeed in 1988 he was given an Honorary Knighthood for his pro-British stance during the Falklands War. I found him a sympathetic interviewee.

* * * * *

The main points made by the first nine interviewees in 'America, Europe and the World' were featured in the BBC World Service publication *London Letter* No 1600, which had on its cover a coloured photo of me interviewing Robert Mugabe. The remaining four interviewees were featured in a later edition of *London Letter*. The series was also noticed in *The Times Saturday Review*, in a column by David Wade, published on 1 August 1981:

> As many listeners have found, the World Service transmits a full mixed programme some of which they prefer to the domestic output – often for the excellent reason that it is as good or better. With one recent series, indeed, Bush House can be said to have stolen a march on Langham Place: *America, Europe and the World* consisted of 13 interviews which have been going out over the last three months and which owe their existence to David Perman, Greek Programme Organiser in the Southern European Service. Leaving the Greeks in other safe hands, Mr Perman went off to interview an immensely distinguished collection of people: Mugabe, King Hussein, Weinberger, Brzezinski, Eban, Vance.... Talk revolved around the likely drift and consequences of Reagan's foreign policy, a topic of some interest, you might say, but one which to my knowledge Radios 3 and 4 have left alone. One of them could repair the omission by repeating this important series.

16.
The Falklands Conflict

Before 1982, all I knew about the Falkland Islands was that they were in the South Atlantic and that Dr. Johnson thought their seizure from Spain by the British in 1770 was ridiculous. The islands, he wrote, were 'a colony that could never become independent, for it could never be able to maintain itself'. So, when on Friday 2 April 1982, the Argentine army invaded and occupied the Falkland Islands – as well as South Georgia and the South Sandwich Islands a day later – I was interested and mildly surprised, but not terribly concerned. Latin America was not one of my fields of interest. The invasion figured in the BBC World Service news and in the news bulletins for the Greek Section, but the main interest Greeks had in the invasion was that it reminded them of how Turkey had invaded and occupied Northern Cyprus in 1974. To push the analogy a little further, both invasions were the result of military coups – the Greek military junta in 1974 had carried out a military coup in Cyprus to unite it with military-controlled mainland Greece, thus provoking Turkey, while the 1982 invasion of the Falklands was a result of General Leopoldo Galtieri seizing power in Buenos Ayres from another Argentine general a few months earlier. Surely the Argentine invasion like that of the Turks would lead to international condemnation, resolutions at the United Nations and a stalemate that would drag on and on.

The real surprise was the reaction of the British government under Mrs Thatcher. The day following the invasion, the Prime Minister set up a War Cabinet to consider ways of bringing the islands back under British control, if necessary by force. All the indications were that Margaret Thatcher considered the invasion a personal affront and was determined to get the Falklands back. The surprise was that it was being done while many well-informed people thought it would be impossible. The Falkland Islands were more than 8,000 miles from London, but only 1,500 miles from Buenos Aires; the British had 42 serviceable aircraft against the Argentines' 122; the Argentine navy was large and some of its ships were armed with French Exocet missiles, which could also be launched from land. And in any case, surely Britain was prepared to come to a compromise with Argentina to save face on both sides. Diplomats may have been considering a compromise – part of the reason why the Foreign Secretary, Lord Carrington, resigned – but Mrs Thatcher was in no mood to compromise.

In the first weeks of April, events began to move at breakneck speed, which underlined the determined mood of Britain and its Prime Minister. But it was all so unreal and scarcely believable. This was Britain in 1982 acting as if it was reliving 1942. Frigates and aircraft carriers set sail from Portsmouth, waved off by crowds of well-wishers. On its return from a cruise, the ocean liner *SS Canberra* was requisitioned to act as a troop ship. Long-range bombers attacked an airfield held by the enemy and special forces retook some islands south of the war zone. Then came the surprising big events – the sinking of the cruiser *General Belgrano* with the deaths of 323 Argentine sailors, the sinking of the destroyer *HMS Sheffield* by an Exocet missile, killing 20 British sailors and severely injuring 24 others, and the attack on the landing ship *Sir Galahad* which left 48 British servicemen dead. All three events were controversial. Meanwhile negotiations were going on between the warring parties at second hand and the United Nations Security Council was passing highly contested resolutions. As of 17 May 1982, the Falklands War was about to move on to another plane and become a land war.

* * * * *

It was on 17 May that I was snatched away from the Greeks and drafted back to my old department, Central Current Affairs Talks. In fact, I was promoted to be Acting Assistant Head or A/AH CCAT under my old friend, Leslie Stone. Leslie had asked for me because the need to keep abreast of all the different strands of the Falklands conflict, to commission Talks on developments and keep issuing updates was too much for one man – Leslie had no assistant. So I became a Talks writer again, a current affairs journalist at the beck and call of the news, very much living on my nerves.

The working day was dictated by events. We would arrive at Bush House early and put out Talks interpreting the overnight news; we would then scrutinize the British Press to see if any developments there merited Talks. Then we would await the Ministry of Defence morning briefing and the return to Bush House of the World Service Defence Correspondent, Andrew Walker, who would file a piece in the Newsroom which would be circulated around the building – preceded by a Tannoy announcement if it merited it.

This was a difficult area to write about. Keeping abreast of the news was vital but what if we and the Newsroom got ahead of the news? Part of the problem was that the briefings at the Ministry of Defence were given by civil service Press Officers on the basis of what was *assumed to be taking place* 8000 miles away, rather than on what had actually happened. Also problematic was the fact that BBC News bulletins and Commentaries were being translated into Spanish and within a short space of time broadcast to Latin America, including Argentina and the Falklands.

The BBC came in for considerable criticism during the Falklands War, most of it unjustified. The commander of the task force, Admiral Sandy Woodward, blamed the World Service for disclosing information that led the Argentines to change the retarding device on their bombs – the World Service had reported the lack of detonations after receiving a briefing from a Ministry of Defence official. The Admiral described the BBC as being more concerned with being 'fearless seekers after truth' than with the lives of British servicemen. There was similar criticism of the BBC by Lieutenant Colonel Herbert 'H' Jones, commanding officer of the 2nd Battalion, Parachute Regiment, who claimed that the World Service had disclosed to the Argentines that a British raid was imminent at Goose Green. This particular criticism was given added weight by Colonel Jones's action at Goose Green and his death, when he was awarded a posthumous Victoria Cross.

Andrew Walker, who was the World Service Defence Correspondent at the time, later gave his version of what actually happened [*A Skyful of Freedom: 60 years of the BBC World Service*, London, 1992]. A senior member of the Ministry of Defence gave Christopher Lee, Defence Correspondent for BBC (domestic) radio, details of the attack on Goose Green, which he thought was already in progress and therefore no secret. By the afternoon of 27 May this story was broadcast and the whole country knew about it, including the fact that there had already been a clash some five miles from Darwin – on the way to Goose Green . . .

The same afternoon (wrote Andrew Walker) *the World Service reported some of these developments – rather cautiously – and a few days later was bitterly criticised in a despatch from a journalist in the Fauklands for allegedly showing 'a reckless disregard for security' in mentioning troop positions. The allegation was investigated and rebutted at the time, by the Ministry of Defence as well as the BBC, but it emerged ten years later in a particularly violent form in the memoirs of the task-force commander, Admiral Sandy Woodward. Of course, the troops in the Falklands could not know what was being reported in London and may well have felt exposed by the broadcast, although the report was actually broadcast after the clash with the Argentine patrol outside Darwin: hardly a breach of security for the Argentinians to be informed by the BBC after the event. The incident, though, is a reminder of the immediacy of radio, particularly noticeable in war.*

Margaret Thatcher also criticised the BBC for 'assisting the enemy during the Falklands War' by reporting the latest developments in the fighting and what the next, 'likely steps' would be. But both of these things originated with the Ministry of Defence briefings. There was no independent news source of what was going on in the Falklands War which was described as 'the worst reported war since the Crimea'. No television cameras were on hand to film the war and journalists on the spot had to negotiate a place on the next military flight home for their dispatches, which were censored anyway.

However, there was one criticism of the BBC to which we in Bush House could plead guilty. In reflections on the war written in 1983, Mrs Thatcher accused the BBC of 'the chilling use of the third person' by referring to the 'British forces' and 'British soldiers', rather than 'Our Boys' which is the term she herself used. Of that, we in Bush House were certainly guilty since the impartiality of our News and Commentaries was at the core of our existence.

* * * * *

The war ended on 14 June with the surrender of the Argentine garrison in Port Stanley – it is said that General Mario Menéndez defied orders to fight on after hearing of British successes on the BBC Spanish service for Latin America. The Falkland Islands were returned to British control and the government could congratulate itself on a victory against all the odds. Mrs Thatcher was certainly triumphant; she was later quoted as saying 'in the struggle against evil, we can all today draw hope and strength' from the Falklands victory. She went on the following June to win the General Election with a decisive Conservative majority. But the cost of the Falklands War was considerable. In the United Kingdom it cost the lives of 255 men, the loss of six ships – with ten others damaged – and 34 aircraft, and a financial bill of £1.19 billion (according to Mrs Thatcher's statement to the House of Commons). For Argentina the cost was much greater: as well as the 649 dead and the destruction of much of its navy, the war produced demonstrations which eventually led to the overthrow of the military dictatorship.

On 26 July 1982 a service of 'Thanksgiving and Remembrance' was held in St Paul's Cathedral, attended by the Queen, the government, MPs and many of those involved in the Falklands affair – though only a few of the servicemen who did the fighting. I was given a ticket by the BBC and sat in one of the side aisles. Mrs Thatcher clearly intended the service to be one of triumph and congratulation for a great victory – St Paul's had had many such services in the past. But, since it was designated a service of 'Thanksgiving and Remembrance', the Archbishop of Canterbury, Robert Runcie, devoted part of his sermon to remembering and honouring the dead of both sides. It seemed to me a fitting thing to say at the time. The next day, however, many of the newspapers reported that Mrs Thatcher had been angered by the Archbishop's sermon and that many Conservative MPs wished to denounce him as a pacifist and a defeatist. Other Conservatives objected to this, pointing out that during the Second World War Runcie had been a tank commander and had won the Military Cross. I knew and admired Runcie: as Bishop of St Albans he had given out the prizes at my daughters' school in Ware.

I met the Archbishop again, briefly in 1987, when he entertained the leader of the Orthodox Church – the Ecumenical Patriarch of Constantinople (Istanbul) His All Holiness Demetrios I – in Canterbury Cathedral. Neither the Greek Section nor the World Service normally gave much space to ecclesiastical visits, but this was special: it was in many ways a *first* and it had an interesting musical accompaniment. The British composer, John Tavener, who had converted to the Orthodox faith, had been commissioned by the cathedral authorities to set to music a Greek-language text welcoming the Patriarch to Canterbury, and I was sent down with a BBC recording engineer to cover the event. It was the 8 December 1987, a Tuesday evening, and in many ways it was a private event without much of a congregation. I recorded interviews with the Dean of Canterbury and with the charismatic John Tavener; I then retreated to the organ loft with the engineer, while the cathedral choir performed Tavener's three-minute 'Acclamation' of welcome.

* * * * *

On 13 June my attachment to Central Current Affairs Talks had come to an end and I had returned to the Greek Section. Leslie Stone told me that he had requested that I stay on as Assistant Head of CCAT, but had been overruled by the Controller who wished to bring in an outside candidate.

But more needs to be said about Leslie Stone who in many ways was one of the 'square pegs' in the BBC External Services. As with Anatol Goldberg, the bosses in Bush House did not really know how to manage a commentator with an Oxford DPhil and personal acquaintance with the leading politicians of Britain and the US. As his obituary in *The Guardian* on 24 October 2001 – by his Oxford contemporary, David McKie – put it:

> *Few analysts of British politics, and certainly no British analyst of US politics, knew more than he did - and his knowledge of American sport was very nearly a match for it. Indeed, the very wealth of his expertise was something of a trial to him, reducing him to seething exasperation as more famous pundits pronounced judgments which he knew to be rotten with error.*

Leslie's time at the BBC became increasingly troubled and in 1991 he took early retirement to devote himself to lecturing – mainly at universities in the United States. Towards the end of the century, he developed motor neurone disease and died in October 2001.

17.
Greeks and Turks

In 1983 Greece and Turkey celebrated the sixtieth anniversary of the Treaty of Lausanne, which brought to an end the last war between them. I say 'celebrated' but in Greece there was less celebration or even recognition of the treaty than in Turkey. Indeed Turks had many reasons for celebration. First, the Treaty of Lausanne provided for the creation of modern Turkey, since the decree establishing the Republic of Turkey on what was left of the Ottoman Empire was officially proclaimed on 29 October 1923 – the BBC had sent me to Turkey in October 1973 for the fiftieth anniversary. But there were further reasons for celebration in Ankara since on 6 November 1983 Turkey had its first parliamentary elections since 1977, in fact since the declaration of martial law in 1980. Those elections resulted in a significant victory for the Motherland Party (ANAP) led by the new Prime Minister, Turgut Özal.

Conscious of how well it would go down in Turkey if the BBC were to feature the new government, the anniversary of Lausanne and Republic Day all in one programme, Andrew Mango proposed that I should produce the feature. There was no Arabic Service money this time, but funds were available, Mango assured me. He said he would like me to interview historians and other experts on the 1923 treaty and try to get an interview with Prime Minister Özal. Reluctantly, he agreed to my trying to get an interview with the controversial Andreas Papandreou, who had been Prime Minister of Greece since 1981. Two of the main experts were very near at hand. Professor Bernard Lewis of SOAS – the School of Oriental and African Studies – in Bloomsbury, was a widely recognised writer on the Ottoman Empire and the establishment of modern Turkey; he later taught at Princeton University in the United States and became an adviser to the White House. Richard Clogg of King's College London was the best-known British historian of modern Greece. I invited them both for interview in Bush House and they substantially agreed on the provisions of the Lausanne treaty, of how and why it was drawn up and what it achieved.

When the First World War ended in 1918, British and French troops occupied Constantinople (Istanbul), capital of the Ottoman Empire which had allied itself in the war with Imperial Germany and

Austria. Between then and 1923 the Western powers used various treaties to begin carving up the Ottoman Empire. Its possessions in the Middle East – Mesopotamia (Iraq), Syria and Lebanon – were shared between Britain and France, Palestine became a British mandate of the League of Nations, while other territories like Yemen and the Hejaz were simply abandoned. Most of the Ottoman territories in Europe were incorporated into Romania, Bulgaria and Greece. All these changes were incorporated in 1920 in the Treaty of Sèvres, but the Kingdom of Greece refused to sign it and the Turkish 'national movement' led by Mustafa Kemal (Atatürk) rejected it. There then followed the Greek-Turkish war of 1919-23 – also known as the 'Turkish War of Independence' – in which Greek forces, inspired by the 'Great Idea' (*Megáli Idéa*) of creating a nation on both sides of the Aegean Sea, invaded Anatolia, capturing Smyrna (Izmir) most of whose citizens were Greek-speaking, and other towns before tbeing decisively defeated and driven back. The sequel to that was an enormous exchange of populations: 1.5 million Christians from Anatolia and Pontus were deported to Greece and 500,000 Muslims were expelled from Northern Greece to Turkey. Once the two governments had regularised the population exchange with their own treaty, the way was clear for the Lausanne Treaty to incorporate all the developments since 1918 and put a final line under the First World War.

Turgut Özal

My trip to Ankara to interview Prime Minister Özal was nearly a disaster. I had booked into a hotel near the Parliament building – not the Bulvar Palas where I stayed in 1973. At supper for dessert I ordered some fruit with milk and was surprised when the waiter brought hot milk. I said I had wanted *cold* milk to go with the fruit, so the waiter took it away and eventually brought back cold milk which I poured on the fruit. At the time I did not suspect that it was the hot milk chilled, but I soon found out. An uncomfortably bilious, incontinent night followed from which I had barely recovered when I was due at the Prime Minister's office for the interview.

Turgut Özal was a friendly, self-confident interviewee. He did not dwell on the provisions of the Lausanne Treaty, but extolled the

Two views of the Treaty of Lausanne from Turgut Özal of Turkey (left) and Andreas Papandreou of Greece.

achievements of the modern Republic of Turkey. The past three years of military rule, he said, had been a corrective, even a necessary corrective, in the political life of his country. He was confident that the return to democratic government would enable Turkey to fulfill all its international obligations, especially within the NATO alliance. When I asked him about a recent report from the Council of Europe highlighting Turkey's use of torture against Kurdish prisoners, he blandly assured me that soon his government would ban the practice. On relations with Greece and its complaints of Turkey's encroachment on Greek territorial waters in the Aegean, he said that such problems could only be solved by negotiation – and so far Greece had refused to negotiate.

Özal's confidence – and ebullience – were well justified. He remained Prime Minister until 1989 when he became President until 1993, bringing in what became known as the 'Özal decade'. His sudden death in 1993 brought back to power Süleyman Demirel, whom I had interviewed back in 1973.

Andreas Papandreou

A week later I flew to Athens to interview Andreas Papandreou at his villa in the upmarket suburb of Kifisia. I came straight from the airport, avoiding any problems in a hotel. In contrast to the blandness of Özal, Papandreou was an engaging, charismatic – some said 'dangerous' – figure. His father, George Papandreou, had been a liberal Prime Minister, regarded as reliable and pro-British, but Andreas created waves from the beginning of his time in politics. In 1965 while serving as Defence Minister in his father's government he became involved in an army officers' conspiracy and was sacked by his father. During the Colonels' dictatorship, he lived in Sweden.

I began by asking Papandreou whether Greeks would celebrate the anniversary of the Treaty of Lausanne, to which he replied that the treaty had created peace between Greece and Turkey for fifty years but was not now taken seriously by Turkey. He spoke of the Turkish invasion of Cyprus in 1974 and its provocative behaviour in the Aegean, by declaring that half the sea was Turkish territorial waters and issuing licences for oil exploration. He said that these were clear breaches of the Lausanne Treaty and illegal in international law. The policy of Turkey was to act in this way and then to call upon Greece to negotiate. He said he was ready to meet with Özal or any other Turkish leader, but would not negotiate about any issue involving the sovereignty of Greece. In February 1982, Papandreou had been the first Greek Prime Minister to visit Cyprus, where he declared his determination to seek a just solution to the island's problems which would be fair to both the Greek majority and the Turkish minority.

My feature on the Treaty of Lausanne was due to go out in January 1984, but I ran into opposition from Andrew Mango. The Head of the South European Service objected to Papandreou's interpretation of the treaty and asked me to edit what he had said or, at least, to include a disclaimer. I objected, saying that to edit the Greek Prime Minister would be bad journalism and very bad public relations. Eventually, I had to include an editorial comment that there were different interpretations of the Lausanne Treaty in Turkey and Greece and also among historians.

The expulsion of Greeks from Asia Minor is always referred to as the *Mikrasiátiki Kastástrophe* (the Middle East Catastrophe) but in many ways it was a blessing for the tiny Hellenic Kingdom of Greece. The influx of a million and a half Asia Minor Greeks enlarged the population, particularly benefitting the north where cities like Thessaloniki had been denuded of their Turkish, Jewish and Bulgarian middle classes and soon became wholly Greek. But the 'Catastrophe' also transformed and enriched the culture of mainland

Greece. When I came to Athens in 1980 to interview Adamantios Pepelasis, the guide he provided for me was an enterprising woman named Anna Kanakáki, who in the evening took me with friends to an *ouzeri* bar in the port of Piraeus where *rebétiko* music was performed. *Rebétiko* – very much in vogue in the seventies and eighties – was the music that the poorest immigrants brought from Smyrna and Pontos, the sad songs of a refugee subculture, reminiscent in many ways of the *blues* in the American south and *fado* in Portugal.

Cyprus

It was not long after the programme on the Lausanne Treaty that I paid my first visit to Cyprus. Tentative talks were going on between the Greek and Turkish-speaking communities – the first since the Turkish invasion of northern Cyprus in 1974 – there were also talks between the Cypriot government and a group from the European Community. The latter talks were significant, since the EEC had avoided taking sides over the division of the island, and yet had recognised the Greek Cypriot government for the purposes of trade and cultural relations and refused to recognise the Turkish Cypriot regime established after the Turkish military invasion. Very much later, in 2004, Cyprus became a full member of the European Union without any sign of reconciliation between the two halves of the island. Also watching the talks with the EEC was our Athens stringer for the Greek Section, Adriana Ierodiakónou – who was in fact Cypriot by birth – but she too found the discussions with the EEC impenetrable.

I had arranged interviews with the two community leaders – Prime Minister Spyros Kypriánou of the Greeks and Rauf Denktash of the Turks – for a World Service feature, but there was no hurry. I had five days in Cyprus and was determined to use them to see as much of the island as possible. I landed at Larnaca and took a bus to Nicosia, where the EEC talks were taking place and where I had an appointment with Radio Cyprus before seeing Mr Kypriánou the following day. I found Nicosia – or *Lefkosía* in Greek – a pleasant, not too frantic city, unlike the port cities of Larnaka and Limassol.

The real pleasure for me, forbidden to Greek Cypriots, was to show my British passport at the Ledra Street crossing on the 'green line' and be able to explore the Turkish-occupied north of the city. I had an appointment with Mr Denktash in the afternoon of the third day and spent the morning exploring northern Nicosia – or *Lefkoşa* in Turkish. There were few tourists and I was able to wander freely, taking photos of the Ayia Sophia Cathedral, the church of Agios Spyridon and the Lala Mustafa Mosque – formerly the Crusaders' Catholic Cathedral of St Nicholas. I wished that I had had the time to explore more of Northern Cyprus.

Back in the Greek part of the city, I hired a car and drove through the Troodos mountain range to Paphos, the delightful, laid-back town on the south-west tip of the island and a centre of incomparable archaeology. In my three days there, I was able to see the wonderful mosaics – then still being excavated – in the villas of Dionysos, Theseus and Aion. Since I still had the car, to be returned at Larnaca airport, I was able to drive out of Patras and see the strange rocks rising out of the sea where Aphrodite, goddess of love and beauty, is said to have been born – the Greek word *'aphros'* meaning foam.

Mario Modiano

In Cyprus I met our Greek Section correspondent, Adriana Ierodiakónou, who was also the Athens stringer for the *Washington Post*, and she told me that she was thinking of giving up journalism. Her sister ran a craft school and workshop in Cyprus and Adriana thought she might join her. She had been a good, reliable correspondent and was young and left-of-centre – very much in tune with the staff of the Greek Section. Back in London, while we were discussing Adriana's replacement, I had a visit from Agape Stasinopoúlou who said that her sister, Arianna, was a writer and journalist and might be interested in working for the BBC Greek Section. I knew Arianna Stassinópoulos (as she was known) through mutual friends in London: she came from a well-known Athens family, had studied at Cambridge where she was President of the Union and had been the girlfriend of the columnist, Bernard Levin. I doubted Arianna's commitment to journalism and so gave her sister a non-committal answer. I was wrong, of course, because Arianna went to the United States where she married a Congressman and founded the immensely successful Huffington Post website.

It was through my predecessor, Paul Nathanail – now retired and living in Athens – that we found a new Athens correspondent in Mario Modiano *(right)*. For some years Mario had been the correspondent of *The Times*, which meant that some members of the Greek Section mistrusted him from the start, but I found his copy perfectly acceptable. He used to file by telex and a member of the section would voice his dispatches. I met Mario and his Turkish wife, Inji, at their apartment in the smart Kolonaki area of Athens and took an instant liking to them both. They were a cultured, cosmopolitan couple with a wide circle of expatriate friends and acquaintances. Mario came from a Jewish family who had left Italy in the sixteenth century and settled in Salonika (the old name for Thessaloniki). Like many of the Jews of Salonika, they were probably refugees from the Spanish Inquisition originally. Shortly before the Germans entered Salonika in 1941, the Modiano family tried to escape to Athens, but they failed and were sent to the Jewish ghetto. But, as Italian Jews were exempt from the Nazi racial laws, Mario's father appealed to the Italian consul to claim Italian nationality for his family. They succeeded for themselves and for 138 other families who in that manner managed to escape from the ghetto. Before the First World War, Salonika had been a majority Jewish city and the unique home of Ladino, the blend of Spanish and Hebrew the refugees from the Inquisition had brought with them.

Display Determination

Greece and Turkey are both members of NATO (the North Atlantic Treaty Organisation); they applied to join at the same time and became members together in 1952. But the relationship is not an easy one, nor an equal one. Greeks have long believed that NATO and its biggest member, the United States, favoured Turkey more than them for strategic reasons – Turkey shared a border with the Soviet Union, it controlled the Bosporus seaway linking the Black

Sea with the Mediterranean, and Turkey's armed forces were among the largest in the alliance. It is for that reason, Greeks believed, that neither NATO nor the United States intervened when Turkey invaded Cyprus in 1974. Nor has their membership always run smoothly. Following the Cypriot crisis, Greece withdrew its armed forces from the military command structure and did not return to the military wing of the alliance until 1980. Then, in 1981, the newly-elected left-wing government of Andreas Papandreou withdrew Greek forces from certain shared commands and that remained the case for some years.

Display Determination was an annual joint exercise, involving the armed services of all the member states in the Mediterranean region. It was due to begin on 1 October 1984 in the Gallipoli area of Turkey and the BBC World Service was invited to send a reporter. Andrew Mango said that I should go to represent the South European Service and suggested I might also take a broader view of the exercise by seeing how it was received in Greece, which in due course I did.

I went first to Naples to interview the Commander-in-Chief Allied Forces Southern Europe, US Navy Admiral William N. Small. I had not been to Naples before and found it attractive and slightly worrying – the worry was Naples' reputation as the crime capital of Italy, home to the Camorro clan of the Mafia. With what little time I had to explore, I avoided the narrow streets of the old part and was browsing a shopping arcade when a middle-aged man in a suit approached and said he would show me round. I was reluctant to take up his offer but, as the streets were thronged with people, I followed him a little way. He asked if I was American and a tourist: I answered 'No' to both. I asked him what he did for a living and he said he was a guide. *'An official guide?' 'Just a guide.'* Eventually we arrived at the place where he was taking me – a large jewelry store where the owner greeted the guide by name. I plucked up courage, said 'Thank you. No.' and walked away.

At the headquarters of AFSOUTH, I told my Public Information contact about my morning and he said in Naples everyone had to be cautious. Then with a smile he told me a story: one of the senior officers had purchased an expensive, high-powered Alfa Romeo but found there was a minor problem with the headlights. So he rang the garage where he bought it and they agreed to fix it if he brought the car in the next day. But the next day he was due to fly to SHAPE headquarters in Belgium, so he drove to the garage, left the car with the key in the ignition and went to the airport. Returning three days later, he was surprised to see his car still outside the garage with the key in the ignition. Then he realised that the garage was not the one where he had purchased the Alfa Romeo. Later he related the incident to a Naples policeman, who said the Camorro would have assumed the car was a police trap and therefore no one touched it.

Admiral Small *(pictured above)* – known to his men as 'Smally' – was a Naval Aviator who had once commanded the US Sixth Fleet. He was also an astute politician who responded with a wide smile when I asked him about Greek-Turkish tensions and how they affected NATO. His answer was that the alliance took no notice of disputes between members, so long as they did not impair the commitment or the readiness of those countries' armed forces. He pointed out that Greece and Turkey were both committed to the alliance and that Greece had the biggest defence budget per capita of any NATO member, including the United States and Britain. He said it was a pity that the socialist government in Athens had withdrawn Greek forces from exercises like *Display Determination*, but that did not mean that Greek forces would be any the less effective in the event of an East-West conflict with the Soviet bloc. When I told him I was going to the Aegean to observe alleged Turkish encroachments of Greek airspace, he said that that would be a good context in which to judge the readiness and effectiveness of the two air forces.

From Naples I travelled to Athens by air and then went down to the port of Piraeus. My plan was to take a ferry to the islands of the Aegean and see how much Turkish military activity there was and what reaction there was to it among the Greek population. The ferry was an old motor vessel, the *MS Kiklades*, going to the Greek island of Limnos with stops at Chios and Mytilene (Lesbos) *en route*. It was a long journey – 12 hours 15 minutes – but I had a cabin and plenty of books, there was a bar selling coffee, *ouzo* and *souvlaki*, and there were plenty of diversions watching the student tourists and older Greeks coming and going – in one case with a trailer full of goats. The ship's final destination, the island of Limnos (or Lemnos), was doubly appropriate for me if I was going to observe military activities by Greece and Turkey. Limnos is situated in the middle of the Aegean Sea at the edge of the maritime boundaries claimed by both states, but it had a unique military history of its own. In the spring of 1915, thousands of Australian, New Zealand and British troops landed at Limnos to prepare for the invasion of the Ottoman shore at Gallipoli; it was from Moudros Bay at Limnos that the invasion fleet set sale and from Moudros that troops were repatriated after the invasion failed. In 1918 the Armistice between the Ottoman Empire and the Allies was signed on a Royal Navy warship in Moudros Bay.

It was the last week of September and the end of the tourist season; the hotels and bed-and-breakfasts that were still open were offering good accommodation at cheap rates. I found a B-and-B in Myrina, the main town, and explored that end of the island, including a 1915 Anzac cemetery. The over-flying began at dawn the next morning – as it did at dawn every morning in the autumn, I was told. Two jet warplanes came in low over the town, close together with barely the length of a fuselage between them. I could see what Admiral Small meant about judging the readiness and effectiveness of the two air forces. The roar of aircraft flying overhead went on for about twenty minutes. At breakfast I asked the B-and-B owner whose planes they were and what he thought about it all. The leading plane would have been Turkish, he said, and the one in pursuit Greek. Of course, it was a violation of Greek airspace and caused major difficulties for commercial flights to and from the Aegean islands, but at least the flights were regular: they did not fly after 9 am and they did not fly in the main tourist months of July and August. I got similar reactions from other townspeople I interviewed: the overflying had been going on in the autumn for two or three years. Mostly the islanders shrugged and said they were now a fact of life, and protests from the Mayor and from the government had had little effect. Only one hotelier seemed angry at the Turkish Air Force, and he was an Athenian, about to pack up and leave for the winter.

From Limnos I took a flight to Athens – in the afternoon, of course – and then another flight in the evening to Istanbul. The next morning

I joined other journalists at a rendezvous with the NATO Public Affairs chief, Captain James Matthews USN, and we set off by coach to the exercise site on the Gelidolu Peninsular – as Gallipoli is now called in Turkish. *Display Determination* was a land and sea exercise on the shores of Saros Bay and also on the three uninhabited islands in the bay. Mock attacks and landings from the sea were accompanied by troop movements coming down from Turkish Thrace, and in 1984 all went according to plan and without incident. Eight years later, however, missiles fired from the aircraft carrier, *USS Saratoga*, severely damaged a Turkish destroyer, causing a number of deaths and many injuries. I found it difficult to do interviews during the exercise: the attitude of the NATO staff was that I had been given an important, high level interview with Admiral Small and further comment would be superfluous. Besides, while everyone regretted the absence of the Greek armed forces, a NATO exercise was not thought to be the proper context for discussing the political dispute between Turkey and Greece. And that was the message I took back to Bush House, to be incorporated in my feature for the World Service on *Exercise Display Determination*.

18.
'Are you really a Communist?'

Andrew Mango retired from the BBC External Services in the summer of 1986, on reaching the age of 60. A dinner party was held in his honour in one of the dining rooms in the Centre Block of Bush House, hosted by Peter Fraenkel, Controller European Services. The other guests included Mrs Mango, Gamon McLellan, the Turkish Programme Organiser, Tony Hughes and Tony Menezes, who had been programme organisers of the Spanish and Portuguese sections until those languages for Europe were axed, and myself. At the table I found myself sitting next to Mrs Mango who – the moment we sat down – asked:

'Are you really a Communist?'
'Goodness,' I replied with surprise. 'Why do you say that?'
'Andrew says you have strong, pro-Communists leanings.'
'I don't think I do. Anyway, I'm a founder member of the Social Democratic Party – the SDP.'

Mrs Mango then turned away and did not speak to me again during the meal. I was quite puzzled by the exchange. Why the assumption or accusation that I was a Communist? Andrew Mango had certainly not wanted me as Greek Programme Organiser in 1979 and we had disagreed about some programme issues, such as my wish to give the Greek socialists under Andreas Papandreou a fair hearing. But I put that down to his Turkish bias. He had been born in Istanbul, had worked during the war for the British Embassy in Ankara, had been Turkish Programme Organiser and in retirement wrote guide books about Turkey and an authoritative biography of Kemal Atatürk. There was some debate about his religious history. Since his family came from Russia, I assumed they were originally Jewish, but I knew somehow that his wife was an enthusiastic Roman Catholic. Mango had often talked of his visits to a university in Pamplona in Spain, but whether that was the public university or the university set up by Josemaria Escriva de Balaguer, the founder of the right-wing Catholic body *Opus Dei*, was not clear.

    I thought little more about the exchange with Mrs Mango until a few months later when Andrew Mango's successor, Benny Ammar, called me into his office. Benny was an old friend and a great practical joker. He directed me to sit down and then opened a drawer and pulled out an Annual Report form: *'This is about you, written by Andrew Mango, but Peter Fraenkel says that you are not to see it on any account.'* Then he laughed and put the paper back in the drawer which he locked. I protested that as he had told me about it I should see the report, but to no avail.

Benny Ammar grew up in a Jewish family in Egypt before moving to Cyprus; he was fluent in Arabic, Greek and other languages as well as English. When I edited *The World Today* in 1974, Benny was one of the producers working under me. Later he came on a holiday in Ithaca, staying in a house belonging to Ariánna Ferentínou, one of the Greek Section producers. I was there with two friends – Chris Bickerton from the African Service and Linda Staines, who brought along her eighteen-month old daughter Chloe: when I wheeled the blonde child around the main town, women would exclaim *'Kúkla'* meaning 'doll'. Anyway, Benny Ammar was there with a girlfriend and hired a moped to drive her round the island, but when he leaned into the first bend.twards and both came off. After the South-East European Service, Benny's balance did not fail him and he progressed in the World Service to become Head of the Europe Regions and then Head of Go Digital.

Posidonia at Piraeus

Piraeus, which had served Athens since the third millennium BC, became the busiest port in the Mediterranean, outstripping even Genoa and Marseille. In the 1980s it was undergoing a comprehensive programme of modernisation and enlargement. This was partly the result of the increase in passenger traffic associated with cruise liners; improvements to the central port were undertaken in 1984 to serve passenger traffic. At the same time plans were made to exploit the Central Passenger Terminal as an exhibition space, particularly for international exhibitions. Then in 1986 work began on expanding the Container Terminal. All of this formed the backdrop to the biannual Posidonia International Shipping Exhibition, organised in association with the Union of Greek Shipowners. *Posidonia 1986*, therefore, promised to be a particularly important event and the BBC World Service decided it would cover the exhibition with me as the producer/manager.

I was there to help with features about Posidonia for two programmes. The World Service had been broadcasting *The Merchant Navy Programme* since the end of the Second World War and the Greek Section had a similar programme in *Théssalla kay Thessallinée* (Sea and Seamen). George Yemenakis was there for the Greek Section and my role was to make sure his recordings were of good enough quality. For *The Merchant Navy Programme,* the presenter, Malcolm Billings, came out and with him I had to arrange interviews, help with the recordings, edit the interviews on my Uher, record Malcolm's introduction and linking script and – finally – take the finished tape to Greek Radio (ERT) for them to send it over to Bush House.

Malcolm, who was an old friend and partner in freelancing, originally trained as an actor in Australia and appeared with Barry Humphries, though not when he was doing Dame Edna Everage. Malcolm then came to London and worked mainly in radio – reporting on the *Today* programme for Radio 4 and undertaking numerous assignments for the World Service. Later he made features about history and archaeology, including a splendid series about the Crusades which he published as a book.

The Merchant Navy Programme was eventually recorded and sent to London. Then I hired a car and, as planned, set out to take Malcolm and his wife, Brigid O'Hara, to Nafplion which I had enthused about on many occasiions. We had not booked hotel rooms, but it was mid-October and there should not have been trouble finding rooms. But we did not get to Nafplion. Just south of Corinth we encountered a serious traffic jam and the road blocked by tractors and farm vehicles (all newly purchased with grants from the EEC) as the conservative members of the Peloponnesan Union of Farmers protested against the agricultural policies of the left-wing PASOK government. It was six in the evening and it was clear we would not get to Nafplion that way and that night. Malcolm with characteristic briskness called on me to take 'executive action!' So I turned the car about and headed back over the bridge of the Corinth Isthmus to the junction of a road which I had not used before, and as much by luck as by judgement we eventually came on to the main highway to Delphi. I was not used to driving at night on Greek roads as they then were, and we had a few near misses, but as we passed by ancient

Malcolm Billings interviewing a seaman for the World Service programme, 'The Merchant Navy Programme', assisted in the background by his wife, Brigid O'Hara.

Thebes I pointed this out to my passengers and Malcolm took our minds off the road with the story of Oedipus and his family. We arrived in Delphi in the late evening and fortunately found rooms at the Delphi Palace Hotel.

I had been to Delphi before, with a girlfriend in 1983, and either Malcolm or Brigid had too – probably Malcolm on a slow, tourist itinerary like many young Australians – but the opportunity to explore the oracular heart of the ancient world at leisure, without bus loads of other tourists, was very welcome. Our enjoyment was all the greater for being unexpected. If we had been in Nafplion as planned, I would have been the know-it-all guide, but in Delphi we were all equal, all seeing things afresh. We walked up the slope to the Temple of Apollo in comparative silence, all thinking – or certainly I was – of the important decisions in our lives on which we might have consulted the Pythia, the Sybil at the sanctuary of Apollo. The Sybil had to be an older woman of blameless life, chosen from the peasants of the area; I commented that Greece does not have any real peasants now, blameless or otherwise, and Malcolm and Brigid were forced to agree.

Monemvasia

In 1987 my brother, Ray, came to Greece and I took him to Nafplion for a night; then we drove south towards Monemvasia at the bottom of the Peloponnese. We had both been reading Patrick Leigh Fermor's books and particularly *Mani,* about his travels in southern Greece. We also knew of his walk across Europe in 1934 and his war service including the kidnap of a German general in Crete – filmed in 1957 as *Ill Met by Moonlight* with Dirk Bogart playing Leigh Fermor. So I drove from Nafplion across the Peloponnese to Kalamata on the west coast and headed for Leigh Fermor country. It was dark by the time we reached Kardomyli, the nearest town to the writer's house, where we stopped at a taverna for a meal. Leigh Fermor was said to be hospitable to English visitors – especially perhaps to a newspaper journalist like Ray though he might have had misgivings about me because he was said to dislike the radio – but it was late, the taverna owner said 'Kyrios Paddy' and his wife retired to bed early, and we wished to press on to Monemvasia that night. So sadly we did not meet our philhellene hero. For a travel writer, he was perhaps unique in having a military OBE and DSO and being knighted in 2004. In 2007 he said he had begun using a typewriter for the first time to write his books. He died in 2011 and is buried next to his wife in the Gloucestershire village of Dumbleton.

Mani is an extraordinary book. It is certainly not a travel guide to southern Greece; more a love poem in prose, extolling the virtues of the *Maniótes,* isolated for centuries from European history, fighting among themselves from their fortified tower houses, but preserving characteristics and virtues that Leigh Fermor traced back to the great days of Byzantium. He met a fisherman in Kardomyli and saw in him the physiognomy of the Byzantine royal family, the Palaeologi, and so went on to imagine that the empire had been restored with the magnanimous gift of Constantinople by modern Turkey. It was a vision of living history that appealed to me, like Enrico Thorn Prikker's fair-haired fisherman in Nafplion who could have been one of King Otto's followers or the plaque commemorating the murder of Kapodistrias by Petros Mavromichalis, last of the *beys* of Mani. These resonances from the not-too-distant past meant more to me than the archaeological treasures of Ancient Greece, which tourists pay so much to visit. And in Monemvasia itself – which we reached

The rock of Monemvasia with the causeway in the foreground.

in the late evening – we were reminded of Yannis Ritsos, poet, patriot and Communist, who believed that the 'Greekness' of the Byzantines was kept alive in codes of honour, loyalty, bravery, love of the land, religious devotion and patriotism. His great poem about this 'Greekness' or *Romiosíni* was published in 1954; Yannis Ritsos was born in Monemvasia. Ray and I stayed in a guest house in Monemvasia – not the one within the castle walls which is now called Ritsos Guesthouse – but we did meet a woman who claimed to be a relative of the poet.

Monemvasia is itself a wonder. Similar to Gibraltar in being built on a huge, steep-sided rock, its connection to mainland Greece is a causeway 200 metres long. Remarkably, most of the modern development is on the mainland side of the causeway and the city itself is unspoiled traditional architecture. This is mainly due to the efforts of an Athenian couple, Alexander and Haris Kalligas, who have been restoring the old buildings since the 1960 and in 1980 were awarded a Europa Nostra heritage medal. But the real wonder of Monemvasia is the steep slope to the summit and the view over the edge to the Aegean and beyond. When I first went there with Kostas Psomadarkis, he told me that at the time of Greek Independence any Turks remaining in the city were brought to this summit and thrown over the edge. It is not a story found in the guidebooks.

From Monemvasia, Ray and I returned to Athens via Mistras, the

Byzantine city rising up a long hillside. This was a peaceful place to be savoured at leisure. Nearby is ancient Sparta, now subsumed in the modern town of the same name. But to get to Sparta from Mistras, one goes through a narrow canyon which symbolised the rigid discipline of that ancient warrior culture.

Family affairs

I thoroughly enjoyed working with the Greek Section and enjoyed being Greek Programme Organiser. They were a varied group of men and woman and they seemed to like being managed by me. Never once in my ten years with them did any member of the section complain about me to Andrew Mango or his successor, Benny Ammar. Indeed any complaints tended to be directed at each other with me as a confidant or referee. But in fact there were very few complaints in the Greek Section, which functioned as a loose-knit family of equals. It occurred to me how different it was from the Arabic Service, where I had little direct contact with the rank-and-file translators and broadcasters, having to deal instead with the 'unit heads' – a bunch of very prickly gentlemen. In fact, my only real contact with the Arabic staff was my leaving party, as I said earlier, when quite unexpectedly they clubbed together to give me a present and turned out in force to drink my health.

A few of the Greek Section had worked for the BBC during the military dictatorship, but the veterans of that period had mainly gone home and been replaced by younger translators. The assistant programme organiser, George Yannoulópoulos, had been in London since at least 1970 when he married the daughter of a Lord Justice of Appeal; George was finishing a PhD on the poet George Seferis and was fairly laid-back about working for the BBC. Among the others, there were two Christinas – Coucounará, who was next in seniority to George, and Koutsoudáki, who after she left the BBC became famous as a character actor on Greek TV. Another veteran, Christos Pittas was a composer who had worked closely with Mikis Theodorakis and, in his own right, developed interpretations of music and drama, including for BBC Radio Three: his composition 'Idola' for a chamber orchestra and dancers was performed at the Queen Elizabeth Hall on the South Bank in 1984 – I had a small hand in arranging that.

Members of the Greek Section photographed outside the front entrance of Bush in 1981. In the centre is my secretary, Pambos Morphitis, with my deputy, George Yannoulopoulos, in the background between Pambos and me.

Members of the Greek Section were in two categories. Some were on pensionable contracts – as I was – while others were recruited for five years, after which they could be transferred to pensionable service, extended or sent back to Greece. The idea was to refresh the output with younger people familiar with the up-to-date language of ordinary Greeks. When I arrived, there was a group of young journalists whom we assigned in 1980 to cover Greece's membership of the European Economic Community (EEC) – Dimítris Petyhákis, Vasílis Kapetanyánnis and Níkos Língris, who were all on short-term

A later and fuller photo of the Greek Section, including part-time staff, secretaries and freelanes.

contracts and left soon after. Lingris said on his website that he found working for the BBC Greek Section 'exciting, but then my wife got sick of the English weather'. In fact when he left the BBC, Nick founded a bookshop near Syntagma Square in Athens, modelled on the Compendium bookshop at Camden Market. It was Nick Lingris who introduced to the section Dr. Agis Tsourós – newly qualified from the Queen's Medical Centre at Nottingham University – to write a review of the 1980 Reith Lectures, entitled 'Unmasking Medicine' by Sir Ian Kennedy QC, founder of the Centre of Medical Law and Ethics at King's College London. We met in the Bush House canteen, George Yannoulopoulos, Nikos, Agis and I – and also a senior medical student named Irene Higginson, who will figure later in this memoir under her poetry *nom-de-plume*, Danielle Hope.

As some Greeks left, others joined the section from Athens or indeed London, including Yannis Karavídas, Víron (Byron) Karídis and Doxa Sivropoúlou. There were two married women, Eirene Arcoumáni and Anna Stamatopoúlou, who worked part-time. A poet, Michalis Mítras – who always referred to me as his *kapitanós* – came from Greece on a short-term contract, along with his partner, Natásha Hadzidákis, another poet. Arianna Ferentínou came first as a freelance, offering to finance herself for a series of features on the Greek diaspora, entitled *Ee Alii Elynes* (The Other Greeks) and later joined the staff. George Yannoulópoulos, Christina Coucounará, Christina Koutsoudáki and Christos Píttas all appeared on cassettes in the BBC Language and People series. And I must not forget our egregious freelance – George Yemenákis, who was a correspondent of ΥΕΝΕΔ, the Greek Armed Forces radio (a left over from the dictatorship), and fronted our merchant navy programme, *Théssalla kay Thessallinée* (Sea and Seamen).

The only occasion when this group of talented and charming people fell out was over a love affair. Two of the programme assistants – one married, the other in a long-term relationship – fell in love and announced to the section that they intended to live together. The news was greeted with concern, neighbouring on outrage, mainly from the other female members of the section, who knew the couple and their existing partners and had exchanged meals and outings with them and their children. Eventually the affair calmed down and the couple brought in their children, who got on well together from the very start.

In addition to the Programme Assistants, there was a changing group of typists, mainly Cypriot, and my own secretary, Pambos Morphitis, who was also Cypriot. When Pambos left, I had a succession of less efficient female secretaries who found it difficult to grasp the Bush House bureaucracy's demand for Ps-as-Bs ('Programmes as Broadcast' reports). A Ps-as-B detailed each programme's duration, use of signature tunes, other music, copyright material, outside contributors, staff and every other detail under the sun. A young woman used to come to the office periodically to chivy or bully my secretary for being late with the section's Ps-as-Bs. I found this disturbing and one day told her that I had interviewed the Ayatollah Khomeini and Margaret Thatcher but she was more objectionable than either of them. She was quieter after that.

The Canteen and the Club

The two institutions that united the diverse disciplines and nationalities of the World Service were the canteen and the BBC Club. The canteen lay under the carpark separating the South-East Wing from the Centre Block and was shaped like a figure '8' lying on its side. Along the bottom of the '8' were two serving counters, one dispensing hot meals, the other salads, sandwiches and snacks. Diners would tend to remain in national grouping, but with the busy crush at lunchtimes a Brazilian could find herself eating with Poles, or a Ugandan with Japanese. With the lack of security in the Seventies, college students would often find their way into the canteen but the story is surely apocryphal that an announcement came over the Tannoy: *'Will the students from the LSE kindly leave as it is time for King's College to dine'*. Security was tightened in about 1980 when student demonstrators invaded the Centre Block and threw papers from the English-by-Radio offices into the Aldwych – the 'Defenestration of Bush House'.

The Club was originally located across the Strand in Surrey Street. Many happy evenings were had there: I remember taking up a challenge to drink champagne from a female producer's shoe, issued by Mark Tully, later BBC correspondent in New Delhi. A well-known seduction ploy was to invite a female member of the Club to see the Roman bath, which did indeed exist on the opposite side of Surrey Street, down a flight of steps, off a dark service lane. The Surrey Street Club closed when the Reading Room of the India Office Newspaper Library – from the time of the East India Company and the Raj before Indian Independence – was moved from the Lower Ground floor of the Centre Block. The move took place in stages and the final shape of the Bush House Club produced two chambers. The management thought it was a good idea to have a long aquarium tank separating the two rooms – I remember taking an Arab visitor to the Club and having difficulty tearing him away from the gyrations of tropical fish in the tank. Then one morning the Club staff found the tank had ruptured and water, weeds and dead fish covered the floor.

Unlike the canteen where staff came, ate and left in quick order, the Club was a place to linger in and be entertained, not only for hardened drinkers – though there were some – but for the generality of staff. A few of the Controllers would hold court at the bar, Austen

Kark and Lance Thirkell who was in charge of 'Personnel' (Human Resources) and was known for his acerbic wit – 'the Vicious Thirkell'. The entertainment quotient was enhanced by Berny, an outrageously gay barman/manager who loved to scandalise the drinkers from foreign parts. While I was in Nafplion learning Greek, Christina Koutsoudáki brought Berny there on a surprise excursion, causing wide-eyed amazement in the Yacht Club. I used to drink in the Club with a select circle which – over time – included Chris Bickerton and William 'Barry' Burgess, the Hausa Programme Organiser, Chris Child, my predecessor as Arabic PO, Christina Koutsoudáki, Laurence Lalanne from the French Service and Abdi, a Somali whose surname I never knew – Abdi was often arrested for violating his student visa by working but then released to interpret for the Immigration Service in the prosecution of other Somalis.

One of the incidental pleasures of working in Bush House was to run into well-known actors in the canteen or the Club. The likes of Anton Diffring or Theodore Bikel between film engagements would be contributing a talk or translation to the European Services. In the Arabic Service I passed the time of day with the actor, Nadim Sawalha, who hailed from Madaba in Jordan; he does not now appear very much on British television, but his daughters Julia and Nadim Sawalha do. In the Club I often drank with the Punjabi actor Saeed Jaffrey, well known for his fluency in various languages and his gift for mimicry – his imitation of Bengalis would attract an appreciative crowd, although not of Bengalis, of course, but as they were mainly Muslim few Bengalis drank in the BBC Club. I can claim to have invented a drink with Saeed - St Clementsky, a St Clement's of orange and bitter lemon, spiced with vodka. Saeed later became an international star after his bravura performance as Billy Fish in *The Man Who Would Be King* and came less often to the Club or Bush House.

There were other familiar faces in Bush House, like Georgi Markov of the Bulgarian Section who was murdered in 1978 by someone wielding a poisoned umbrella. I knew his wife, Annabel Dilke, rather better for she was a fine novelist and also the daughter of Christopher Dilke, a frequent contributor to *Commentary*. The Bulgarian I knew best was Teo Lirkoff, a typist in the Bulgarian Section (and also part-time at the Bulgarian Embassy) who was a drinking companion of my Turkish colleague, Feyyaz Fergar. Teo had a serious drinking problem and also a wooden leg; on one occasion he was 'let go' by the Head of the East European Service who kindly awarded him severance pay 'in view of your disability'. Teo showed the letter to a trade union official who was outraged to think the BBC had sacked someone because they had a wooden leg.

* * * * *

When I joined the World Service, Bush House was a gargantuan consumer of paper. Reams of paper were expended on News bulletins, Commentaries, memos, reports and every other type of communication, however brief or transitory. Even though the BBC was a pioneer in providing computers for schools – in 1982 *The Computer Programme* on television led to most schools in Britain being supplied with Acorn 'Micro' computers – Bush House was slow to go paperless.

The first step was the introduction of screens in editors' and translators' offices so that News bulletins could be flashed up for programme makers; but paper bulletins were still being brought round and deposited in trays in the corridor, and most programme assistants seemed to prefer to work from paper. It was only at the end of the 1980s that I was supplied with a computer, capable of word-processing but not as yet emails.

After Andrew Mango's retirement, his pet scheme of retaining a few Italian, Portuguese and Spanish staff to supply features to the domestic radios of the three states was discontinued, and a reorganisation took place. Under Benny Ammar it became the South East European Service and included the Bulgarian, Romanian and Yugoslav sections as well as us Greeks and Turks. This introduced a whole new culture to our lives.

As yet the Iron Curtain had not fallen and the three new sections were broadcasting to pro-Soviet Communist countries, but there were ominous signs of future trouble. Eireni Arcoumani, who had a Serbian mother and understood the language, told of disturbing xenophobia she heard in the canteen or corridors – a few years before the Balkan crisis and the terrible wars that took place between the constituent parts of Yugoslavia.

Crete

I do not recall the reason for my first visit to Crete. It may have been a World Service feature about the Battle of Crete in 1941 because I visited only Chania in the west of the island, the scene of most of the fighting. But it may also have been a feature about Greek politics since the right-wing challenger to Andreas Papandreou was Constantine Mitsotakis, who was born in Chania. Mitsotakis of the New Democracy party became Prime Minister from 1991-93.

The Battle of Crete in May 1941 was significant because in just ten days the *Wehrmacht* defeated large units of British, Greek and New Zealand forces. The Allied forces were swollen by troops evacuated from mainland Greece – mainly through the ports of Kalamata and Nafplion – many of whom had had to leave their weapons behind. It was also the first major attack by airborne forces – German paratroopers (*Fallschirmjäger*) and gliders – in the Second World War. By capturing the main operational airfield at Maleme, east of Chania, the paratroops were able to outmanoeuvre and demoralise the Allies who either surrendered or withdrew to the south of the island and then were evacuated to Egypt. During my stay in Chania, I visited Maleme airfield and the war cemeteries around the city. But 1941 was significant also in being the first time the German armed forces had encountered serious resistance from the civilian population, leading to widespread executions.

A few hundred British and Commonwealth soldiers remained in Crete, harassing the Germans with the aid of the very active Cretan Resistance. One of the officers sent to Crete by SOE – Special Operations Europe – was C.M. ('Monty') Woodhouse, who was later parachuted into mainland Greece to blow up the strategic Gargopotamos rail bridge. After the war, he worked in the British Embassy in Teheran as an intelligence officer and was the instigator of 'Operation Boot' to remove the democratically elected government of Mohammed Mossadegh, who had nationalised the British-owned oil fields, and make Reza Shah the unchallenged ruler. Incidentally, Woodhouse used fake BBC World Service broadcasts to undermine Mossadegh, which is a counter argument to the later accusation that the BBC was always against the Shah. In 1959 Monty Woodhouse became the Conservative MP for Oxford and I interviewed him for the *Oxford Mail* at the elections of 1964 and

1966, when he was defeated by Evan Luard for Labour. He later succeeded to his father's title as the 5th Baron Terrington.

Crete became part of independent Greece as late as 1898. Then it had been an important Venetian and Genoese base before being conquered by the Ottomans in 1669. Those were just its more recent occupations, of course, for the island's distant past had seen Minoan, Mycenaean, Hellenistic, Roman, Byzantine and Arab rulers, but in Chania it was the more recent past that was most evident. The older part of Chania, with its cafés overlooking the harbour to the Venetian lighthouse, was a good place to sit and read my notes. Narrow streets filled with shops and more cafés radiated from the harbour. In a back street I found a synagogue, boarded up but undamaged, with a sign directing enquirers to the municipality. Greece is careful to preserve the buildings of other cultures and religions: in Nafplion there is a *hammam* or Turkish bathhouse, next to the Church of St Spyridon. Chania lost its Muslim citizens in the great expulsion of 1923. Its Jewish citizens stayed on, only to be rounded up by the Nazis in 1941 and shipped out on a steamer, which was tragically sunk by a Royal Navy torpedo.

I had explored Chania and had a few days spare, so I decided to go to the south coast of Crete. I would have liked to walk the scenic gorge of Samaria in the White Mountains east of Chania, but a ten miles (16km) hike which was said to take seven to nine hours was beyond me. Instead I took a bus to Paliokóra (*Palióchora*) on the south-western tip of the island. The bus was filled with backpackers and so was the resort. A long stretch of beach, lined with tavernas, ended with a crowded nudist reserve. It was a resort for hedonism and the young. I chatted with a taverna-owner who bemoaned the fact that older, freer spending tourists no longer came to *Palióchora*. I asked him what lay in the hinterland of the resort and he pointed out a track which went up into the mountains.

The next day, before returning to Chania, I set off up the track winding through woodland and scrub. After an hour and at some elevation from the coast I came across a cottage on the right of the track and a small group of tables and chairs opposite. Assuming this was an apology for a rural taverna, I sat at one of the tables and waited. A small, stocky woman with a swarthy complexion emerged from the cottage and came across. I asked her in Greek if there was food. She said there was and then asked:

Eeste Yermanós? (Are you German?)
Ochi. Ingláizos eeme. (No, I'm English.)
Inglázos! Thavmátio! (English! Wonderful!)

She then told me – at first in Greek, then increasingly in German – how she had been in the Cretan Resistance during the war, how she hated the Germans and yet had spent eight years in Germany with her husband as *Gastarbeiter* but still disliked them, and would bring me food with pleasure. She went back to the cottage and re-emerged not with food, but with a box containing papers and three medals. They were the British 1939-45 Star and two Kingdom of Greece medals, one of them called the Cretan Medal. She said she had received them from a British general.

The encounter with the woman – let's call her Eleni – set me thinking about the way we remembered and portrayed the war. Most films about the Cretan resistance featured the daring deeds of allied commandos, landed on the island by submarine, with male Greek peasants in supporting roles. The women in these dramas would be either a love interest or maybe secretly working for the Germans. On my return to London, I began to research the role of women in the Cretan resistance and was astonished to find they had been at the very centre of the struggle, and spontaneously involved in fighting the invader, whatever assistance they also gave to the Allies. Many of them had worked as wireless operators, like the splendidly named Terpsichóri Chryssouláki-Vláchou, who before she was shot scrawled a defiant message on the wall of her cell: *Ζήτω η Ελλάδα. Ζήτω η Κρήτη – Long live Greece! Long live Crete!* She was only 18 years of age. Or there was the widow, who sheltered two British soldiers and, when they were discovered and arrested, stood outside the German commander's office and harangued him for his inhumanity. I wondered what Eleni had done to earn her medals.

Thessaloniki

Thessaliniki is the second city of Greece, after Athens, and every September it hosts the Thessaliniki International Fair (TIF) which has been described as the most important trade and cultural event in south-eastern Europe. In 1988 it was decided that the BBC would have a stand at the fair with the Greek Section fronting the display. So I went with Ariana Ferentínou from the section as my assistant and fixer.

It was my first visit to Thessaloniki and I was impressed by its grandeur. I knew something of its commercial importance, as a major port and trade and industrial centre – a sort of Liverpool of Greece. But I did not expect to see the extensive array of the docks, and least of all the rail hub connecting Greece to the Balkans; at the time my only experience of Greek railways was the funny little trains of the Peloponnese narrow gauge line from Corinth to Kalamata via Argos, with a defunct branch line to Nafplion. East of the docks was the long sweep of the residential seafront, beginning at the White Tower and curving round to Kasamaria at the top of the Chalkidiki peninsular – a more leisurely area then, now crowded with tower blocks. Another surprise was to discover that the main thoroughfare of Thessaliniki was called the *Via Egnatia*, the name of the main route of the Roman Empire in the East, running from the Adriatic to Constantinople. But then Thessaliniki – or Salonika – was a Roman and Byzantine city before it became Venetian and Ottoman, finally joining independent Greece as late as 1912.

It took a few days to set up the BBC stand at the international fair, since display boards and furniture were being shipped out from Britain and erected by a local contractor. This gave me the chance to explore the city and find relics of the Ottoman period, including the birthplace of Mustafa Kemal (Atatürk), leader of the Young Turks, and relics of the Jewish community which I had learned about from Mario Modiano. It was a fine and warm September day and in the evening Ariana Ferentinou and I had supper *al fresco* near the White

Tower: with us was Timuçen Ertan, a friend from the Turkish Section. During the meal a young girl came to our table, selling roses. Tim bought one for Ariana and a few minutes later got up from the table and followed the girl. He came back fifteen minutes later and told us how he had found a Turkish man with an old van filled with flowers, which his children were taking from restaurant to restaurant – he intended to write a piece about it for *Cumhuriyet*. On the strength of his connection with the Turkish paper, Ariana and I arranged for Tim to take a ferry to Mount Athos on the far side of Chalkidiki – the monks never allow a woman, or anything female, to land at their sanctuary but there was no bar to Turks or Muslims.

'Your BBC'

The BBC stand at the international fair was extensive, consisting of twenty panels and tables containing books and leaflets, also two television receivers, and above them the rubric '*to BBC sas*' ('*your BBC*'). Ariana and I managed the stand with help from a few former members of staff and their children. Listeners of every age came by to chat in English or Greek or sometimes both. On one occasion, a Greek gentleman in a suit came to the stand and spoke to me. I answered him in Greek, but Ariana nudged me and whispered that the man was the principle of a *frontistírion*, a crammer, and was actually speaking English rather poorly – *frontistíria* were common in Greece where the quality of state-run education was low and any student wishing to go to university had to attend a *frontistírion* or have a private tutor.

Every public exhibition or conference in Greece has to have a brains-trust type of panel, where a group of experts or worthies sit at a high table and pontificate – and often contradict each other. The BBC stand at the Thessaloniki International Fair was no different. At the centre of our brains trust was the British Ambassador, Sir Jeremy Thomas KCMG, who had been accompanied from Athens by the Consul General and an interpreter. Sitting next to the ambassador was Stelios Papathemelis, a member of the PASOK government who that very year had had his title changed from Minister for Northern Greece to Minister of Macedonia and Thrace. They were joined by the chairman of the Thessaloniki Chamber of Trade at one end of the table and myself at the other end.

The British Ambassador, Sir Jeremy Thomas, speaking at the brains trust, with Perman on the left and Stelios Papathemelis, the new Minister of Macedonia and Thrace, on the right. Behind is the man in cavalry uniform.

The mayor of Thessaloniki was not invited since he was a member of the opposition New Democracy party. The brains trust drew a large audience and was considered a success. Photographs were taken, which showed a Greek in bearskin hat and British cavalry uniform standing behind the ambassador. The ambassador thanked me afterwards and said he would report back to London most favourably – this was Sir Jeremy's last posting and in retirement he became chairman of the Chichester Harbour Trust, for which he recorded a blog, still available online.

He was not invited to the brains trust, but the mayor, Sotiris Kouvelas, was not to be denied a presence. He came on the final day of the fair, bringing with him his children and a large bunch of flowers for Ariana. Kouvelas then gave a speech, repeating the announcement he had made earlier in the day about progress on plans for a Thessaloniki Metro underground line and his plan to set up Thessaloniki TV. He also invited me to join him at the municipality the following day to discuss possible rebroadcasting of the BBC

The Mayor of Thessaloniki, Sotiris Kouvelas, and the Greek Opposition Leader, Constantine Mitsotakis, visit the BBC stand. Next to Perman is Ariana Ferentinou from the Greek Section.

Greek Section's output on local Thessaloniki FM. I agreed to the meeting and then Kouvelas produced his trump card, a visit to the BBC stand by the Leader of the Opposition, Constantine Mitsotakis. More colour photographs were taken with Mitsotakis holding one of the Kouvelas children, another child holding Ariana's bouquet and everyone smiling.

The following morning Ariana and I went to the municipality to meet the mayor. His desire for simultaneous rebroadcasting of our Greek Section output had become economically viable through an offshoot of satellite television. Satellite TV had become well-nigh universal by the 1980s, but it was realised that uploading a TV programme did not use the whole bandwidth of the carrier signal: there were sidebands that could be used for other purposes, such as radio. All that was needed to receive such a radio signal was a piece of technology similar to the low-noise block downconverter found in the ordinary satellite dish. Such a converter was available in London though not then in Greece, so when Kouvelas and I made our agreement I undertook to buy a downconverter and send it to Thessaloniki. So the mayor and I made an agreement and another photograph was taken of us shaking hands.

Back in Bush House my agreement with Kouvelas received a mixed reception. The Controller European Services, Andrew Taussig, and the new MDXB, John Tusa, were delighted – Taussig had concluded a similar deal for rebroadcasting with a radio station in Austria. I was awarded my fifth BBC bonus of £100. However, the news that I had done a deal with the New Democracy mayor of Thessaloniki and had shaken hands with the party leader, Constantine Mitsotakis, did not go down well within the Greek Section. It was all to the good that we were being rebroadcast but some members of the section felt they would be unable to face their friends in Greece once the news got out. One colleague even called me 'an opportunist and capitalist', which I regarded as a compliment.

I attempted to be even more 'opportunist' by making contact with London Greek Radio (LGR), the former pirate station broadcasting to the mainly Greek Cypriot community in North London. LGR was given a license by the Independent Radio Authority in 1989. I visited their offices and studio in Finchley and interested them in taking the Greek Section's news and some of the features, such as *Ee Alii Elynes* (The Other Greeks). Before attempting to receive our broadcasts by satellite, LGR were prepared to take them by phone. I discussed this with Benny Ammar and we drew up a draft contract. Then BBC Radio London stepped in and vetoed the plans – they were not then broadcasting in Greek, but reserved the right to do so in the future.

The Wall comes down

In 1989 the Cold War began to thaw and by the end of the year the international divide was positively warm. The thaw had really begun some years earlier in the Soviet Union where the new Communist Party boss, Mikhail Gorbachev, began reforming the system with his policies of *Perestroika* (reconstruction) and *Glasnost* (openness). These policies applied within the Soviet Union and at that time did not apply to Eastern Europe. In a famous summit between President Reagan and Gorbachev in 1987 in Berlin, the American leader pointed at the nailed up Brandenburg Gate and the Berlin Wall and issued a challenge:

Secretary General Gorbachev, if you seek peace, if you seek prosperity for the Soviet Union and Eastern Europe, if you seek liberalization: come here, to this gate. Mr. Gorbachev, open this gate. Mr. Gorbachev, tear down this wall.

That did not happen for another two years and it was not the Russians who tore down the wall but the Germans themselves. In the meantime, widespread industrial strikes in Poland had forced the Communist Party to allow free elections in April 1989 in which the Solidarity movement won power. In Hungary, new leaders took over and dismantled the electric fence along the border with Austria. This provided an escape route to the West not only for Hungarians, but also for thousands of East Germans. But not all East Germans wished to leave and in November 1989 half a million gathered in East Berlin chanting *'Wir bleiben hier!'* ('We're staying here') and demanding political changes. Thousands leaving and thousands more demonstrating led the East German politburo to allow some crossing through the Berlin Wall to the West, but they bungled the announcement. At a press conference a party boss was asked when the changes would take effect, and answered that as far as he knew 'immediately, without delay'. This led to the guards at the Wall allowing people to cross. By eleven o'clock on 9 November people were passing through the Wall in both directions, without hindrance, and others were dancing on top of the Wall to celebrate. Within days people were using picks to begin dismantling the infamous Berlin Wall – they became known as *mauerspechte* or wall woodpeckers.

It was one of the great events of the twentieth century. Sadly I was not in Berlin to see the Wall come down, but I did watch it on television – the hundreds of young Berliners, who had not been born when the Wall went up, climbing, sitting and dancing on the infamous Wall which was already being chipped away. And then there was the great celebratory concert on Christmas Day, with Leonard Bernstein conducting a choir and orchestra with performers from Berlin, Leipzig, Munich, London, Paris and New York in Beethoven's Ninth Symphony; and Bernstein had modified the text of the Schiller poem so that it was no longer an Ode to Joy, *An die Freude*, but *An die Freiheit*, an Ode to Freedom. I was working at Bush House but also in Ware planning the restoration of the eighteenth-century grotto, built by the Quaker poet, John Scott of

Amwell. In the early months of 1990, my friend, the poet Danielle Hope, went to Berlin and brought back a fragment of the Berlin Wall, which we incorporated in the new porch for the grotto – as a time marker.

Cessated

In early 1990 everyone in any management role in Bush House was required to begin preparing a 'zero-based' budget of their department. It was a new discipline for me and, I imagined, for most of my colleagues in the World Service. We were called to meetings of the various divisions – ours was the European Service, chaired by the Controller, Andrew Taussig, and addressed by a member of the Finance Department, who explained the process of zero-based budgeting. It started, he said, from a 'zero base' and every function within an organisation was analysed for its needs and its costs. Budgets were then built around what was needed for the next accounting period, regardless of whether that budget was higher or lower than the previous one. The reason why we were undertaking this exercise was that the National Audit Office required it, so that the House of Commons could review the way in which the World Service managed and spent its grant-in-aid from the Foreign and Commonwealth Office. The World Service and the FCO reviewed the grant-in-aid every three years and during the current triennial period, we were told, the World Service received £143 million for broadcasting with another £16 million for the Monitoring Service at Caversham. Zero-based budgeting would set the parameters for the next three years.

I went away and began preparing a zero-based budget for the Greek Section, working on figures I received or was able to ferret out for staff salaries, studio use, travel, etc., etc. They were not sums I was able to verify – not that I really wished to – and the whole process became for me an exercise in imaginative accounting. I had worked quickly, perhaps too quickly; there were sure to be mistakes, there always were, but I was glad to have the job done. So I submitted my returns to the Controller via Bennie Ammar, Head of the South East European Service, and waited.

It was a week or so before Benny called me in to his office. He asked me to sit down and took the Greek Section's zero-based return from a drawer.

'David, you've done it again – the first zero-based budget we received in the South East European Service and the most complete – or almost complete. You've included everything except your own salary. Why is that? I can't imagine it was a simple oversight. Are you trying to tell us something by any chance?'

Was I trying to tell them something, or was it my habitual carelessness? To tell the truth, I was not sure. I had raced through the budgeting exercise, trying to get it done and off the agenda. On the other hand, perhaps I had made an unconscious – or perhaps semi-conscious – decision to find a way out, to apply for early retirement as other colleagues had done already. I had been with the World Service for twenty years, ten of them as Greek Programme Organiser, and while I enjoyed the job, enough was surely enough. There were plenty of things I wished to do with the rest of my life other than attending morning editorial meetings and sitting in an office, waiting for Greeks to tell me their troubles. I would miss the travel but I could always go to Greece on holiday. The other things I wished to spend more time on included restoring Scott's Grotto and working as Hon. Secretary and curator at the Ware Museum, which I had helped to set up in 1986. And there was publishing – I had been publishing small books and pamphlets about local history for years and thought I might expand on that.

So I answered 'yes' to Benny's question: I *was* telling them something. I would like to take early retirement if that could be arranged. Benny said he had mentioned the possibility to the Controller and they felt it might be possible. Without making any promises, he would arrange for me to spend time with Personnel and a representative from the BBC Pension Scheme. And so that is what happened. Discussions were held over a matter of weeks and on 23 March 1990 I was officially declared 'Cessated'. The leaving note said that I had served 7,494 days with the World Service, or 20 years, 6 months and 14 days. The reason for my leaving was 'Premature retirement in the Management interest'.

* * * * *

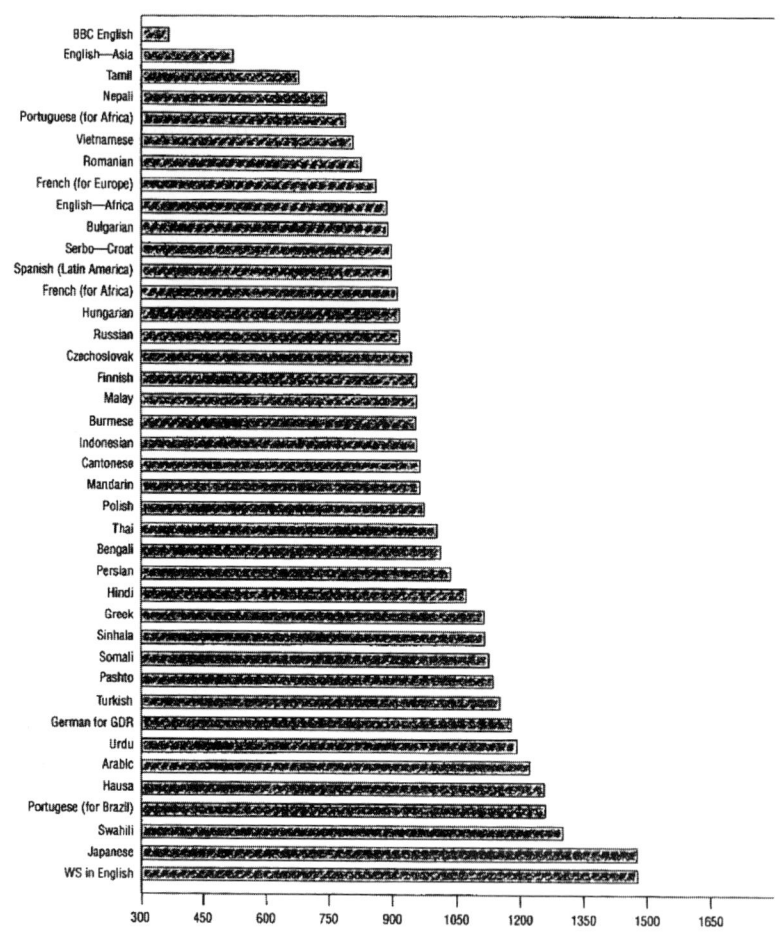

Fig.5 of the National Audit Office report, comparing the relative costs of the BBC's language services, as a unit cost of per hour broadcast. The Greek Section was 13th from the most expensive, between Hindi and Sinhala.

I did not think anything more about zero-based budgeting until, some years later, I found online a report from the National Audit Office entitled 'Management of the BBC World Service'. It was the project for which we had all been working in early 1990, an enquiry into the way the World Service managed its grant-in-aid to see if it did so 'economically, efficiently and effectively'. A number of improvements in financial management were recommended, but what struck me as central to the whole report was this paragraph:

Providing high quality worldwide broadcasts is expensive and there are many factors which can influence the cost of programmes, ranging from the use of studios to transmissions' requirements and the sophistication of the target audience. Nevertheless there was a wide range in the cost of broadcasting for each of the 37 output services, from between £500 to £1500 an hour. Apart from its annual budget review the World Service did not undertake internal comparisons to justify such differences. More attention might be paid to the implications of these varying costs in determining the balance of output

A little further on the report contained a table, comparing the unit costs per hour for broadcasts by the World Service in English and the 37 foreign language services. The lowest unit cost was for Tamil and the highest for the World Service in English and the Japanese Section. The Greek Section ranked No. 31 and the Turkish Section No.29. If I had not retired and my salary had been included, I wondered: perhaps programmes in Greek would have been as costly as those in Turkish. Overall it seemed to me a largely irrelevant exercise. What decisions by management could possibly be made by comparing the unit costs per hour for Romanian (No. 6) with those for Polish (No. 22) or Nepali (No. 3) with Urdu (No. 33)? As for the most costly services – well, if the Foreign Office decreed that the BBC must broadcast in Japanese, the BBC was forced to pay the market rate for reliable Japanese translators, was it not?

Hopefully the National Audit Office added 'there seems to be scope for further reductions in the production costs of the English Current Affairs service'. But World Service current affairs programmes were cut-price bargains compared with comparable programmes on Radio 4. I was once told that 'File on 4' were going to use a World Service feature I had made, so would I send the insert tape to Broadcasting House for the interviews to be transcribed? I did so and was later called to BH to record the programme, which took over three hours of studio time with a recording engineer, a producer and a secretary working from scripts – which I had never done – and numerous retakes of my linking oration. I calculated that the Radio 4 broadcast cost four-to-five times that of the World Service original, made by me alone in a self-op studio.

19.
Two Bush House Poets

The World Service nurtured a rich variety of creative literature, sometimes overtly for use in radio features, often covertly – in the dead of night the offices of Bush House were the perfect companion for poets and novelists. I was only dimly aware of this underground stream, even though my two non-fiction books had been written on BBC typewriters. But at my leaving party, it seems, I committed myself to publishing one of the most remarkable poets ever to work in Bush House – I say 'it seems' because I was plied with drink throughout the evening and the next day my friend Danielle Hope said: 'You know you promised Feyyaz last night that you will publish his poems, don't you?' Feyyaz was Feyyaz Fergar, a former Turkish programme organiser, long-term drinking companion and great fund of stories, but I did not recall our conversation of the night before or the fact that he wrote poetry. And as for publishing his work – for a few years I had been producing slim books about local history, focusing on Ware and surrounding parts of Hertfordshire, and hoped to expand on that in retirement from the BBC, but I had not planned on publishing poetry. But a promise is a promise, and Danielle for one seemed delighted at the new turn in my life.

Feyyaz Kayacan Fergar

Feyyaz had been writing poetry for most of his adult life. He was educated in Istanbul at a French *lycée* run by Jesuits and his first poems, as he told me, were imitations of Paul Valéry, the French symbolists or Hölderlin and Kleist. While still at school he published a slim volume entitled *Les Gammes Insolites*, which was reviewed in the local French-language newspaper with the prophecy: 'a new poet is born along the shores of the Bosphorus – watch him, he'll go far'. Feyyaz joked that he had gone far because he was sent to Paris to study politics and, when the Second World War began, went to a college in Newcastle-upon-Tyne, then part of Durham University. His second poetry collection, *Gestes à la Mer*, was published by the Grey Walls Press run by Alex Comfort. As a result, Feyyaz was labelled a surrealist and later appeared in a television documentary about the surrealists alongside Roland Penrose and the jazz singer

George Melly. He joined the BBC Turkish Section, married and lived in Forest Hill, South London, in the later years of the war. He then began writing prose and fiction in Turkish over the pen name, Feyyaz Kayacan.

While at the BBC he was invited by Danielle Hope, then a medical student in Nottingham, to send translations of some Turkish poets for inclusion in the poetry magazine, *Zenos,* which she edited. He sent her 40 translations which she published in two editions of the magazine, and included some poems of his own. Danielle said she liked his 'stuff' – an expression he said that made him feel good. Their friendship continued and he invited her to Bush House. When at last he put together a collection for me to publish, the dedication was 'to Danielle Hope, all these, as installments of my gratitude for her bright friendship and her inspiring faith in my voice'.

The collection was entitled *A Talent for Shrouds*. It was the first venture in poetry for Rockingham Press (named after my mother's family) and a product of my inexperience. I made two misjudgments which I was careful not to repeat in other publications. One was the decision to give the book an Introduction: it was written by William Oxley, a poet and critic I had not then met but who had praised Feyyaz's poetry, but William was also the editor of a polemical magazine called *Litack* and in his Introduction he praised Feyyaz as embodying the hope that 'the romantic poet is coming into his own again, after the excesses of the 1940s'. Not that William's judgment was wrong, but it would have been more suitable as a review than an Introduction. My other mistake was to include a long biographical interview which, although worthwhile in itself, distracted readers' attention from the poems. In fact reviews mainly commented on the interview, and especially the part where Feyyaz had discovered that his father was a *muhtedi,* a convert to Islam. His grandfather and brother had been the first photographers in Constantinople– later the poet Anne Born told me she had a photograph taken by the Abdullah Brothers, photographers to the Sultan.

A Talent for Shrouds whetted my appetite for more by Feyyaz. The following year, 1992, I published *Modern Turkish Poetry* edited by Feyyaz Kayacan Fergar - his selection of 58 Turkish poets from Aşik Veysel (1893-1973) and the great Nazım Hikmet (1901-63) to Necati Polat (born 1962). Not all the translations were his – he included some by Richard McKane, Ruth Christie, Talat S. Halman

Feyyaz Kayacan Fergar in reflexive mood.

and Mevlut Ceylan. But what made this anthology outstanding was Feyyaz's notes on each poet and his idiosyncratic 13-page introduction on the glories and special characteristics of Turkish poetry:

> *'We have the Magna Carta but no cuisine,' said an English friend of mine some years ago. He came back from a visit to Turkey smacking his lips in memory of all the succulent dishes with which he had 'enlightened' his palate. He added: 'I met an extraordinary man in Istanbul. He wore glasses, false teeth and a toupet. But there was nothing false about his dazzling mastery of the art of Turkish cooking. He said he could cook for me lunch and dinner for three months without repeating himself once. I believed him implicitly. Items like "nightingle's nest", "beloved lip" and "woman's thigh" have an exciting poetic aura and their recipes should be rewritten by a modern John Donne or Andrew Marvel.' When I told him that Turkey had its own Donnes and Marvels and a rich poetic tradition kept alive today by the works of outstanding poets, he gave me such a voluminous look of utter disbelief that I*

decided not to pursue the matter any further. I had a different man, a different person in front of me.'

Feyyaz's *Modern Turkish Poetry* was made the Recommended Translation of the Poetry Book Society.

Rockingham published two further books by him – both posthumously. Feyyaz died in April 1993 leaving a stack of unpublished work in both Turkish and English. Danielle Hope – his long-term friend and literary executor – made the selection and edited *The Bright is Dark Enough*, which was published later in 1993. They were mostly poems he was working on before his death: he told a friend that he had written or reworked over twenty poems within a month. For the previous two years, he had put aside his own work to edit and translate the anthology, *Modern Turkish Poetry*, and a collection by his friend Can Yücel. But Feyyaz was urgently concerned by the 'massacre of nature' and gave his final book the subtitle *a cycle of poems of dark ecological introspecti*

It was some years before Feyyaz's 'Shelter Stories' were translated and published in English. They had been written while his first wife was being treated for a terminal cancer and recalled their time together in Forest Hill,- during the Second World War, sheltering with other Londoners from the V1 flying bombs – Mrs Valley, 'the mistress of dirty jokes'; Mr Ellis, the gardener; Gareth, the tobacconist; and Vera his daughter with the shapely legs'. The doodle-bugs, flying bombs or V1s represented the threat of instant death but also the subject of a hundred jokes, stories and curses.

Loaded with metaphors, the stories when published were a revolution in Turkish literature – extending the possibilities of the Turkish language and continuing with the same concentrated richness on every page of every story. They revolutionised Turkish fiction and won for Feyyaz the distinguished Turkish Language Academy prize. In 2007 for the first time they were translated into English by Ruth Christie and Selçuk Berilgen, and published by Rockingham Press as *Mrs Valley's War: the Shelter Stories of Feyyaz Kayacan Fergar*. The translation was financed by the Turkish Ministry of Culture and promoted by some of Feyyaz's admirers. The cover illustration was from Henry Moore's second *Shelter Notebook*, in which he sketched people sleeping in the Underground during the London Blitz.

Mahmud Kianush

In August 1993 – quite out of the blue – I received a letter and a typescript for a book in a format similar to *Modern Turkish Poetry*, although it did not mention Feyyaz's work:

> *Please find enclosed the typescript of "Modern Persian Poetry", an anthology of poems by the Iranian contemporary poets, from Nimâ Youshij, the leading pioneer of modern poetry in Iran, to the youngest generation of poets today. It consists of a short history of Persian poetry and the translation of about 150 poems by 41 poets. As far as I know no such anthology has appeared in this country. I hope you will consider it for publication in your Poetry in Translation series, and I look forward to hearing from you shortly.*

The letter was signed by Mahmud Kianush, a name unknown to me. He expected a reply 'shortly' but that I could not provide. The delay was partly due to my wish to get a second opinion, something I had not felt necessary with Feyyaz Fergar. And so I sent the typescript to two Iranian academics, one of whom sat on it and did not reply for months: retrieving it, I then sent it to Parvin Loloi, the Iranian-born wife of Glyn Pursglove, reviews editor of the poetry magazine *Acumen*, whom I had met when I published a collection by William Oxley, author of the introduction to Feyyaz's first book. Parvin replied in April 1994. Then there was further delay caused by my illness – Danielle and I had taken a package holiday in The Gambia, where I fell off a bicycle and got a wound which went septic: throughout that summer I went from hospital to hospital being treated for a virulent African variety of septicemia. As a result, I did not give a detailed reply to Kianush until November 1994.

Mahmud Kianush, it turned out, had lived in London for twenty years and was a contributor on cultural affairs for the BBC Persian Section. In Iran he had been a school teacher and then a civil servant in the Ministry of Education, before taking early retirement in 1974 and moving to London with his family. In Iran he had gained a reputation for his translations of American and European literature and for children's poetry, of which he was a leading practitioner; he was also the editor of two literary magazines and a magazine for

Mahmud Kianush

children. I met Mahmud at his home in Ealing, West London, and immediately liked him although I learned quite early on that he was a tremendous self-publicist. He was also non-political and one of the few Iranians I had met who seemed immune to the effects of the Islamic Revolution.

Modern Persian Poetry was published in May 1996 and launched at the prestigious Library for Iranian Studies in Acton. I had judged Kianush to be something of a loner, but the Iranian community in West London turned out in force to greet his poetry anthology – academics, broadcasters, business people, poets and artists. I was introduced to Bahman Forsi, whose illustration 'A Page of a History' – showing an angry moon behind a prison grill – we had used on the cover of the book: he thanked me and said I had used the illustration upside-down, but it did not really matter. Kianush gave a reading which was enthusiastically applauded, and we sold a large number of books. In such friendly Iranian company, I refrained from owning up to my role in the fateful interview with Ayatollah Khomeini of 1978.

Although it was modelled on *Modern Turkish Poetry*, *Modern Persian Poetry* was a more substantial volume in many respects. Its 212 pages included a 40-page introduction, a further 15 pages of notes on the poets and two pages describing how the Arabic script of

Persian had been transliterated in English. The final selection of 43 poets ranged from Iran's great innovator, Nimâ Yushij, through the poets who had flourished or suffered under the Shah to the well-known feminist writer, Forugh Farrokhzâd, who was also a film director, and Ahmad Shâmlu, the real star of the collection. His poem 'In This Dead End' referred to the early days of the Islamic Revolution when young fanatics enforced the moral code of *shari'a* by sniffing people's mouths to see if they had been drinking or forcibly wiped lipstick from women's mouths, even using razors:

Behold! Butchers are on guard at thoroughfares
With their bloodstained cleavers and chopping boards
Such a strange time it is, my dear!
They cut off the smiles from lips,
And the songs from throats!
  We must hide our Emotions in dark closets!

Kianush included a number of his own poems, though it was unclear whether they were translations from Farsi originals or poems written in English. A similar question arose when some years later he asked me to publish separate books of his poetry, only one of which seemed to have its roots in Iran – *Of Birds and Men: Poems from a Persian Divan* (2004).

* * * * *

Publishing the poetry anthologies edited by Feyyaz Fergar and Mahmud Kianush was a cultural sequel to my twenty years in broadcasting. I had worked alongside Feyyaz in Bush House – he with the Turks, I with the Greeks – and drank with him in the BBC Club or his favourite watering hole, Hennessy's in the Strand. I did not know Kianush in Bush House and by the time I was publishing his later work, the Persian Section had moved to Broadcasting House. Broadcasting and publishing poetry were for me two facets of the same noble structure, the communication of ideas in words – and not just any words but the best words, whether original or in translation, to convey meaning and enlighten the listener. To quote Coleridge's famous definition of poetry: 'the best words in the best order'.

20.
Then and Now

Working in Bush House was for me a great adventure and a privilege: there was no other broadcaster which could compare with the BBC. It was particularly important at that time – in the sixties, seventies and eighties – when much of our international audience was struggling to achieve freedom of expression, freedom to tell the truth in any medium, and when radio, even short-wave radio, was a prime source of news and comment not yet pushed aside by social media and the belief that everyone and anyone can generate news. I made mistakes, certainly, and at times failed to recognise that the milieu of foreign broadcasting demanded personal diplomatic skills not necessary in Fleet Street. But I believe I used my talents to the best of my ability and made a valuable and valued contribution to the institution that employed me, the BBC World Service.

Working for the World Service was also enormous fun. The many nationalities and cultures in Bush House enjoyed a palpable community spirit, despite the many irksome problems with which we all worked – the crowded offices, the scarce studio time, the poor pay. African and Asian 'programme assistants' would emerge with triumphant smiles on their faces, after spending hours editing recorded tapes with a razor blade and stop-watch. Such small triumphs would be shared in the canteen or the Club with others working under similar conditions. Friendships were formed across cultural boundaries, romances blossomed; wives, husbands and children would appear at times to appreciative cries of recognition. There was always some celebration, probably a leaving party, taking place somewhere in the building. After I had retired, I was invited to a party which had transformed the carpark between the South-East Wing and Centre Block into a vast marquee of reminiscing, laughing men and women: I cannot now recall what the occasion was, perhaps an important World Service anniversary. I saw many people I recognised and was recognised – much to my surprise – by many other people.

It is tempting and very easy to be nostalgic and starry-eyed about my twenty years working for the World Service in Bush House. In a cooler frame of mind, perhaps, I can identify interesting contrasts and similarities between the Then and the Now of broadcasting and the world at large. The vast advances in information technology over the past three decades have made news and ideas almost universally available, with an immediacy and at far lower costs than we could have imagined. When events can be captured and shared on a smart phone within minutes, the time-consuming, cumbersome and expensive business of flying back from Dublin with the prime minister's words – as I did in 1975 – becomes an historical curiosity. Indeed, the sort of broadcasting we did is now studied as history: in December 2019 I attended a symposium held in the History Department of Panteion University in Athens where three of my former colleagues were joined by academics in analysing the structure and impact of the BBC Greek broadcasts we made. Further advances in technology will surely make our style of broadcasts even more obsolete and strange. The obverse of the new immediacy is, of course, the danger of 'false news', of reports which may be just innocently inaccurate or mendacious and politically manipulated.

While the technology and broadcast journalism have changed, the political world seems destined to repeat itself and its mistakes. The Soviet Union fell apart in 1990 and the Cold War came to an end, but a resurgent Russian Republic now threatens the West, not with tanks but with spying and hacking technology. In the United States, reactions to the policies of Donald Trump, the 45th President, echo the reactions and fears that greeted the 40th President, Ronald Reagan. In Britain, the economic belt-tightening of government policies which went under the name of 'monetarism', was repeated after 2010 in the name of 'austerity'.

In my twenty years working for the World Service, I cannot remember conducting an interview on global warming. It was not a common headline in the British Press and indeed most reporting on the environment in 1980-90 was about the potential dangers of global warming. How things have changed. It is not the potential but the actual danger that now figures in the Press – the melting of Greenland's glaciers, the Siberian heatwave, micro-plastic pollution of the oceans, wildfires, tornados and unprecedented extremes of climate. Politicians and world leaders have been slow to recognise these dangers and even slower to form policies that could contain global warming, but surely this must be the dominant concern of the next generation of broadcasters in the BBC World Service and elsewhere in the world at large.